הגדה סיפור החיים

THE NARRATIVE OF FAITH

a father-to-son haggadah

by Ephraim Nisenbaum

FELDHEIM PUBLISHERS
Jerusalem / New York

FELDHEIM PUBLISHERS
POB 35002/Jerusalem Israel
200 Airport Executive Park, Nanuet, NY 10954

Typeset by
STAR COMPOSITION SERVICES, INC
New York, NY
212 684 4001

לזכרון עולם בהיכל ה׳

This Haggadah is dedicated
to the eternal memory of

HaRav Chaim Schmelczer זצ״ל
הרב חיים בן משה יוסף זצ״ל

beloved Rosh Yeshiva, mentor, father, and friend to
thousands of Talmidim and admirers. His מסירת נפש
for אהבת ישראל, אהבת התורה and אהבת חסד, as seen
through the prism of his quiet and unassuming
manner, will always remain as a guide to me.

Ephraim Nisenbaum

In loving memory of

ר׳ מרדכי בן הרב אפרים
חנה בת הרב יעקב אייזיק
חשא בת ר׳ יצחק איסר

dedicated by
Yaakov and Karen Nisenbaum

In loving memory of
my grandparents

David Harris

דוד בן יחיאל

Yetta Harris

יטא בת שמעון מאיר הכהן
whose strength, kindness, and self-sacrifice
helped mold the next generation,
and future links in the chain.

In loving memory of my Aunt

Sylvia Rotner

שרה בת דוד
a model of selflessness and concern for others

In loving memory of my father

Dr. Herbert Harris

חיים בן דוד

whose integrity, kindness, and selflessness in
both his personal and professional life continue
to be a source of strength and inspiration. I am
forever grateful to him.

Moshe and Sydney Harris
and Family

Dedicated in loving memory of

חיים אברהם יונה בן אפרים אליעזר הכהן ז״ל
נפ׳ ז׳ תמוז תשד״מ

Alvin E. Schottenstein

Alvin E. Schottenstein was a much- loved and respected business leader in Columbus, Ohio. As busy as he was in the world of commerce, he was a humanitarian and philanthropist with a humble spirit and generous heart. He was always available to those seeking help. His devotion to his family, his community and to Eretz Yisrael was his precious legacy.

Irving Altman

יצחק אייזיק בן עקיבה הכהן ז״ל
נפ׳ ר״ח אב תשכ״ח

Irving Altman was an אוד מוצל מאש, "a firebrand saved from the fires" of the Holocaust. He came to America with his faith in Hashem intact, and imbued with the learning he received in his parents' home in Bardejov, Slovakia. His sterling character and warm nature, his humility and piety, and his acts of kindness, were his hallmarks. His Torah values and pride in Yiddishkeit was the legacy that he transmitted to his family.

Dedicated by
Beverly Schottenstein, Helen Altman,
Robert M. and Caroline Altman Schottenstein
and sons Isaac, Ephraim and Avi

Letter of Approbation from
HaRav Avrohom Chaim Levin שליט״א
Rosh Yeshiva Telshe – Chicago

אברהם חיים לוין
RABBI AVROHOM CHAIM LEVIN
5104 N. DRAKE AVENUE • CHICAGO, IL 60625
ראש הישיבה\טלז-שיקגו • ROSH HAYESHIVA/TELSHE-CHICAGO

ב"ה

בס"ד יום ועש"ק

כבוד ידידי רב חביבי הרב הג[אן] ל' אברהם ניסנבוים
שליט"א מגדולי ראשי שיעורי לסדר וישב וישב
לגלות הגדות ומאמרים וכמה הוא רב ואשרי
צונ כאני קליון ולצ', דרגו להגדיס כיון
 על תפ[לה] ומסרו הקונטרסים שעיין כהם,
ואמרתי אתם שלמים מלאיות שורות
והכל גם צאקות ויגרות כפי כחו הקלן
כהכנת המארי חל לשאמרם, ול אות
ולתם כין הנתן כין הלך ודלויות קהל
הרבת תולת אפ[סבר, ולין לאיין קהל
לבהל יואר, ווליית רבל ברכין ולצבה
להאניק צדוגתו הקצה לצדות אל
כרהים.

לצדר הכת חיים ול[וין]
ידי' ל' אברהם הגס

Letter of Approbation from
Rav Moshe Eisemann שליט"א
acclaimed author and Rebbe in
Yeshiva Ner Israel – Baltimore

Vaad L'Hatzolas Nidchei Yisroel

of Stam Gemilas Chesed Fund, Inc.   Tax Exempt #22-2371275

401 Yeshiva Lane • Baltimore, Maryland 21208 • Tel: 410-484-7396

Fax: 410-486-8810 • E-Mail: eisemann@juno.com

Rabbi Moshe M. Eisemann

January 12, 2000

Rabbi Ephraim Nisenbaum
2362 Milton Road
Cleveland Ohio 44118-3940

Dear R' Ephraim:

Thank you so much for allowing me to see some samples of your Hagada Commentary. One would have thought that by this time there really is nothing new to be discovered in those beloved pages. So much has been written, so much told. But wonder of wonders! You have coaxed unsuspected treasures from every single page.

The beauty of your approach is that your discoveries are no, ממרחק תביא לחמה. You read the text, carefully, thoughtfully and with an eye unjaded by constant exposure. Your insights were there all along, waiting to be uncovered. It seems to me that the value of your book goes well beyond the boundaries of the Hagada. All of us can benefit from reading texts which we have known since childhood, the Sidur, the Chumash and so much more, with a willingness to slip just one notch beneath the surface and end up in a dazzling world of insight and instruction of which we never knew.

In my opinion your Hagada deserves to be studied seriously and lovingly by everyone seeking depths and experiences which are in the reach of us all.

Keep doing your great work. Many will be grateful.

Best wishes:

Moshe M. Eisemann

MAKING UP TO THE JEWISH YOUTH OF THE FORMER SOVIET UNION FOR 70 YEARS OF EMPTINESS & SORROW

The Narrative of Faith
A Father-to-Son Haggadah

Introduction

More commentary has been written on the Haggadah than any other part of the Torah. Undoubtedly, this is because of the Torah's mandate to every person to discuss the Exodus from Egypt with his children every year on Pesach night. Indeed, the Haggadah itself encourages this proliferation of commentary: "The – "כל המרבה לספר ביציאת מצרים הרי זה משובח" more one elaborates upon the Exodus, the more praiseworthy it is."

What exactly is the purpose of this elaboration? The commentators explain that the mitzvos associated with each holiday are actually tools through which one can draw its spiritual essence. (See R. Moshe Chaim Luzzatto, *Ma'amar Hachochma*). It is important, therefore, not to lose the essence of the holiday through its more extraneous details and customs.

We sometimes become so involved with the minor customs associated with the holidays – for example flowers for Shavuos and latkes for Chanukah – we forget the essence of the holiday. But it is the essence of the holiday that is the ultimate goal of all the customs and mitzvos. Similarly with Pesach, we can become so involved in elaborating on the Haggadah, that the ultimate purpose of the mitzvah of discussing the Exodus may be forgotten.

The goal of the Haggadah is to help one gain a better appreciation of G-d's great kindness and miracles during the Exodus from Egypt. The *Sefer HaChinuch* explains the importance of the mitzvah of discussing the Exodus: It is the foundation of a Jew's belief in G-d's omnipotence and involvement in the day-to-day affairs of the world. It is therefore understandable that there is a special mitzvah in elaborating on the Exodus: By doing so, one can strengthen his belief and faith in the Al-mighty.

Rav Shlomo Wolbe, the esteemed Mashgiach and Mussar personality from Jerusalem, explains that the Haggadah is a tool through which one can feel as if he had personally experienced the Exodus. Through this experience, G-d takes each person by the hand, as it were, bringing him closer to His service. As it says in the Haggadah, "At first, our fathers served idolatry, and *now* G-d has brought us close to His service." This implies that *now*, during the Seder, G-d brings us close to His service. This is the ultimate goal of discussing the Pesach narrative (*Alei Shur* vol.2, p.390).

However, the Haggadah lends itself to a wide variety of interpretations. It is easy, then, to forget the focus of these goals and become entangled in a web of homiletic *vertlach*, scholarly discourse, and ethical insights. Many of these insights do not even relate to the actual Exodus itself; rather, they explain and interpret some of the peripheral parts of the Haggadah. As enjoyable as it may be to share these insights at the Seder, they actually contribute very little to the goals of the mitzvah.

This is especially true where children are concerned. Discussing the Exodus is presented by the Torah as a means of instilling basic Jewish beliefs and ideals in one's children on Pesach. It is stated, "והגדת לבנך ביום ההוא": "And you should tell your child on that day." Yet at many Seder tables, the adults exchange insights that, although beautiful, are beyond a child's comprehension.

Even in many schools, the emphasis seems to be more on the child's being able to recite a notebook full of choice *vertlach* at the table, rather than on the parents' transmitting fundamentals to their children. It is as though the Torah said "והגדת לאביך" – "Speak to your father" – rather than "והגדת לבנך" – "Speak to your child."

I have spoken with people who were present at the Seder tables of great Roshei Yeshiva and Torah scholars. They had gone to these Sedarim with expectations of hearing deep, intricate, and scholarly insights on the Haggadah, and they left sorely disappointed. These great people would lead a Seder on an almost elementary level, reading and illuminating the Haggadah with different Midrashic accounts of the Exodus, in a manner simple enough for a child to understand.

Yet therein lies the profundity of the Haggadah. Some of the most important principles of Judaism are conveyed in a deceptively simple manner, to be understood on a variety of levels, by each person according to his or her capacity. It is well known that Rav Yechezkel Levenstein, the Mashgiach of the Ponovezh Yeshiva, put great effort into trying to experience the Exodus from Egypt personally[1]. He felt that the fulfillment of this mitzvah was necessary for the proper development of one's belief in G-d.

Over the past ten years I have had the fortunate experience of leading the Pesach Sedarim, not only with my own children, but also with adults, many of whom were not familiar with some of the basic principles of Judaism. I have always tried to use our Seder as a vehicle to present some of the Torah's important ideals of faith, in a manner palatable to my students. At the same time, I try to remain mindful of the directive to focus on teaching my children the lessons of the Exodus.

This Haggadah is the result of these efforts. Many of the interpretations and ideas expressed here may be familiar, for they are based on concepts and thoughts that I have read or heard in other places. However, I have been careful to pres-

---

1. A reliable source reported that Reb Chatzkel, as he was known, was once seen marching back and forth in the Beis Medrash. He explained to a curious observer that he was trying to imagine crossing the Sea at the Exodus.

ent all of the commentary in a way that is both simple and short enough for an astute child to comprehend, yet sufficiently thought-provoking to satisfy the more mature mind.

In an effort to make the Haggadah more user-friendly, instructions and basic halachos have been cited in their respective places throughout the Haggadah.

I pray that my efforts will be successful in contributing, in some measure, to the enhancement of the mitzvos of the Pesach Seder.

Acknowledgements

"*Hoda'ah*," the Hebrew word for "thanksgiving," is also used to mean "admission" – implying that there is some connection between these two seemingly unrelated ideas. The explanation offered is that every thank-you is actually an admission of sorts: "I couldn't have done this without your help!"

My primary debt of admission and appreciation is, of course, to *HaKadosh Baruch Hu*. I am humbled to have been chosen as a beneficiary of so much of His kindness – a wonderful supportive family, great Rebbeim, the opportunity to teach and spread Torah to His nation, and much more. I hope I will be able to show some measure of appreciation by realizing my potential in sanctifying His Name.

ı owe a debt of gratitude to many people without whom this book could never have been written. My parents, Yaakov and Karen Nisenbaum, have always imbued their children with a love of Torah and a responsibility for others. Their encouragement and assistance have been constant. They are role models for our entire family. May *HaKadosh Baruch Hu* grant them good health and much nachas from the whole mishpacha.

My parents-in-law, Rav Chaim Tzvi and Gittel Goldzweig, are exemplary models of *mesirus nefesh* for the Klal. My father-in-law's superhuman efforts on behalf of Kashrus throughout the world, and his selflessness and generosity are legendary. I thank them for their love and support. May *HaKadosh Baruch Hu* grant them the good health to enjoy much nachas from the whole mishpacha.

I would also like to thank my brothers and sisters and my wife's brothers and sisters and their families for their words of encouragement.

I have had the zechus of learning in the Telshe Yeshiva, both in Cleveland and Chicago. I can never repay the Torah and the *Halichos Chaim* I received from my Roshei Yeshiva in Chicago, HaRav Avraham Chaim Levin שליט״א and HaRav Chaim Dov Keller שליט״א.

HaRav Chaim Schmelczer זצ״ל, the Menahel of Telshe Yeshiva-Chicago, was a role model for me. His recent passing has left a great void, but his sterling character, fatherly concern, and keen insights continue to inspire me and so many others. I am also personally indebted to him for having introduced me to my wife. The title of this Haggadah, ״סיפור החיים״, is dedicated to his everlasting memory[2].

I have also enjoyed the great *zechus* of drinking from the waters of the Mashgiach, HaRav Shlomo Wolbe שליט״א, both in Yeshivas Be'er Yaakov and in the Beis HaMussar in Yerushalayim. His personal greatness and wisdom have profoundly influenced my life and my way of thinking.

I extend heartfelt gratitude to all of my students at the Jewish Learning Connection. Their many questions, comments, and insights inspired and enhanced many of the Divrei Torah in this book. I am both amazed and proud of our students' fiery enthusiasm, and their desire to grow and understand Torah properly. I constantly appreciate having been given the opportunity to teach such a fine and dedicated group of people.

My sincere appreciation is due to the mentors and chaverim who reviewed and commented on parts of the manuscript: Rabbis Menachem Feifer, Aharon Levitansky, Yitzchok Miller, and Moshe Stoll, who is my partner at the Jewish Learning

---

2. As I indicate elsewhere, I have tried to keep the focus in this Haggadah on the development of fundamentals of Jewish faith. The title is also a reference to the passage in Chabakuk (2:4), וצדיק באמונתו יחיה: "The righteous person lives by his faith." ״סיפור החיים״ also has the same numerical value as the author's name, אפרים נחם (חסר).

Connection. Rav Nachman Bulman שליט"א also offered constructive advice, for which I am grateful. Rabbi Doniel Neustadt reviewed the halachos. All of the above contributed much to the book. Any mistakes, however, are solely my responsibility.

I thank Rabbi Hanan Minkowich for graciously allowing me to use his *Haggadah Berurah* as a resource and format for the halachos.

Sincere thanks are also due Rabbi Menachem Wagshal of Maznaim Publishing for allowing me to use the translation from *The MeAm Lo'ez Haggadah*.

My gratitude is also owed to Rabbi Hillel Yarmove and Ms. Jill Brotman for their meticulous editing, and to Mrs. Esther Goodman, my mother Mrs. Karen Nisenbaum, and my wife Chanie, as well, for both proofreading and editing the manuscript. My daughters Nechama Rivka and Malkie assisted in the typing.

My major debt of gratitude is, of course, reserved for my dear wife Chanie, truly the greatest gift G-d has granted me. Her patience, support, total devotion, and extraordinary kindness, both to our family and to others, leave me in awe. May we be deserving of having all of our *tefillos* answered and merit much *nachas* from all of our dear children.

ביעור חמץ ❖ Biur Chametz

Search for Chometz

(The numbers in parentheses refer to the chapter and halacha in Shulchan Aruch Orach Chaim. The numbers in brackets refer to the Mishna Berura.)

• The *bracha* is recited before beginning the *bedikas chametz*. If one begins the search without saying the *bracha*, it can still be said at any time during the *bedikah*. However, once the *bedikah* has been completed, no *bracha* should be recited (432:1). Some authorities say that if one forgets to recite the blessing, it may be said the next morning before burning the chametz (ibid.,[4]).

• One should not speak after reciting the *bracha* until the search for chametz begins. If one does speak, as long as the interruption concerns the search, the *bracha* need not be repeated; otherwise, the *bracha* must be repeated (ibid.,[6]).

• If possible, one should not interrupt the *bedikah* with

❖ **The Definition of Freedom**

The prohibition of chametz on Pesach is unique. With no other food does the Torah prohibit *both* its consumption, *and* having it in one's possession; one also may not derive from it any physical benefit or financial remuneration. Why is the Torah so stringent with this proscription?

It is generally assumed that the prohibition of chametz is linked to the mitzvah of eating matza, because the dough did not have time to rise when the Jews left Egypt. This conclusion, however, is problematic. First, the ban on chametz receives very little mention at the Seder. If the prohibition of chametz were linked to the eating of matza, it would likely receive greater attention. Second, it seems illogical for the Torah to be more stringent regarding the prohibition of chametz, which commemorates only what the Jews *did not* eat, than it is with matza, which commemorates what they *did* eat — especially since the prohibition against chametz commences half a day before Pesach begins. What, then, is the reason for the Torah's strict interdiction?

Perhaps the ban on chametz

matters that do not pertain to it, in order to pay serious attention to searching for chametz (ibid.).

Before the search, we light a candle and say the following blessing.

בָּרוּךְ אַתָּה יְיָ אֱלֹהֵינוּ מֶלֶךְ הָעוֹלָם, אֲשֶׁר קִדְּשָׁנוּ בְּמִצְוֹתָיו, וְצִוָּנוּ עַל בִּיעוּר חָמֵץ.

Blessed are You G-d, our Lord, king of the world, Who has commanded us on the burning of chametz.

• After the *bedikah* is completed, any chametz that was found or that will be eaten the next morning should be put in a secure place to prevent its becoming lost or scattered (434:2).

• כל חמירא should be recited immediately after the *bedikah* to nullify any undetected chametz. This is referred to as *bitul chametz*. Although a somewhat different version of the *bitul* is recited the next morning after the burning of the chametz, it is nonetheless recited at night after the search for chametz, as a precautionary measure, in case it is forgotten the next day (ibid.,[11]).

---

has nothing to do with the circumstances of the actual Exodus itself, as much as with the general concept of freedom from slavery. In order to celebrate freedom on Pesach, we must first understand what freedom is, and why it deserves celebration. The prohibition of chametz facilitates this understanding.

Slavery is not limited to subservience to another human being. A prisoner who refuses to submit to a captor's demands, despite threats of torture and persecution, is less a slave than a weak-willed person, who cannot control the desire for, say, some physical pleasure. The prisoner may be enslaved in body, but has an independent spirit. The other individual, however, although free to move about and make choices, cannot appreciate freedom, due to a lack of self-discipline.

Rav Noach Weinberg, Dean of Yeshiva Aish HaTorah in Jerusalem, relates an incident con-

• In order for the nullification of unknown chametz to take effect, one must understand the meaning of כל חמירא. It must therefore be spoken in a language that one understands, as it is a legal declaration, not a prayer (434:2).

After the search is over, we make the following declaration:

כָּל חֲמִירָא וַחֲמִיעָא דְּאִיכָּא בִרְשׁוּתִי דְּלָא
חֲמִתֵּיהּ וּדְלָא בְּעַרְתֵּיהּ וּדְלָא יְדַעְנָא לֵהּ
לִבָּטֵל וְלֶהֱוֵי הֶפְקֵר כְּעַפְרָא דְּאַרְעָא.

All bread and leaven that is in my possession, that I have or have not seen, that I have or have not destroyed, shall be nullified, and shall be public like the dust of the earth.

• The following morning, the *bitul* must be made before the sixth hour. After that time, according to the Torah, the chametz is no longer one's own, and the nullification cannot take effect.

cerning a young man who stumbled into the Yeshiva and attended classes for a couple of days. When he was ready to leave, the young man bade Rav Weinberg good-bye. He said that he had really appreciated the classes and found them to be very stimulating. The rabbi asked him if he would consider staying a little longer. The young man replied that he could not. He had a ticket for a flight back to the States the next day, and his family was waiting for him.

Rav Weinberg said, "Steve, you know I can't stop you from going. But at least be honest with yourself. Don't say you *can't* stay. If you wanted to, you could change your flight to one leaving at a later date. Maybe it would cost you a hundred dollars, no more. You could call your family and say you need to stay a little longer than planned. In all likelihood, they would understand. So it is possible for you to stay. If you don't *want* to stay, say you don't *want* to stay – not that you *can't* stay."

Steve understood what the rabbi was getting at, but still was unwilling to change his plans. "O.K., Rabbi. It's not that I *can't* stay. I don't *want* to stay."

"But Steve," Rav Weinberg con-

• The chametz must be burned before reciting כל חמירא in order to fulfill the mitzvah of burning the chametz with one's own chametz. Once the *bitul* has been recited, the chametz saved for burning is no longer considered one's own (434:2,[12]).

• The *bitul* recited in the morning, following the burning of chametz, differs from the *bitul* recited the previous evening after the *bedikah*. Whereas the evening *bitul* nullifies only undetected chametz, the morning *bitul* includes **all** chametz: both the known chametz– chametz found during the *bedikah* and any chametz saved for the morning meal that was not eaten–and the unknown chametz – chametz not found during the *bedikah* and missed during the preparatory cleaning for Pesach (434:3).

---

tinued, "You admit how stimulating you found the classes. You really *do* want to stay. Say, rather, that you don't *feel* like staying!"

Steve smiled. "All right, Rabbi. I really do *want* to stay, but I don't *feel* like staying!"

"Ah, Steve," the rabbi concluded, "When was the last time you *felt* like getting out of bed early on a cold morning? Every one of us would rather stay under the nice warm blanket. And when was the last time you *felt* like taking an exam in school? We don't do these things because we *feel* like doing them. We do them because we want to succeed in life, and that's the only way we are going to succeed. Let me tell you an important principle in life. Never do what you *feel* like doing. Do what you really *want* to do!"

True freedom is to do what one *wants* to do, not just what one *feels* like doing. The purpose of the redemption from Egypt was not merely to free the Jewish people from their slave masters. It was also to give them complete freedom to choose what would be good for them – that is, what they truly wanted.

Eating matza and refraining from eating chametz provide a metaphor for the understanding of freedom. Matza and chametz share the same ingredients; they look alike when the dough is first made. However, whereas the matza comes out of the oven looking much as it did when it went in, the chametz rises and grows into a loaf with an appealing appearance and fragrance. In truth, they are one and the same. Yet the chametz stimulates the desire for something

After the chametz is destroyed, we make the following declaration:

כָּל חֲמִירָא וַחֲמִיעָא דְּאִיכָּא בִרְשׁוּתִי,
דַּחֲזִתֵיהּ וּדְלָא חֲזִתֵהּ דַּחֲמִתֵּהּ וּדְלָא חֲמִתֵּהּ,
דְּבִעַרְתֵּיהּ וּדְלָא בִעַרְתֵּהּ, לִבָּטֵל וְלֶהֱוֵי הֶפְקֵר
כְּעַפְרָא דְאַרְעָא.

All bread and leaven that is in my possession, that I have or have not seen, that I have or have not destroyed, shall be nullified, and shall be public like the dust of the earth.

that is perhaps more than what it is, and that is greater than the sum of its parts. Our desire for the loaf of bread comes from what we perceive and *feel*, not from what we *want* or need. We can say, therefore, that matza represents freedom – what the person really wants to do; chametz represents what the person feels like doing, against his better judgment – in other words, slavery.

This may be why the Torah is so emphatic about forbidding any contact whatsoever with chametz. In order to appreciate freedom, it is necessary to distinguish between what is only fanciful desire and what is real. The Torah prohibits chametz half a day before Pesach, in order to give the Jew a period of separation, a time when he can enter the Yom Tov of Freedom, while exercising his free will and making a choice to do what he really wants to do.

❖ The Constraints of Freedom

Another lesson regarding the meaning of freedom may be gleaned from the prohibition of chametz. Freedom requires vigilance and order. There is always the potential for freedom to erode and erupt into chaos. The most independent person must live a structured life to keep from becoming unruly and wild.

The difference between chametz and matza is this structure. Matza is guarded carefully from the moment the grain is harvested until the time baking is completed. Throughout the entire baking process, it is never unguarded, even for a moment. This vigilance represents a proper attitude towards freedom. But with chametz, the reverse is true. The dough is deliberately left to rise without human assistance, and it spreads amorphously. Again, it is made of the same ingredients as

Some include the following prayer while the chametz is burned:

יְהִי **רָצוֹן** מִלְפָנֶיךָ, יְיָ אֱלֹהֵינוּ וֵאלֹהֵי אֲבוֹתֵינוּ
כְּשֵׁם שֶׁאֲנִי מְבַעֵר הֶחָמֵץ מִבֵּיתִי וּמֵרְשׁוּתִי כַּךְ
יְהוָֹה אֱלֹהֵינוּ וֵאלֹהֵי אֲבוֹתֵינוּ תְּבַעֵר כָּל
הַחִיצוֹנִים וְאֶת רוּחַ הַטֻּמְאָה תְּבַעֵר מִן הָאָרֶץ,
וְאֶת יִצְרֵנוּ הָרַע תַּעֲבִירֵהוּ מֵאִתָּנוּ, וְתִתֶּן לָנוּ
לֵב בָּשָׂר לְעָבְדֶךָ בֶּאֱמֶת, וְכָל הַסִטְרָא אַחֲרָא
וְכָל הָרִשְׁעָה כֻּלָּהּ כְּעָשָׁן תִּכְלֶה וְתַעֲבִיר
מֶמְשֶׁלֶת זָדוֹן מִן הָאָרֶץ וְכָל הַמַּעֲיקִים לִשְׁכִינָה
תְּבַעֲרֵם בְּרוּחַ בַּעֵר וּבְרוּחַ מִשְׁפָּט כְּשֵׁם
שֶׁהֶעֱבַרְתָּ אֶת מִצְרַיִם וְאֶת אֱלֹהֵיהֶם בַּיָּמִים
הָהֵם וּבִזְמַן הַזֶּה, אָמֵן.

May it be Your will, O G-d my Lord and Lord of my fathers, that just as I have removed all leaven from my house and property, so may You destroy all evil forces and remove the spirit of wickedness from Your world. May You wipe out all our evil desires and grant us a pure heart. May all that is against You, all that prevents good, and all forces of evil, vanish like smoke, and may You remove all sin from the earth. May all the evil thoughts that keep us far from You be taken away in a spirit of destruction and judgment, just as You destroyed the Egyptians and their idols a long time ago at this season. Amen!

the matza, but it represents an unfettered freedom that results in chaos.

The Torah therefore prohibits any benefit from chametz – to help prepare the Jews before Pesach, the Holiday of Freedom, with the knowledge that the proper use of this "newfound" gift requires vigilance, discipline, and order.

עירוב תבשילין ❧ Eruv Tavshilin

*When either day of Yom Tov falls on a Friday, an Eruv Tavshilin
should be made before Yom Tov in order to allow cooking and
other preparations on Friday for the Shabbos meals.*

*A piece of matza and a piece of cooked food, such as meat or fish,
should be put aside, indicating that with this the preparation for
Shabbos has begun. This is called Eruv Tavshilin, or Blending of
the Cookings.*

The foods should be lifted, and the following is said:

בָּרוּךְ אַתָּה יְיָ, אֱלֹהֵינוּ מֶלֶךְ הָעוֹלָם, אֲשֶׁר
קִדְּשָׁנוּ בְּמִצְוֹתָיו, וְצִוָּנוּ עַל מִצְוַת עֵירוּב:

בְּדֵין עֵירוּבָא יְהֵא שָׁרֵא לָנָא לַאֲפוּיֵי
וּלְבַשּׁוּלֵי וּלְאַטְמוּנֵי וּלְאַדְלוּקֵי שְׁרָגָא
וּלְתַקָּנָא וּלְמֶעְבַּד כָּל צָרְכָנָא מִיּוֹמָא טָבָא
לְשַׁבַּתָּא לָנָא וּלְכָל יִשְׂרָאֵל הַדָּרִים בָּעִיר
הַזֹּאת:

Blessed are You, G-d our Lord, King of the
world, who has made us holy with His commandments and instructed us to keep the Laws
of Eruv.

With this Eruv, we shall be allowed to bake,
cook, roast, keep food warm, light a fire, and do
all that is necessary for the Shabbos, on this
coming holiday. This goes for us and for every
other Jew living in this city.

סדר הדלקת הנר ❧ Candlelighting

- As on every Shabbos and festival, it is customary for the woman of the house to light at least two candles.

- On the second night of Pesach, one should be careful to light the candles from a pre-existing flame. One may not strike a match on Yom Tov (502:1,[4]). The candles on the second night may not be lit until nightfall (Introduction to Perisha, Yorah Deah).

- When Pesach falls on Motzei Shabbos, the candles may not be lit until nightfall. Before lighting the candles, one should say:

בָּרוּךְ הַמַּבְדִיל בֵּין קֹדֶשׁ לְקֹדֶשׁ:

"Blessed is He who divides between holy and holy" (299:10,[36])

- After lighting the candles, the following bracha is said. When the holiday falls on Friday evening, the words in parentheses are added.

בָּרוּךְ אַתָּה יְיָ, אֱלֹהֵינוּ מֶלֶךְ הָעוֹלָם, אֲשֶׁר קִדְּשָׁנוּ בְּמִצְוֹתָיו, וְצִוָּנוּ לְהַדְלִיק נֵר שֶׁל (שַׁבָּת וְ) שֶׁל יוֹם טוֹב.

בָּרוּךְ אַתָּה יְיָ, אֱלֹהֵינוּ מֶלֶךְ הָעוֹלָם, שֶׁהֶחֱיָנוּ וְקִיְּמָנוּ וְהִגִּיעָנוּ לַזְּמַן הַזֶּה.

Blessed are You, G-d our Lord, King of the world, who has made us holy with His commandments, and commanded us to light the candles (for Shabbos and) for the Festival.

Blessed are You, G-d our Lord, King of the world, who has granted us life, kept us, and let us reach this season.

יְהִי **רָצוֹן** מִלְּפָנֶיךָ, יְיָ אֱלֹהֵינוּ וֵאלֹהֵי אֲבוֹתֵינוּ, שֶׁיִּבָּנֶה בֵּית הַמִּקְדָּשׁ בִּמְהֵרָה בְיָמֵינוּ, וְתֵן חֶלְקֵנוּ בְּתוֹרָתֶךָ, וְשָׁם נַעֲבָדְךָ בְּיִרְאָה, כִּימֵי עוֹלָם וּכְשָׁנִים קַדְמוֹנִיּוֹת: וְעָרְבָה לַיְיָ מִנְחַת יְהוּדָה וִירוּשָׁלָיְם, כִּימֵי עוֹלָם וּכְשָׁנִים קַדְמוֹנִיּוֹת:

יְהִי **רָצוֹן** מִלְּפָנֶיךָ, יְיָ אֱלֹהַי וֵאלֹהֵי אֲבוֹתַי, שֶׁתְּחוֹנֵן אוֹתִי [וְאֶת־אִישִׁי, וְאֶת־בָּנַי, וְאֶת בְּנוֹתַי, וְאֶת־אָבִי, וְאֶת־אִמִּי] וְאֶת־כָּל־קְרוֹבַי; וְתִתֶּן לָנוּ וּלְכָל יִשְׂרָאֵל חַיִּים טוֹבִים וַאֲרוּכִים; וְתִזְכְּרֵנוּ בְּזִכְרוֹן טוֹבָה וּבְרָכָה; וְתִפְקְדֵנוּ בִּפְקֻדַּת יְשׁוּעָה וְרַחֲמִים; וּתְבָרְכֵנוּ בְּרָכוֹת גְּדוֹלוֹת; וְתַשְׁלִים בָּתֵּינוּ; וְתַשְׁכֵּן שְׁכִינָתְךָ בֵּינֵינוּ. וְזַכֵּנִי לְגַדֵּל בָּנִים וּבְנֵי בָנִים חֲכָמִים וּנְבוֹנִים, אוֹהֲבֵי יְיָ, יִרְאֵי אֱלֹהִים, אַנְשֵׁי אֱמֶת, זֶרַע קֹדֶשׁ, בַּיְיָ דְּבֵקִים, וּמְאִירִים אֶת הָעוֹלָם בַּתּוֹרָה וּבְמַעֲשִׂים טוֹבִים, וּבְכָל מְלֶאכֶת עֲבוֹדַת הַבּוֹרֵא. אָנָּא שְׁמַע אֶת תְּחִנָּתִי בָּעֵת הַזֹּאת, בִּזְכוּת שָׂרָה וְרִבְקָה וְרָחֵל וְלֵאָה אִמּוֹתֵינוּ, וְהָאֵר נֵרֵנוּ שֶׁלֹּא יִכְבֶּה לְעוֹלָם וָעֶד, וְהָאֵר פָּנֶיךָ וְנִוָּשֵׁעָה. אָמֵן.

The Seder/ סדר ליל פסח

קַדֵּשׁ. וּרְחַץ. כַּרְפַּס. יַחַץ. מַגִּיד. רָחְצָה.
מוֹצִיא. מַצָּה. מָרוֹר. כּוֹרֵךְ. שֻׁלְחָן עוֹרֵךְ. צָפוּן.
בָּרֵךְ. הַלֵּל. נִרְצָה.

Seder Preparations

• The table should be set before nightfall, so the Seder may begin promptly (472:1).

• The Seder table should be set with one's most elegant utensils and dishes as a way of portraying freedom and royalty (472:2,[6]).

• The *Ke'ara,* or Seder plate, is placed before the leader (473:4). The plate consists of:

❖ The Essence of Order

The Pesach meal is called the Seder, meaning "order," because fifteen steps are followed throughout the evening. Although some of these steps are mitzvos unique to Pesach night, many of them – such as Kiddush, washing before the meal, and Hamotzi – are standard practice for the Shabbos and Yom Tov meals. Why, then, did the Rabbis find it necessary to give a special name to the Pesach table service? Furthermore, some families follow the custom of announcing each step before proceeding with that part of the Seder. Is there a connection between the order and the mitzvos themselves? Some explanation is necessary.

When we think of the Jews leaving Egypt, the image that likely comes to mind is one of a mass of humanity jostling forward to freedom. It is hard to conceive of any semblance of order, in a population escaping its pursuers. Yet the Rabbis paint quite a different picture: A nation moving forth with a sense of purpose, protected by the Clouds of Glory. Even in their flight from the Egyptians, the Jewish nation is described as being divided into twelve different tribes. They entered the split Sea in their respective columns.

The Torah relates that on the night of the Exodus – while the Plague of the Firstborn was taking its toll throughout Egypt– among the Jews, not one dog raised its voice (*Shemos* 11:7). This seeming-

(1) the *zeroa*, a roasted shankbone or some other roasted piece of meat, to recall the *Korbon Pesach*, the Pesach offering;

(2) the *beitzah*, a roasted egg, to recall the *Korbon Chagiga*, the holiday offering brought in the Temple on each holiday;

(3) the *marror*, or bitter herbs (usually horseradish and/or Romaine lettuce), to recall the bitter slavery in Egypt;

(4) the *charoses*, a mixture of apples, nuts, cinnamon and wine, which represents the mortar the Jews were forced to make in Egypt; and

ly insignificant detail is important, because dogs ordinarily bark in agitation or warning, when their customary environment is upset. Although pandemonium broke out among the Egyptians, calm and order prevailed among the Jews. Because there was no break in the routine, even the dogs were not disturbed and hence did not bark. The Jewish nation would receive the Torah in just a few weeks. It was crucial that the Jews leaving Egypt not give the appearance of a band of wild fugitives. The people themselves had to feel they were on an important mission, not just escaping pandemonium.[3]

For this reason, whenever the nation traveled or camped in the desert, they did so in an organized manner, each tribe with its own location. Certain tribes were juxtaposed with others, and they could not change places. At Mount Sinai, too, the people had assigned areas where they could stand, and boundaries they could not cross. Rav Shlomo Wolbe suggests that *each individual* had to stand in a designated place at Mount Sinai

---

3. In a similar vein, Rav Elya Meir Bloch once commented that when Yonasan, King Shaul's son, arranged to signal David to indicate whether David was in danger, Yonasan said, "If I tell the lad, 'Behold, the arrows are beyond you,' then go, because G-d has sent you." Why did Yonasan say "Go," instead of the more grammatically correct, "Flee"? Rav Bloch explained that a person who recognizes G-d's Divine Providence knows that even when escaping from danger, one is on a guided mission and not just in flight.

(5) the *karpas*, the vegetable that is dipped in salt water, which represents the tears and suffering in Egypt.

Most people place the *marror* used for *Korech* separately on the plate. This *marror* is often referred to as *chazeres*. Three matzos are also placed before the leader, one on top of each other.

• If horseradish root is used for *marror*, it should be grated before the Seder. Different customs determine whether or not the grated horseradish may be left uncovered to weaken its potency (473:5,[36]).

• If Romaine lettuce is used for the *marror*, each stalk must be checked carefully for insect infestation (ibid.,[42]).

• The obligation to eat *marror* cannot be fulfilled with cooked, or otherwise prepared, *marror*. Accordingly, one may

---

(*Kuntres Yemei Haratzon*, Be'er Yaakov, 1973).

The Torah could be given only to a single nation, comprised of many separate tribes – each with its own place and with its own way of contributing to the common goal. Perhaps for this reason, as well, emphasis is placed on structure, when we celebrate the Exodus from Egypt. Even those mitzvos common to every Shabbos and Yom Tov table are arranged on Pesach evening in a new order – the Seder. Order was integral to the Exodus, and must remain integral to our everyday lives.

This orderliness also parallels the coherence demonstrated by G-d's actions during the Exodus. Every miracle and every plague took place in a precisely calculated manner. Each plague affected only the specific people for whom it was meant, to the degree intended. Recognition of this underlying precision and cohesion is necessary for a fuller appreciation of G-d's greatness. According to the Torah, it was this recognition that convinced Yisro to accept the G-d of Israel over the other gods he had worshipped (*Shemos* 18:11).

We may now understand another curious point. The Haggadah later quotes Rabbi Yehuda as designating an acronym, *Detzach, Adash, and BeAchav*, as a mnemonic device for remembering the Ten Plagues. The commentaries question the necessity of this acronym. What was Rabbi Yehuda adding that we did not already know? Perhaps Rabbi Yehuda was trying to convey the idea of order, of a pattern to the punishments

not soak the lettuce in salt water, even for a short time, or in plain water for twenty-four hours or longer (ibid.,[38]). For this reason, commercially prepared horseradish may not be used.

• It is customary for married men to wear a *kittel*, a white robe, at the Seder.

afflicted on the Egyptians, when he classified the plagues in three distinct categories. Although Rabbi Yehuda does not explain what the categories[4] represent, he clearly understood that G-d had ordained a distinctly defined order, in accordance with an organized plan.

The significance of order may also underlie two other puzzling parts of the Haggadah. The commentators question the connection of the last two songs of the Seder – *Echad Me Yodaia*, "Who knows One?" and *Chad Gadya*, "One little kid" – with the rest of the Haggadah (see *Seder HeAruch*, ch.160). Given a cursory glance, *Echad Me Yodaia* seems merely to explain the religious meaning of the first thirteen numbers (that is "1,2,3, etc."). *Chad Gadya*, too, although obviously a metaphor for something deeper, is ostensibly a children's tale of successive tri-

umphs and losses. What is the connection between these two songs and the Exodus?

Perhaps, through the songs, the Haggadah once again emphasizes the need for order – a message that will remain with us long after the Seder is over. *Echad Me Yodaia* relates the amazing symmetry and perfection of every event in Jewish history, as well as the perfection of Nature itself. The number of matriarchs, the days of the week, the months of gestation – each is accounted for in the overall scheme of things. *Chad Gadya* shows the complex interrelationships among seemingly unrelated occurrences. The isolated incident of a cat's eating a little goat is a link in a chain of events that lead to the annihilation of death. Every event and component of existence is but a detail in the great master plan that encompasses

---

4. See Ritva who explains that the first three plagues proved the existence of G-d, the second three proved His constant involvement with nature, and the third group proved the validity of prophecy. Rav S. R. Hirsch explains the three categories as three stages of punishment for the Egyptians: The first group made the Egyptians experience a sense of insecurity in their land; the second made them experience feelings of submission; and the third brought them actual affliction.

Kadesh

• *Kiddush* must be said after nightfall and not during twilight (472:1).

• The leader of the household should preferably have somebody else pour the wine for him as a symbol of freedom (473:1).

• The *Kiddush* cup must hold at least a *revi'is* (between 3.3 and 4 fluid ounces) (472:9). The cup should be filled to capacity (271:10). Although the whole cup should preferably be drunk, if most of a *revi'is* is drunk, the mitzvah is fulfilled (472:9, [33]).

• The majority of the *revi'is* must be drunk within a few minutes – if possible, in two sips. If longer than nine minutes elapses, the cup must be drunk again, with a new bracha (472:9,[34]).

• Red grape wine is preferable for the Four Cups. However, if one is unable to drink straight wine, it may be diluted, or grape juice may be substituted (472:10,[37]). A Rav should be consulted regarding the ratio and other details for diluting the wine.

• If the Seder falls on Motzei Shabbos, *Havdala* is said during the Seder *Kiddush*. If one forgets to say *Havdala*, it must be said on one of the other cups of wine drunk during the Seder. If *Havdala* is not remembered until the meal, it should be said immediately on a cup of wine, without making a *bracha* on the wine. If it was not remembered until after finishing the fourth cup, *Havdala* should be made on a fifth cup **with** a *bracha* (473:1,[4]).

• One should recline on his left side while drinking the wine. However, if one forgets to recline while drinking the wine, it need not be drunk again (472:7,[21]).

1. קַדֵשׁ /Kadesh

הֲרֵינִי רוֹצֶה לְקַיֵּם מִצְוַת כּוֹס רִאשׁוֹן שֶׁל אַרְבַּע כּוֹסוֹת לְשֵׁם יִחוּד קוּדְשָׁא בְּרִיךְ הוּא וּשְׁכִינְתֵּיהּ עַל יְדֵי הַהוּא טָמִיר וְנֶעֱלָם בְּשֵׁם כָּל יִשְׂרָאֵל. וִיהִי נוֹעַם אֲדֹנָי אֱלֹהֵינוּ עָלֵינוּ וּמַעֲשֵׂה יָדֵינוּ כּוֹנְנָה עָלֵינוּ, וּמַעֲשֵׂה יָדֵינוּ כּוֹנְנֵהוּ.

On Friday night, one should hold the cup of wine in his right hand, and say:

(וַיְהִי עֶרֶב וַיְהִי בוֹקֶר)

יוֹם הַשִּׁשִּׁי, וַיְכֻלּוּ הַשָּׁמַיִם וְהָאָרֶץ וְכָל צְבָאָם: וַיְכַל אֱלֹהִים בַּיּוֹם הַשְּׁבִיעִי מְלַאכְתּוֹ אֲשֶׁר עָשָׂה, וַיִּשְׁבֹּת בַּיּוֹם הַשְּׁבִיעִי מִכָּל מְלַאכְתּוֹ אֲשֶׁר עָשָׂה: וַיְבָרֶךְ אֱלֹהִים אֶת יוֹם הַשְּׁבִיעִי וַיְקַדֵּשׁ אֹתוֹ, כִּי בוֹ שָׁבַת מִכָּל מְלַאכְתּוֹ אֲשֶׁר בָּרָא אֱלֹהִים לַעֲשׂוֹת:

the whole of Creation.

Both these poems, then, serve to underscore the theme of orderliness that recurs throughout the Haggadah. One of the aims of the Seder night is to instill an awareness of the care that G-d and the Jewish people displayed during the Exodus, and then to stimulate the Seder participants to imitate this precision in their day-to-day lives.

קַדֵשׁ / KADESH

❖ The Source of Belief

This is the first of the four cups of wine that are drunk during the Seder. The Jerusalem Talmud

(*Pesachim* 10:1) states that the four cups correspond to the four expressions of redemption in the Torah:

G-d spoke to Moshe... I am Hashem... Say to the Children of Israel: 'I shall take you out from under the burdens of Egypt; I shall save you from their service; I shall redeem you with an outstretched arm and with great judgments. I shall take you to Me for a nation and I shall be a G-d to you; and you shall know that I am Hashem your G-d, Who has taken you out from under the burdens of Egypt" (*Shemos 6:6*).

1. **Kadesh/** Recite Kiddush

I am ready and prepared to keep the commandment of drinking the first of the four cups of wine, for the sake of the One G-d and His presence, may it be counted as done in the name of all of Israel.

On Friday night, one should hold the cup of wine in his right hand, and say:

It was evening, and it was morning –

The sixth day! Finished were the heaven and earth and all that was in them. On the seventh day G-d had finished all the work He had done, and on the seventh day He rested from all the work He had done. G-d blessed the seventh day and made it holy, for He then rested from all His work, which G-d created to make.

Each of these expressions represents another, progressively higher, stage of redemption. With each cup we drink we should try to appreciate the advantages of the corresponding stage of redemption.

Ramban (loc. cit.) explains the different stages of redemption. In the first stage, the Children of Israel were freed from the oppression, but they remained enslaved to the Egyptians. In the second stage, they were freed from slavery, although they remained strangers in Egypt. The third stage was heralded by their departure from Egypt, and the fourth, when

G-d took the nation as His own at Mount Sinai.

The above passages, however, seem to follow a circular reasoning: G-d will take the Jews out of Egypt, in order that they should know that He took them out of Egypt. What does this mean? *Rambam* (*Yesodei HaTorah* 8:1) writes that the belief in Moshe and his prophecy did not result from the miracles that Moshe performed when the Jews left Egypt. A belief grounded solely in miracles is shallow: Doubts will always accompany it. The real source of the Jews' belief in Moshe was the Divine Revelation at Sinai: There, every

On Friday night continue with the following, including all the
words in parentheses.
On weekdays nights, begin here, disregarding the words in
parentheses.

סַבְרִי מָרָנָן וְרַבָּנָן וְרַבּוֹתַי:

בָּרוּךְ אַתָּה יְיָ, אֱלֹהֵינוּ מֶלֶךְ הָעוֹלָם,
בּוֹרֵא פְּרִי הַגָּפֶן.

בָּרוּךְ אַתָּה יְיָ, אֱלֹהֵינוּ מֶלֶךְ הָעוֹלָם, אֲשֶׁר
בָּחַר בָּנוּ מִכָּל עָם וְרוֹמְמָנוּ מִכָּל לָשׁוֹן וְקִדְּשָׁנוּ
בְּמִצְוֹתָיו, וַתִּתֶּן לָנוּ יְיָ אֱלֹהֵינוּ בְּאַהֲבָה (שַׁבָּתוֹת
לִמְנוּחָה וּ) מוֹעֲדִים לְשִׂמְחָה, חַגִּים וּזְמַנִּים לְשָׂשׂוֹן,
(אֶת יוֹם הַשַּׁבָּת הַזֶּה וְ) אֶת יוֹם חַג הַמַּצוֹת הַזֶּה, זְמַן
חֵרוּתֵנוּ, (בְּאַהֲבָה) מִקְרָא קֹדֶשׁ, זֵכֶר לִיצִיאַת
מִצְרָיִם. כִּי בָנוּ בָחַרְתָּ וְאוֹתָנוּ קִדַּשְׁתָּ מִכָּל
הָעַמִּים, (וְשַׁבָּת) וּמוֹעֲדֵי קָדְשֶׁךָ (בְּאַהֲבָה וּבְרָצוֹן)
בְּשִׂמְחָה וּבְשָׂשׂוֹן הִנְחַלְתָּנוּ. בָּרוּךְ אַתָּה יְיָ,
מְקַדֵּשׁ (הַשַּׁבָּת וְ) יִשְׂרָאֵל וְהַזְּמַנִּים.

Jew experienced G-d's word and saw that Moshe was acting solely as an envoy of G-d.

This, then, is the meaning of the four expressions of redemption: "I will take you out of Egypt and save you and redeem you" – but that will not be enough to make you believe beyond a doubt, that I was the One Who sent Moshe. However, when "I take you to me for a nation" – through the experience of Divine Revelation at Mount Sinai – then you will know, for sure, that G-d is indeed the One Who took you out of Egypt.

❖ **The Significance of Being Chosen**

ברוך... אשר בחר בנו מכל עם
Blessed are You. . . Who chose us from every nation. . . and sanctified us with His commandments

On Friday night continue with the following, including all the words in parentheses.
On weekdays nights, begin here, disregarding the words in parentheses.

Blessed are You, G-d our Lord, King of the world,Creator of the fruit of the grapevine.

Blessed are You, G-d our Lord, King of the world, who chose us from every nation, raised us over every language, and sanctified us with His commandments. You gave us, G-d our Lord, with love, (Sabbaths for rest,) festivals for happiness, holidays and seasons for joy; (this Sabbath day, and) this feast day of Matzos, the time of our freedom, (with love,) a holy assembly, recalling the Exodus from Egypt. For it is us You have chosen, and it is us You have made holy, above all nations, and Your holy (Sabbath and) festivals with happiness and joy You granted us. Blessed are You G-d, Sanctifier of (the Sabbath,) Israel, and the seasons.

The Jewish Nation enjoys a special relationship with G-d, as His chosen people. However, this concept of chosenness is often misunderstood. Some actually think of it as a form of genetic superiority – that Jews are somehow intrinsically superior to other people. This supposition is racist; it differs little from the Aryan claim of being a "master race." Although Jewishness is passed down through a Jewish mother, and in that sense it is genetic, biological inheritance does not mean biological superiority.

G-d chose the Jewish people to follow His Torah, live a sanctified existence, and become a role model and teacher to the rest of society. Anyone who desires may join the Jewish people, live by this standard, and ultimately be rewarded for doing so. This is what it means to be chosen. It is not the people who are superior: It is the mission. When Jews do not live up to what is expected of

בָּרוּךְ אַתָּה יְיָ, אֱלֹהֵינוּ מֶלֶךְ הָעוֹלָם, שֶׁהֶחֱיָנוּ
וְקִיְּמָנוּ וְהִגִּיעָנוּ לַזְּמַן הַזֶּה:

On Saturday night, the following is substituted.

סַבְרִי מָרָנָן וְרַבָּנָן וְרַבּוֹתַי:

בָּרוּךְ אַתָּה יְיָ, אֱלֹהֵינוּ מֶלֶךְ הָעוֹלָם,
בּוֹרֵא פְּרִי הַגָּפֶן.

בָּרוּךְ אַתָּה יְיָ, אֱלֹהֵינוּ מֶלֶךְ הָעוֹלָם, אֲשֶׁר בָּחַר
בָּנוּ מִכָּל עָם וְרוֹמְמָנוּ מִכָּל לָשׁוֹן וְקִדְּשָׁנוּ
בְּמִצְוֹתָיו, וַתִּתֶּן לָנוּ יְיָ אֱלֹהֵינוּ בְּאַהֲבָה מוֹעֲדִים
לְשִׂמְחָה, חַגִּים וּזְמַנִּים לְשָׂשׂוֹן, אֶת יוֹם חַג
הַמַּצּוֹת הַזֶּה, זְמַן חֵרוּתֵנוּ, מִקְרָא קֹדֶשׁ, זֵכֶר
לִיצִיאַת מִצְרָיִם. כִּי בָנוּ בָחַרְתָּ וְאוֹתָנוּ קִדַּשְׁתָּ
מִכָּל הָעַמִּים, וּמוֹעֲדֵי קָדְשֶׁךָ בְּשִׂמְחָה וּבְשָׂשׂוֹן
הִנְחַלְתָּנוּ. בָּרוּךְ אַתָּה יְיָ, מְקַדֵּשׁ יִשְׂרָאֵל וְהַזְּמַנִּים

them, they have no right to take pride in their status as a chosen people. Only when we understand the responsibilities of being chosen, and take our responsibilities seriously, are we justified in taking pride in our status.

❖ Appreciating Being Chosen

אשר בחר בנו מכל עם

. . . Who chose us from every nation, . . .

Imagine someone who has bought a ticket in the state lottery.

The prize of $8 million seems quite tempting, but this person knows that statistically the chance of winning is very small. Were the person to win, the sheer joy of being chosen from millions of others would be indescribable.

There are approximately six billion people in the world. Fewer than fifteen million are Jews. The chance of a child's being born Jewish, on any given day, is quite slim. The chance of being born a Jew who appreciates what it means to be a Jew

Blessed are You, G-d our Lord, King of the world, who has granted us life, kept us, and let us reach this season.

On Saturday night the following is substituted.

Blessed are You, G-d our Lord, King of the world, Creator of the fruit of the grapevine.

Blessed are You, G-d our Lord, King of the world, who chose us from every nation, raised us over every language, and sanctified us with His commandments. You gave us, G-d our Lord, with love, festivals of happiness, holidays and seasons for joy; this feast day of Matzos, the time of our freedom, a holy assembly, a commemoration of the exodus from Egypt. For it is us You have chosen, and it is us You have made holy, above all nations, and Your holy festivals, with happiness and joy, You granted us. Blessed are You G-d Sanctifier of Israel and the seasons.

are even slimmer – not much different from the chance of winning a lottery. The prize, however, is worth more than all the money in the world.

This is how we should appreciate what it means to be chosen from all the nations. A Jew should feel the exhilaration of winning a lottery, when he or she realizes the great fortune to be among those people selected to represent G-d before the rest of the world.

קדש ורחץ
KADESH U'RCHATZ

❖ **Pesach and G-d's Trust in Israel**

Some of the commentaries explain that Kiddush ("sanctification") represents channeling positive energy toward holiness. (Reb Aharon M'Koidnov: *see Slonimer Haggadah* and *HaSeder HeAruch*) U'Rchatz ("to wash") on the other hand, represents cleansing oneself

*One should then pass the cup of wine to his left hand, and
stretch forth his right hand toward the festival candles,
opening his fingers. One then says:*

בָּרוּךְ אַתָּה יְיָ, אֱלֹהֵינוּ מֶלֶךְ הָעוֹלָם, בּוֹרֵא מְאוֹרֵי
הָאֵשׁ:

[The cup is replaced in the right hand, and one continues:]

בָּרוּךְ אַתָּה יְיָ, אֱלֹהֵינוּ מֶלֶךְ הָעוֹלָם, הַמַּבְדִּיל
בֵּין קֹדֶשׁ לְחוֹל, בֵּין אוֹר לְחֹשֶׁךְ, בֵּין יִשְׂרָאֵל
לָעַמִּים, בֵּין יוֹם הַשְּׁבִיעִי לְשֵׁשֶׁת יְמֵי הַמַּעֲשֶׂה.
בֵּין קְדֻשַּׁת שַׁבָּת לִקְדֻשַּׁת יוֹם טוֹב הִבְדַּלְתָּ.
וְאֶת יוֹם הַשְּׁבִיעִי מִשֵּׁשֶׁת יְמֵי הַמַּעֲשֶׂה קִדַּשְׁתָּ.
הִבְדַּלְתָּ וְקִדַּשְׁתָּ אֶת עַמְּךָ יִשְׂרָאֵל בִּקְדֻשָּׁתֶךָ:
בָּרוּךְ אַתָּה יְיָ, הַמַּבְדִּיל בֵּין קֹדֶשׁ לְקֹדֶשׁ:]

בָּרוּךְ אַתָּה יְיָ, אֱלֹהֵינוּ מֶלֶךְ הָעוֹלָם, שֶׁהֶחֱיָנוּ
וְקִיְּמָנוּ וְהִגִּיעָנוּ לַזְּמַן הַזֶּה:

from sin. Generally speaking, a person must first clean away the soil of sin, before being able to make positive change. As King David states (*Tehillim* 34:15): סוּר מֵרָע וַעֲשֵׂה טוֹב: "Turn from evil and do good." Pesach, however, is an exception to this rule.

The Rabbis teach that there are fifty levels of spiritual ascent, and a corresponding fifty levels of descent. The Jews in Egypt sank to the forty-ninth level of spiritual degeneration. Had they spiritually deteriorated any further, they would have reached the nadir – a point from which they could never have been retrieved. For this reason, G-d took the nation out of Egypt "*b'chipazon*," in a great hurry. Had the Jews had to wait even a little longer, they might have been trapped at a point of no return.

This, then, is the essence of Pesach. In His great kindness, G-d was willing to overlook the inadequacies of the nation and take the

One should then pass the cup of wine to his left hand, and stretch forth his right hand toward the festival candles, opening his fingers. One then says:

Blessed are You, G-d our Lord, King of the world, Creator of the lights of the fire.

[The cup is replaced in the right hand, and one continues:]

Blessed are You, G-d our Lord, King of the world, who divides between holy and plain, between light and darkness, between Israel and the nations, and between the seventh day and the six work days. Between the holiness of the Sabbath and the holiness of a festival You divided, and You sanctified the seventh day above the six work days. You separated Your People Israel and made them holy with Your own holiness. Blessed are You G-d, who divides between holy and holy.

Blessed are You, G-d our Lord, King of the world, who has granted us life, kept us, and let us reach this season.

people out of bondage, *before* it was deserved. He trusted that if they experienced all the miracles of the Exodus, they would willingly accept the Torah. Salvation would be earned retroactively.

For this reason, on Pesach one can climb spiritual heights, even before cleaning off the stain of previous sins. The placing of Kadesh before U'Rchatz is symbolic of "sanctification" before "washing." Just as G-d made an allowance at the time of the Exodus, so, too, He continues to make this allowance on Pesach today.

This is the deeper reason why the holiday is called Pesach, or Passover. We have always been taught that the name recalls the great miracle of G-d's skipping over the Jewish homes in Egypt, sparing the Jews from the Plague of the Firstborn. It is unclear, however, why this miracle is emphasized more than the many other miracles of the Exodus. The importance of the passing over may be that it symbolizes G-d's willingness to "pass over" the people's deficiencies and take them out of Egypt— despite their not

2. **Urchatz/** Wash Hands

• The hands are washed in the same manner as before eating bread, pouring water from a cup twice on the right hand and then twice on the left. However, no *bracha* is made on this washing (158:4,[20]).

3. **Karpas/** The Celery

• Each person should take a small piece of vegetable (for example, celery, radish, potato or parsley) and dip it into salt water (473:6).

yet deserving redemption. Thus, the name "Pesach" expresses the central idea of the holiday.

We can now also understand another puzzling passage in the Torah. G-d tells Moshe to instruct the Jews to smear the blood of the Pesach offering on their doorposts. Moshe says to the elders of Israel, "G-d will pass through to smite Egypt, and He will see the blood that is on the lintel and the two doorposts; and G-d will pass over the entrance and He will not permit the destroyer to enter your homes . . . " (*Shemos* 12:23) The "destroyer" clearly does not refer to an angel: The Haggadah later explains that G-d Himself passed over the houses of the Jews, and that G-d Himself slew the Egyptian firstborn. The Torah may be saying that, through the blood on their doorposts, G-d

arranged a signal that permitted Him to skip over the deficiencies of the Jews and redeem them. He would not let them sink to the fiftieth level of spiritual impurity, which would have precluded their return. This would have ultimately destroyed them.

This kindness is expressed in other ways during the Seder, too. The *Shulchan Aruch* (472:16) indicates that the very first mitzvah performed at the Seder is the distribution of sweets and nuts to the children, to encourage them to ask questions. It seems a bit strange that the Rabbis found it necessary to use candy to stimulate discussion of the Exodus. Couldn't they have found something more appropriate to Pesach?

The issue here may not be the sweets so much as it is the timing.

- One should have in mind that the *bracha* on the vegetable also covers the *marror* that will be eaten later (ibid.,[55]).

- Although custom varies, generally we do not recline while eating *Karpas* (*Kol Dodi*).

בָּרוּךְ אַתָּה יהוה, אֱלֹהֵינוּ מֶלֶךְ הָעוֹלָם,
בּוֹרֵא פְּרִי הָאֲדָמָה:

Blessed are You, G-d our Lord, King of the world, Creator of the fruit of the soil.

Why are the sweets, which are always served as a dessert after the meal, now served before the child has eaten anything at all? This may be another allusion to the miracle of Pesach: G-d also began the redemption before the appropriate time. The distribution of sweets and nuts is an excellent means of illustrating the story of the Exodus.

כרפס / KARPAS

❖ The Relevance of Mixed Emotions

The Talmud (*Pesachim* 114a) explains the reason for dipping the vegetable in saltwater. Dipping is a privilege enjoyed by wealthy people. Thus it will usually arouse the curiosity of the children. Yet it still remains unclear, if indeed it is meant as an expression of luxury, why is the vegetable dipped in plain saltwater – hardly a liquid representing affluence.

But there is more to this dipping than a mere show of wealth. The freedom that is celebrated this evening is one that has come at a great price, through much suffering. The mitzvos of the Seder night express both the pain and difficulty of slavery and the joy and opulence of freedom. The Jew is entrusted with the unique responsibility of experiencing conflicting emotions – both joy and pain – at the same time. It is important that both these emotions be conveyed to the child, in order to ensure a proper appreciation of the freedom from Egypt. For this reason, the Rabbis suggested combining the dipping of luxury with the saltwater of slavery.

4. Yachatz/ Divide the matza

• The middle matza is taken and broken in two unequal pieces. The smaller piece is returned to its place between the two whole matzos. The larger piece is wrapped up and set aside, to be eaten later as the Afikoman (473:6). There is a widespread custom that the children steal the Afikoman and hide it until it is redeemed for a gift. The purpose of this custom is to encourage their involvement in the Seder.

5. Maggid/ Tell the Passover Story

• The matzos are lifted up while הא לחמא עניא is said to draw the participants' attention to them (ibid.).

הָא לַחְמָא עַנְיָא דִי אֲכָלוּ אַבְהָתָנָא בְּאַרְעָא דְמִצְרָיִם. כָּל דִכְפִין יֵיתֵי וְיֵכוֹל. כָּל דְצָרִיךְ יֵיתֵי וְיִפְסַח. הָשַׁתָּא הָכָא, לְשָׁנָה הַבָּאָה בְּאַרְעָא דְיִשְׂרָאֵל. הָשַׁתָּא עַבְדֵי, לְשָׁנָה הַבָּאָה בְּנֵי חוֹרִין:

• The matzos are removed and placed at the end of the table, to arouse the children's curiosity, after which the second cup is filled (473:6-7).

יחץ / YACHATZ

❖ True Trust

The commentaries explain that the matza is broken during the Seder, as a reminder that the matza is called "lechem oni," poor man's bread, in the Torah. (See *Mishnah Berurah* 473:57.) A poor person does not know where his next meal will come from. When he is able to procure some food, a little is eaten and the rest put away for later – in case no more food can be found for the next meal. Breaking the matza, and putting away the larger piece for later, is thus reminiscent of the poor person's conduct.

The *Sefas Emes* (Pesach 5637)

This is the poor man's bread that our fathers ate in the land of Egypt. All who are hungry, come and eat! All who are needy, come and celebrate Passover! This year we are here; next year may we be in the land of Israel! This year we are slaves; next year may we be free men!

sees, with the breaking of the matza and the saving of the greater part for later, an allusion to the future redemption of the Jews. The redemption from Egypt was a precursor to the final redemption of the Messianic Era. The exodus from Egypt was the first part of the redemptive process, that is, the smaller piece of matza. The delayed consumption of the larger piece of matza represents waiting for the future.

By combining these two interpretations, we can understand Yachatz a little better. Even a person who is enslaved and lives in abject poverty carries the dreams, hopes, and preparations for redemption in his or her heart. Even before we begin talking about the slavery in Egypt, we must show our faith in the final redemption. This is an important lesson for the Jew in exile. Despite all the difficulties the Jew encounters, he or she cannot become disillusioned. The Jew must continue to survive through, and by, clinging to the belief in the coming of the Mashiach.

מגיד / **MAGGID**

❖ **The Seder as a Thanksgiving Celebration**

כל דכפין ייתי וייכול
All who are hungry, come and eat!....

The commentaries question the placing of this statement at the beginning of Maggid. (See *Ma'asei Nissim, Birchas Hashir, et alia.*) If the intention were truly to invite the hungry, would it not have made more sense to make the invitation before the Seder actually began? Furthermore, why is this invitation emphasized more on Pesach than on Shabbos or Yom Tov?

The Vilna Gaon explains the significance of the recurrence of the number four throughout the Seder: four questions, four cups, four sons. Four people were obligated to bring the *Korban Todah*, the thanksgiving offering to G-d during the time of the Temple: one who was sick and had recovered; one who had crossed the sea; one who had traveled through the wilderness; and one who had been released from prison.

מַה נִּשְׁתַּנָּה הַלַּיְלָה הַזֶּה מִכָּל הַלֵּילוֹת.

The Gaon explains that when the Jewish people left Egypt, as a result of their experiences, every individual would have met the qualifications of the four persons: They had been released from slavery; healed from their beatings; crossed the Sea; and traveled through the wilderness. They were therefore obligated four times over to celebrate thanksgiving to G-d. The Seder serves as a form of thanksgiving offering. This, then, is the source of the obligation to drink the four cups of wine. Each one is a separate expression of thanksgiving.

We may add an insight from the Netziv (*Ha'emek Davar, Vayikra* 7:13) regarding the *Korban Todah*. The Torah requires forty loaves to be brought with this offering. The Netziv questions the need for so many loaves, especially since they must be eaten within a day and a night – it would be difficult to consume so much food in so short a time. He answers his own question, saying that a fitting demonstration of appreciation requires a public expression before friends. In the *Hallel*, King David says, "*L'cho ezbach zevach Todah. . . negdah na l'chol amo,*" "I will bring thanksgiving offerings to You before His whole nation." Thus it is that thanksgiving must be public. The Torah therefore required a large amount of food to be brought with the thanksgiving offering, and to be consumed in a short time span, to ensure that each person would invite friends to join in this public expression of gratitude.

We can now understand the need to make the invitation ("Let all who are hungry come and eat. . . .") *before* beginning Maggid. In Maggid, we express our appreciation to G-d for all the miracles of the Exodus. It is important to make this invitation before friends, not necessarily to invite anyone, but as a means of drawing attention to the need for a public forum, while expressing sincere appreciation to G-d.

השתא הכא לשנה הבאה בארעא דישראל

This year we are here; next year may we be in the land of Israel! This year we are slaves; next year may we be free men!

Even before discussing the exile in Egypt, we mention our hope and prayers for the final redemption. This may have nothing to do with the mitzvah of discussing the Exodus, but is nonetheless important. It mirrors the elements of hope and delayed redemption that underlie Yachatz.

One of the lessons to be

The Four Questions

Why is this night different from all other nights?

learned from the story of the Egyptian exile and the Exodus, is that we must cling to our belief and trust in the Mashiach in the midst of the trials and tribulations of the exile. Throughout the Egyptian exile, there were those who encouraged the nation and reminded them of G-d's promise to Avraham, made hundreds of years earlier, that his children would be redeemed from bondage. This prevented their falling into total despair, and helped lift their spirits. During the present exile, we also remember G-d's promise to the prophets regarding the Mashiach. This gives us the fortitude to face future difficulties.

❖ Teaching the Exodus

מה נשתנה הלילה הזה מכל הלילות

Why is this night different from all other nights?

On Pesach night we discuss the Exodus in a question-and-answer format. The interaction is more stimulating and more easily retained than a monologue would be. [5] The questions are asked by a child, and they preface the discus-

sion. Four questions are posed. The questions revolve around four practices specific to the Seder: eating matza; eating bitter herbs; dipping food twice; and reclining. Why are these behaviors supposed to capture the children's attention, when other practices are also unique to this night?

Moreover, why does the Haggadah indicate *which* questions the child should ask? The Talmud states (*Pesachim* 116a) that the *child* should ask these questions. Only when the child lacks understanding, should the father teach the child what to ask. Isn't that odd? How difficult would it be for the child to realize what is different about this night?

Perhaps the four questions are not just those of a curious child wanting an explanation of practices peculiar to this night. Rather, the Rabbis "planted" these four questions for the child to ask, in order to guide the discussion, so that ideas essential to understanding the exile and Exodus would be preeminent. We will try to explain some concepts alluded to in the four questions.

---

5. See Minchas Chinuch (21)

שֶׁבְּכָל הַלֵּילוֹת אָנוּ אוֹכְלִין חָמֵץ וּמַצָּה.
הַלַּיְלָה הַזֶּה כֻּלּוֹ מַצָּה:

שֶׁבְּכָל הַלֵּילוֹת אָנוּ אוֹכְלִין שְׁאָר יְרָקוֹת.
הַלַּיְלָה הַזֶּה מָרוֹר:

שֶׁבְּכָל הַלֵּילוֹת אֵין אָנוּ מַטְבִּילִין אֲפִילוּ פַּעַם
אֶחָת. הַלַּיְלָה הַזֶּה שְׁתֵּי פְּעָמִים:

The Necessity of Haste

שבכל הלילות אנו אוכלים
חמץ ומצה

On all other nights we eat chametz or matza

The first question concerns the obligation to eat matza, coupled with the prohibition against eating chametz. Although the mitzvah of eating matza can be explained as commemorative of the hurried nature of the Exodus, this does not explain the prohibition of chametz. Why does the Torah not permit eating chametz *with* matza? (In fact, an argument can be made for a mitzvah to eat both chametz and matza. The Haggadah calls matza "*lachmo ania,*" the bread of affliction. Since many actions on Pesach night represent the dichotomy of slavery *and* freedom, would it not make sense to eat both matza *and* bread, thus commemorating both affliction *and* comfort?)

The first question might be better stated, or elaborated on, as follows: Why on this night do we eat only matza, which represents haste and affliction, and not chametz, which represents relaxation and luxury?

The question presents us with an opportunity to discuss the necessity of "*b'chipazon,*" in haste. Here, "haste" does not refer merely to circumstances precluding the time needed for dough to rise, but rather, to the Jews' being saved by G-d just in the nick of time: Had they lingered in Egypt even a moment longer, they would have fallen to a spiritual nadir from which they could not have been retrieved. (See our earlier discussion regarding Biur chametz).

Recognizing Slavery

שבכל הלילות אנו אוכלים
שאר ירקות

On all other nights we eat all kinds of vegetables

The second question involves the eating of marror, the bitter herbs. The question is *not* "Why are bitter herbs eaten *at all* this night?" It is sensible for something

On all other nights we eat bread or matza, but on this night only matza.

On all other nights we eat all kinds of vegetables, but on this night bitter vegetables.

On all other nights we do not dip even once, but on this night [we must dip] two times. (celery in salt water, and the bitter herb in charoses)

bitter to be eaten to commemorate the bitterness of exile. There is nothing unique about eating herbs in any case, since other vegetables (including herbs) are also eaten on this night.

The Mishnah (*Pesachim* 39a) mentions the preferred type of marror as "*chazeres*," or Romaine lettuce. The Jerusalem Talmud (*Pesachim* 2:5) states that the mitzvah of eating marror should be fulfilled only with lettuce: the other types of vegetables allowed – for example, horseradish – are acceptable only because they share characteristics with lettuce. Lettuce, however, is preferred, because it parallels the Jewish experience in Egypt.

When the Jews first came to Egypt, they were treated as guests of honor, as befit the family of the Viceroy, Yosef. Later, when they were enticed to work for the Egyptians, it was through "sweet talk" and promises of great reward. Once they began working, they found themselves locked into a sit-

uation, and were forced to labor for Pharaoh. Romaine lettuce is expressive of this idea. When it begins to grow, it is actually quite sweet. Only after it remains in the earth for a while, does it become bitter.

The second question, therefore, is this: If on other nights we eat all different types of vegetables, many of which could represent slavery, why is it that on this night, the vegetable used to commemorate bitterness is also somewhat sweet? Would it not make more sense to use a very bitter vegetable? This question leads us into a discussion of how the Jewish people became, and can become again, enslaved, while living in a seemingly pleasant environment.

Keeping Emotions in Balance
שבכל הלילות אין אנו מטבילים

On all other nights we are not required to dip even once

The Rabbis instituted two dips

שֶׁבְּכָל הַלֵּילוֹת אָנוּ אוֹכְלִין בֵּין יוֹשְׁבִין וּבֵין מְסֻבִּין. הַלַּיְלָה הַזֶּה כֻּלָּנוּ מְסֻבִּין.

- The matzos are returned to the head of the table. Because the discussion revolves around them, the matzos should be visible throughout the recitation of the Haggadah, except when the cup of wine is lifted (473:7).

for the Seder evening: the *karpas* in saltwater and the bitter herbs in *charoses*. We understand the significance of dipping as a display of luxury and delicacy. However, we need to understand why it would not suffice to have just dipped once. The third question, therefore, is this: If on all other nights we do not dip at all, why on this night do we dip twice, when dipping once would have been sufficient, to signify the experience of luxury?

Perhaps this can be understood in light of our explanation above (see page 31). *Karpas* sends a mixed message: The dipping represents luxury; yet the *karpas*, a vegetable, is dipped in saltwater, which represents tears and slavery. With the marror, it is the reverse: The bitter herb, representing slavery, is dipped in the sweet-tasting *charoses*, which represents the promise of a good future.(See the discussion of *Marror*, page 134.) Thus the Seder discussion should now focus on the Jews' acceptance of the dichotomy in what G-d has decreed: maintaining trust in redemption during servitude, and

remembering the pain of exile, even in freedom.

We can explain the third question yet another way. The Rema (476:2) cites the Maharil, who says that during the Seder, a person should not dip any other foods besides *karpas* and *marror*, so as not to add to the number of dips required by the Rabbis. If the dipping is meant to signify luxury, the third question may also be, "Why is the dipping done *only* twice?" Is there a special importance attached to the two dips?

The *Ma'asei Hashem* understands the two dips as representing two memorable events in Jewish history, involving the dipping of an object in blood: Yosef's brothers' dipping his coat in blood; and the dipping of grass in blood by the Jews in Egypt, in order to smear the blood on their doorposts as a signal to G-d to pass over their homes. The first event marked the beginning of the Egyptian exile; the second marked its end. This may also help us understand why the Rabbis decided that the first dip should be in saltwater, and the

On all other nights we eat sitting or reclining, but on this night we all recline.

second in sweet-tasting *charoses.* The first dip, at the beginning of the Seder, recalls the beginning of the suffering of the exile; the second dip, performed after the story of the Exodus has been told, recalls the restoration of freedom and G-d's bringing the Jewish people out of Egypt.

Limitations of Freedom

שבכל הלילות אנו אוכלים בין יושבים

On all other nights we eat either sitting or reclining

The fourth question concerns reclining, which was considered an expression of freedom and comfort. The Rabbis required each person to recline during the Seder, as a means of celebrating freedom. However, it is odd for a truly free person to be coerced into behaving a certain way. If a person wants to recline, he should be able to do so; but if a person does not want to recline, then it should not be required.

This, then, may really be what the child is asking: Why on this night, which marks freedom, must we sit in a specifically prescribed manner, when on all other nights we can choose how we wish to sit

or recline? The purpose of this question is to stimulate a discussion about the meaning of freedom. Freedom, as we have said above, does not give license to do whatever one wants, but comes instead with clearly defined boundaries and responsibilities as to how one may act.

This interpretation of the question, as a lead into a discussion of the obligations of freedom, may also explain why it is that the Four Questions cited in the Mishnah (in *Pesachim*) conclude with a different fourth question from that asked in the Haggadah. Instead of asking about sitting and reclining, the fourth question in the Mishnah asks, "Why is it that on all other nights we may eat meat prepared any way we like, but on this night, we can eat only roasted meat as the Pesach offering?"

The *Sefer HaChinuch* (7) explains that the Pesach offering must be roasted, because roasting brings out the full flavor and aroma of the meat. This, too, is a practice of wealthy people, because a poor or hungry person cannot afford enough meat to be able to roast it. The poor person would rather sacrifice the flavor of the meat by simmering it, since it then has absorbed the water and is

עֲבָדִים הָיִינוּ לְפַרְעֹה בְּמִצְרַיִם, וַיּוֹצִיאֵנוּ יְיָ
אֱלֹהֵינוּ מִשָּׁם בְּיָד חֲזָקָה וּבִזְרוֹעַ נְטוּיָה. וְאִלּוּ
לֹא הוֹצִיא הַקָּדוֹשׁ בָּרוּךְ הוּא אֶת אֲבוֹתֵינוּ
מִמִּצְרַיִם, הֲרֵי אָנוּ וּבָנֵינוּ וּבְנֵי בָנֵינוּ מְשֻׁעְבָּדִים
הָיִינוּ לְפַרְעֹה בְּמִצְרָיִם. וַאֲפִילוּ כֻּלָּנוּ חֲכָמִים,

more filling. The purpose of roasting the meat, then, is the same as that of reclining – to portray wealth and freedom. The question asked about reclining can also be asked about roasting the meat: How is freedom expressed by requiring the meat to be prepared in a specific way? The answer, once again, is that freedom brings with it boundaries.

Finally, why is the question about reclining omitted in the Mishnah?[6] Our answer is that it was not necessary for the Mishnah to mention the question about reclining, since it is subsumed under the question about roasting the meat.

The four questions serve as catalysts for much of the ensuing discussion during the Seder.

❖ The Complete Redemption

עבדים היינו לפרעה במצרים
ביד חזקה ובזרוע נטויה . . .

We were slaves to Pharaoh in Egypt, and G-d our Lord took us out of there with a strong hand and with an outstretched arm

What is the significance of G-d's strong hand and outstretched arm? Was there some difficulty on G-d's part, as it were?

As we have said earlier, at the time of the Exodus, the Jews had sunk to a very low spiritual level: Despite their slavery and affliction, the people actually had become so accustomed to Egyptian culture, they had no desire to leave. The Midrash indicates that, as a result, four fifths of the nation perished during the Plague of Darkness.

---

6. Some commentaries (see Vilna Gaon Haggadah) explain that in the time of the Mishnah, it was common practice to recline every day. Thus, it would not have been something unusual that attracted a child's attention. This, however, is difficult to understand. If it were common practice for everyone to recline, including poor people and servants, how could reclining ever have been considered a sign of freedom and affluence?

We were slaves to Pharaoh in Egypt, and G-d our Lord took us out of there with a strong hand and with an outstretched arm. If G-d had not taken our fathers out of Egypt, then even we, our children and our children's children would still be slaves in Egypt. Even if we are all wise, all clever, and all expert in the Torah, we are

Redeeming the remaining Jews from Egypt was not merely a matter of releasing them from their slave masters; they had to be released emotionally and psychologically, as well. Cutting their psychological bonds was more difficult than accomplishing their physical release. Hence, the use of the expression "G-d's strong hand," to forcibly remove them. An "outstretched arm" conjures up the image of someone's pulling out an object that has fallen far, almost out of reach. A "strong hand" connotes "firmly grasping." The Jewish people had fallen so low, they were almost beyond reach.

The Haggadah continues, if G-d had not taken our fathers out of Egypt, we would still be enslaved to Pharaoh today. Some of the specifics of this are, of course, improbable, since the Egyptian empire no longer exists. However, if G-d had not freed the nation when He did, the psychological and spiritual influences of the Egyptian culture would have been so powerful, that the Jews could never have recovered to become G-d's Chosen People. They would have remained instead the people of Pharaoh.

The "outstretched arm" may also be an allusion to Pharaoh's daughter, who reached out to retrieve the infant, Moshe, from the reeds that grew at the river's edge. In the Talmud (*Sotah* 12b) it is related that the basket that held the baby was actually too far from shore for her to grasp it. Miraculously, she was assisted by G-d, and her arm stretched further than it could have normally. When a person puts forth the best effort, it will often merit special Divine assistance.

Because of the special effort of Pharaoh's daughter, the infant Moshe was saved. This event was an essential link in a chain of events that culminated in the redemption of the Jews from Egypt. Perhaps G-d's outstretched arm is meant to remind us that if we, too, stretch out our arms – that is, try to the best of our ability – G-d will respond in kind.

כֻּלָּנוּ נְבוֹנִים, כֻּלָּנוּ זְקֵנִים, כֻּלָּנוּ יוֹדְעִים אֶת
הַתּוֹרָה, מִצְוָה עָלֵינוּ לְסַפֵּר בִּיצִיאַת מִצְרָיִם.
וְכָל הַמַּרְבֶּה לְסַפֵּר בִּיצִיאַת מִצְרַיִם הֲרֵי זֶה
מְשֻׁבָּח.

מַעֲשֶׂה בְּרַבִּי אֱלִיעֶזֶר וְרַבִּי יְהוֹשֻׁעַ וְרַבִּי
אֶלְעָזָר בֶּן עֲזַרְיָה וְרַבִּי עֲקִיבָא וְרַבִּי טַרְפוֹן
שֶׁהָיוּ מְסֻבִּין בִּבְנֵי־בְרַק, וְהָיוּ מְסַפְּרִים בִּיצִיאַת
מִצְרַיִם כָּל אוֹתוֹ הַלַּיְלָה, עַד שֶׁבָּאוּ תַלְמִידֵיהֶם
וְאָמְרוּ לָהֶם, רַבּוֹתֵינוּ, הִגִּיעַ זְמַן קְרִיאַת שְׁמַע
שֶׁל שַׁחֲרִית.

אָמַר רַבִּי אֶלְעָזָר בֶּן עֲזַרְיָה הֲרֵי אֲנִי כְּבֶן
שִׁבְעִים שָׁנָה, וְלֹא זָכִיתִי שֶׁתֵּאָמֵר יְצִיאַת

וכל המרבה לספר ביציאת מצרים הרי זה משובח
Whoever discusses the Exodus at length should be praised

Mishlei (27:21) reads "איש כפי מהללו" – "A man according to his praises." Rabbi Avigdor Miller (*Awake My Glory*, p.247) explains this passage as meaning that a man can be understood best by what he praises. Rabbi Miller describes three people talking about a Shalosh Seudos they had all attended. One man praises the Rabbi's words of Torah. The second man admires the beautiful songs that were sung. The third man raves about the herring that was served. The essence of a person is revealed by the things that excite him.

When a person elaborates upon the Exodus, an important part of his nature is revealed: an excitement about G-d, the desire to know more about G-d and His great kindness. The value of a diamond can be appreciated only if its every facet is carefully examined, from every angle. G-d's kindness, too, can be appreciated only if His actions are carefully studied. Elaboration on the Exodus is a manifestation of a concerted effort to try to appreciate G-d's munificence.

still obliged to speak of the exodus from Egypt. Whoever discusses the Exodus at length should be praised.

It happened that Rabbi Eliezer, Rabbi Yehoshua, Rabbi Elazar ben Azariah, Rabbi Akiva and Rabbi Tarphon were reclining [at a Seder] in B'nei Berak. They were discussing the Exodus all that night, until their students came and told them, "Masters! It is time for the morning prayer Shema!"

Rabbi Elazar son of Azariah said: Behold! I am like a man of seventy years old, but I had not

---

The next few paragraphs do not really deal with the actual story of the Exodus, itself; rather we review details of fulfilling the mitzvah of discussing the Exodus. In keeping with our goals for this Haggadah – to explain the lessons of the Exodus – we do not analyze the Haggadah sections cited, but instead briefly explain the purpose of each section.

מעשה ברבי אליעזר ורבי יהושע
It happened that Rabbi Eliezer, Rabbi Yehoshua, . . .

The Haggadah relates this story, so that the events described provide a model for our own lives. These great rabbis took so seriously the directive to elaborate on the Exodus, they literally stayed up the entire night fulfilling the mitzvah. We look to our leaders to see

which ideas are meant to be taken literally and more seriously.

Incidentally, *Ibn Ezra* (*Shemos* 12:42) indicates a source for staying up all night. The words "*lail Sh'murim,*" mean "a night of watching": The entire night should be "watched," while discussing the miracles of the Exodus.

אמר רבי אלעזר בן עזריה
Rabbi Elazar ben Azariah said: "Behold! I am like a man of seventy years old . . . "

The section of the Exodus is recited by Jews twice each day throughout the year.

Because so many fundamentals in Judaism are tied to the Exodus, it would be insufficient to mention it just one night a year. Although the mitzvah of discussing the Exodus *at length* is limited to the

מִצְרַיִם בַּלֵּילוֹת, עַד שֶׁדְּרָשָׁהּ בֶּן זוֹמָא.
שֶׁנֶּאֱמַר, לְמַעַן תִּזְכֹּר אֶת יוֹם צֵאתְךָ מֵאֶרֶץ
מִצְרַיִם כֹּל יְמֵי חַיֶּיךָ. יְמֵי חַיֶּיךָ הַיָּמִים. כֹּל יְמֵי
חַיֶּיךָ הַלֵּילוֹת. וַחֲכָמִים אוֹמְרִים, יְמֵי חַיֶּיךָ
הָעוֹלָם הַזֶּה. כֹּל יְמֵי חַיֶּיךָ, לְהָבִיא לִימוֹת
הַמָּשִׁיחַ.

בָּרוּךְ הַמָּקוֹם, בָּרוּךְ הוּא, בָּרוּךְ שֶׁנָּתַן תּוֹרָה
לְעַמּוֹ יִשְׂרָאֵל. בָּרוּךְ הוּא. כְּנֶגֶד אַרְבָּעָה בָנִים
דִּבְּרָה תוֹרָה. אֶחָד חָכָם. וְאֶחָד רָשָׁע. וְאֶחָד
תָּם. וְאֶחָד שֶׁאֵינוֹ יוֹדֵעַ לִשְׁאוֹל.

חָכָם מָה הוּא אוֹמֵר, מָה הָעֵדֹת וְהַחֻקִּים

Seder night, we have an obligation to recite at least one verse about the Exodus each day, once in the morning and once in the evening. The verse chosen to recite is from the third paragraph of the *Shema*, the section about tzitzis. This recitation throughout the year, should bring to mind many of the lessons discussed on Pesach night. The repetition allows us to internalize their important message.

ברוך המקום ברוך הוא

Blessed is the Omnipresent! Blessed is He!....

In this section of the Haggadah, we are shown how the Torah concerns itself with every child, regardless of his or her nature or capabilities. Each child must be given the opportunity to absorb the important lessons of the Exodus.

Four times the Torah mentions the mitzvah of discussing the Exodus with one's children, each time with a slightly different wording. From this, the Haggadah gives us to understand that the Torah is addressing four different types of children: the wise child, the wicked child, the simple child, and the child who does not know to ask the appropriate questions. Each child must be addressed in a way that is best suited to that child's needs.

been able to show that the Exodus must be recited at night until Ben Zoma explained it. It is said, "That you may remember the day you left Egypt all the days of your life". "The days of your life" [alone] would indicate the days; "all the days of your life" [also] indicates the nights.

The [other] sages said that "the days of your life" [alone] indicates our present world. "All the days of your life" [also] indicates the age of Mashiach.

Blessed is the Omnipresent! Blessed is He! Blessed is He who gave the Torah to His people Israel! Blessed is He!
The Torah speaks of four children: One is wise, one is wicked, one is simple, and one does not know how to ask.

The wise child, what does he say? [He asks],

The wise child, who is interested in learning about the Exodus – and has the capacity to understand it in great depth – is taught not only the story of the Exodus, but also the Halachic details of the Pesach offering.

The child who displays a wicked attitude, does not seem interested in learning at all. He is answered simply and sharply. He should not be ignored, but must be shown that a bad attitude is not acceptable.

The simple child has an inter- est, but lacks the intellect to understand very much. This child must be spoken to simply and to the point.

The child who does not know how to ask appears not to be very interested in learning. However, whereas the wicked child has no interest out of rebelliousness, this child has not been sufficiently exposed to experience curiosity. This child, then, should be spoken to warmly, with words that will draw the heart closer, thereby increasing his interest (see Rashi, *Shemos* 13:5).

וְהַמִּשְׁפָּטִים אֲשֶׁר צִוָּה יְיָ אֱלֹהֵינוּ אֶתְכֶם. וְאַף אַתָּה אֱמָר לוֹ כְּהִלְכוֹת הַפֶּסַח, אֵין מַפְטִירִין אַחַר הַפֶּסַח אֲפִיקוֹמָן.

רָשָׁע מָה הוּא אוֹמֵר, מָה הָעֲבוֹדָה הַזֹּאת לָכֶם. לָכֶם וְלֹא לוֹ, וּלְפִי שֶׁהוֹצִיא אֶת עַצְמוֹ מִן הַכְּלָל, כָּפַר בְּעִיקָר. וְאַף אַתָּה הַקְהֵה אֶת שִׁנָּיו וֶאֱמָר לוֹ, בַּעֲבוּר זֶה עָשָׂה יְיָ לִי בְּצֵאתִי מִמִּצְרָיִם. לִי וְלֹא לוֹ, אִלּוּ הָיָה שָׁם לֹא הָיָה נִגְאָל.

תָּם מָה הוּא אוֹמֵר, מַה זֹּאת. וְאָמַרְתָּ אֵלָיו, בְּחוֹזֶק יָד הוֹצִיאָנוּ יְיָ מִמִּצְרַיִם, מִבֵּית עֲבָדִים.

וְשֶׁאֵינוֹ יוֹדֵעַ לִשְׁאוֹל אַתְּ פְּתַח לוֹ, שֶׁנֶּאֱמַר וְהִגַּדְתָּ לְבִנְךָ בַּיּוֹם הַהוּא לֵאמֹר, בַּעֲבוּר זֶה עָשָׂה יְיָ לִי בְּצֵאתִי מִמִּצְרָיִם.

יָכוֹל מֵרֹאשׁ חֹדֶשׁ. תַּלְמוּד לוֹמַר בַּיּוֹם הַהוּא. אִי בַּיּוֹם הַהוּא יָכוֹל מִבְּעוֹד יוֹם. תַּלְמוּד לוֹמַר

יכול מראש חודש

One might think that he must begin on the first day of the month....

Here, too, the Haggadah shows how to maximize the benefits of discussing the Exodus. The discussion must take place at a time when it can make the greatest impression — and that is *only* when the matza and marror are present to reinforce the discussion. To talk about the Exodus a couple of weeks earlier on Rosh Chodesh, or even a day earlier, would not be as powerful as it is on the Seder night.

In the paragraphs below, we

"What are the symbols, rules, and laws that G-d our Lord has commanded you?" (Devarim 6:20). *Then you shall tell him [all] the laws of Passover, [up to], "we do not taste anything after the Passover Afikoman."*

The wicked child, what does he say? [He asks,] "What is this service to you?" (Shemos 12:26). *"To you, but not to me!" Since he takes himself out of the group, he denies everything. You should also give him a blunt answer and say, "Because of this, G-d did [things] for me, when I left Egypt". For me – but not for you! If you had been there, you would not have been saved!"*

The simple child, what does he say? [He merely asks], "'What is this?' You shall say to him 'With a strong hand G-d took us out of Egypt, from the house of slaves'" (Shemos 13:14).

And for the one who does not know how to ask, you must begin for him, as it is written, "You shall tell your child on that day, 'Because of this, G-d did [things] for me when I left Egypt'" (Shemos 13:8).

One might think that he must begin on the first of the month. The Torah therefore continues, "on that day,". If the Torah had only said, "on that day," one might think that [the Seder is begun] during the day. The Torah therefore

return to the actual story of the Exodus in the Haggadah, and the historical events that led up to the Exodus.

בַּעֲבוּר זֶה. בַּעֲבוּר זֶה, לֹא אָמַרְתִּי אֶלָּא בְּשָׁעָה
שֶׁיֵּשׁ מַצָּה וּמָרוֹר מוּנָחִים לְפָנֶיךָ.

מִתְּחִלָּה עוֹבְדֵי עֲבוֹדָה זָרָה הָיוּ אֲבוֹתֵינוּ,
וְעַכְשָׁיו קֵרְבָנוּ הַמָּקוֹם לַעֲבוֹדָתוֹ. שֶׁנֶּאֱמַר,
וַיֹּאמֶר יְהוֹשֻׁעַ אֶל כָּל הָעָם, כֹּה אָמַר יְיָ אֱלֹהֵי
יִשְׂרָאֵל, בְּעֵבֶר הַנָּהָר יָשְׁבוּ אֲבוֹתֵיכֶם מֵעוֹלָם,

❖ **Growth Through Adversity**

מתחלה עובדי

עבודה זרה היו אבותינו

**At first our fathers were idol
worshipers. But now G-d has
brought us close [to Him, that
we may] serve Him....**

The Talmud (*Pesachim* 116a)
states that a person should begin
the discussion of the Exodus from
Egypt by talking about the disgrace
of our people. Subsequent talk
should then lead to their praise.

Two opinions in the Talmud
differ as to whether this disgrace
refers to our enslavement in Egypt
or rather to our idolatrous origins.
Both opinions are incorporated
into the Haggadah, and both are
instructive regarding why we begin
the discussion of the Exodus by
referring to our earlier, diminished
status.

The simple explanation of
beginning with our disgrace is that
a person must first experience slavery in order to be able to appreciate freedom. We must also remember our lowly spiritual origins, in
order to appreciate our spiritual
gains. This explanation, however,
seems insufficient.

The Haggadah mentions the
pagan practices of Avraham's family, as connected with the origin of
the Jewish people. But Terach,
Avraham's father, was not considered a Jew, since the Jewish people actually began with Avraham
himself. (And many sources attest
that Avraham never served idols.
See, for example, Ritva). Thus,
recalling idolatry practiced by
Avraham's father, *before* the beginning of the Jewish people, is not
the equivalent of remembering the
idolatry of the Jewish people themselves. Someone else's misbehavior
—even that of one's relatives —
when juxtaposed with one's own
spiritual gains, does not make one
appreciate his own accomplishments, as does recognizing one's
own former misconduct.

Michtav M'Eliyahu (vol.3,
p.349) explains that Terach's idolatry played a role in the origin of

stresses, "because of this.*" I cannot say [this]
unless matza and the bitter herb is standing
before you.*

*At first our fathers were idol worshipers. But
now G-d has brought us close [to Him, that we
may] serve Him [alone]. It is thus written,
"Yehoshua said to the people: Thus said G-d,
the Lord of Israel, 'Your fathers had always lived*

the Jewish nation, *not because he
was our ancestor,* but because his
idolatry provided an impetus for
Avraham's recognition of G-d. As
Terach's son, Avraham witnessed
the hypocrisy and absurdity inherent in idol worship. This strength-
ened Avraham's belief in an
Omnipotent Being.

This understanding is illustrat-
ed in the famous Midrash
(*Bereishis Rabba* 38:8), which tells
of Avraham's having to tend his
father's idol store, when Avraham
was a young boy. The Midrash
relates that people would enter the
store to bring offerings to the idols
and to pray to them. Avraham
would engage the petitioners in
discussion, and try to show them
the folly of their ways.
Subsequently, he smashed all of
the idols, except for the biggest
one. When his father returned and
saw the broken idols, he was very
angry. Avraham explained that the
idols had been bickering: The
biggest one had broken all the oth-

ers. Terach accused Avraham of
lying, and asserted that the idols
could not speak, let alone fight.
Avraham retorted that it made no
sense to believe in the supreme
power of a piece of wood or stone
that could not move and had no
ability to articulate. Thus
Avraham's beliefs were solidified
through his own experiences and
conclusions. And thereby Terach
can actually be credited with some
of Avraham's accomplishments.

This, then, may be the reason
for beginning the discussion about
our people's history by referring to
their early disgrace –and *then* leading up to their praise. It is necessary to give some credit for the
ultimate "praise" to the original
"disgrace."

❖ A Prerequisite of Leadership

The idolatrous practices of
Avraham's family may also be
described in the Haggadah, as a
way of explaining *why* G-d

תֶּרַח אֲבִי אַבְרָהָם וַאֲבִי נָחוֹר, וַיַּעַבְדוּ אֱלֹהִים
אֲחֵרִים:

וָאֶקַּח אֶת אֲבִיכֶם אֶת אַבְרָהָם מֵעֵבֶר הַנָּהָר
וָאוֹלֵךְ אוֹתוֹ בְּכָל אֶרֶץ כְּנָעַן, וָאַרְבֶּה אֶת זַרְעוֹ,
וָאֶתֶּן לוֹ אֶת יִצְחָק: וָאֶתֶּן לְיִצְחָק אֶת יַעֲקֹב
וְאֶת עֵשָׂו, וָאֶתֵּן לְעֵשָׂו אֶת הַר שֵׂעִיר לָרֶשֶׁת
אוֹתוֹ, וְיַעֲקֹב וּבָנָיו יָרְדוּ מִצְרָיִם.

בָּרוּךְ שׁוֹמֵר הַבְטָחָתוֹ לְיִשְׂרָאֵל, בָּרוּךְ הוּא,
שֶׁהַקָּדוֹשׁ בָּרוּךְ הוּא חִשַּׁב אֶת הַקֵּץ, לַעֲשׂוֹת

brought us close to His service. In the Talmud (*Yoma* 22b), it is written that a person may be appointed to a position of authority only if he has, as they say in the vernacular, "skeletons in the closet." The shameful things in a person's past keep the power or status of a position from going to his head.

Perhaps, the Haggadah is suggesting that G-d was willing to bring the Jewish people close to His service, because the Jews, too, have shortcomings in their history – dating back to Avraham's father. Although Terach himself might not have been a Jew, his idolatrous practices were nonetheless a source of embarrassment to the Jewish people, and could prevent them from becoming haughty.[7]

Yet, it is still hard to understand why it is said in the Haggadah that our fathers served idols, if only a reference to Avraham's father, Terach, is intended. Perhaps the statement "our fathers served idols" refers to our fathers in Egypt. The Midrash (*Shemos Rabba* 16:2) relates that many of the Jews in Egypt had fallen under the influence of the Egyptians and had begun to worship the Egyptian idols. The Haggadah then cites proof for this notion from a passage in *Yehoshua:* Because Avraham came from a family of idolaters across the

7. See Maharsha (Pesachim 116a), who explains this a little differently: The reason for mentioning the idolatrous origins is to prevent the great joy of Pesach evening from turning to arrogance.

on the other side of the [Euphrates] River. [They included] Terach, father of Avraham and Nachor, and they served other gods.

I took your father Avraham from over the river, and led him through the whole land of Canaan. I increased his family and gave him Yitzchak. To Yitzchak, I gave Ya'akov and Esau, and to Esau I gave Mount Seir to keep. Ya'akov and his children went down to Egypt'".

Blessed is He who has kept His promise to Israel! Blessed is He!

Euphrates River, he ran the risk of falling under their influence. G-d therefore took him away from his homeland and brought him to the land of Canaan, where he could develop his spiritual potential (see Malbim on *Yehoshua* 24:3).

Later, however, Yaakov and his sons left Canaan and went down to Egypt. Outside of the Holy Land, living in a culture plagued with depravity, the Jewish people reverted to the practices of their ancestors. It was from this low level that G-d redeemed the Jews and brought them close to His service.

❖ **Reasons for the Exile and the Exodus**

ברוך שומר הבטחתו לישראל
Blessed is He Who has kept His
promise to Israel! Blessed is He!
For G-d had calculated that the
end would come just as He had
told Avraham....

G-d had foretold Avraham that his children would be strangers in a foreign land for 400 years. The Rabbis calculate, however, that in reality the Jews were in Egypt for only 210 years. The Rabbis resolve this discrepancy in two ways. One explanation has it that the exile actually began from the birth of Yitzchak, which was exactly 400 years before the Exodus. The other Rabbinic interpretation is that the Egyptians oppressed the Jews more than they were supposed to suffer, thereby compressing 400 years' worth of suffering into 210 years. This is what is meant by the phrase "G-d calculated the end." G-d calculated the 400 years of the

כְּמָה שֶׁאָמַר לְאַבְרָהָם אָבִינוּ בִּבְרִית בֵּין
הַבְּתָרִים, שֶׁנֶּאֱמַר, וַיֹּאמֶר לְאַבְרָם יָדֹעַ תֵּדַע כִּי
גֵר יִהְיֶה זַרְעֲךָ בְּאֶרֶץ לֹא לָהֶם וַעֲבָדוּם וְעִנּוּ
אֹתָם, אַרְבַּע מֵאוֹת שָׁנָה: וְגַם אֶת הַגּוֹי אֲשֶׁר
יַעֲבֹדוּ דָן אָנֹכִי, וְאַחֲרֵי כֵן יֵצְאוּ בִּרְכֻשׁ גָּדוֹל:

exile, in such a way, that 400 years of suffering could be fulfilled within only 210.

The Brisker Rav says that these two explanations are not mutually exclusive. G-d had foretold two different decrees: (1) that Avraham's children would be strangers in a foreign land; and (2) that they would be enslaved and oppressed. The calculation of 400 years applied to both these decrees. The notion that the decree begins from the birth of Yitzchak explains only the decree of sojourning in a strange land. Indeed, from the time of Yitzchak's birth, the children of Avraham dwelled in a strange land. This could not, however, explain the decree of oppression, because no oppression existed until long after Yitzchak's birth.

The notion of the oppression's being condensed into 210 years, on the other hand, explains only the decree of the nation's being enslaved and oppressed. This could not explain the decree of being strangers, however, since regardless of their hard labor, the Jews were strangers for only 210

years. It is therefore necessary to offer both interpretations.

Based on the Brisker Rav's interpretations we can perhaps explain another contradiction. We have already quoted the Midrash regarding G-d's saving the Jewish people, at the last moment, from reaching a point from which they could not have been redeemed. The implication here is that the people were not saved through their own merits at all; rather, it was an act of undeserved kindness on G-d's part.

From other sources, however, it appears otherwise. The Talmud (Sotah 11b), for example, mentions that the Jews were redeemed from Egypt in the merit of the righteous women. Likewise, the Midrash (Bamidbar Rabba 20:21) mentions that the people were saved, because of a few special and positive behaviors: They did not change their names or language; they did not act immorally; and they did not divulge their secrets. These sources imply that the people were, in fact, saved for reasons that were to their credit, and that

For G-d had calculated that the end would come just as He had told Avraham in the Promise between Halves. It is written, "[G-d] said to Avram, 'Know that your children will be strangers in a land that is not theirs. [The people of that land] will make them slaves and be cruel to them for 400 years. But then I will judge the nation whom they will serve, and after that they will leave with great wealth'". (Bereishis 15:13,14).

salvation was not totally unde-served.

Perhaps we can say, however, that the various sources refer to different aspects of the exile. The decree of being strangers had to be fulfilled, regardless of the peo-ple's conduct, since G-d had deemed it necessary for them to experience 400 years of exile. This was a prerequisite for receiving the Torah. However, when it became clear that if the nation were not redeemed in less than 400 years, there *would be* no nation to receive the Torah, G-d calculated the 400 years from the birth of Yitzchak. This allowed the Jews to leave Egypt 190 years earlier than was originally foreordained.

Nevertheless, the decree of oppression may have been dependent upon their behavior. Because of the righteous women and because of the Jews' other meritorious conduct, G-d was will-ing to count the 210 years of hard labor and persecution as sufficient

for 400 years of slavery. Thus, the abortive ending of the oppression was not merely a stopgap measure, to prevent their slipping into obliv-ion, but rather a reward for good behavior. As the Rabbis explain, this is also suggested by the oppression's actually ending when the Ten Plagues first began – almost a year before the actual Exodus. The end of the enslave-ment was not concomitant with the hasty departure of the Jews from Egypt.

❖ Rewards and Consolation Prizes

ואחרי כן יצאו ברכוש גדול

. . . and after that they will leave with great wealth

Before the Jews left Egypt, G-d asked Moshe to please have the people request valuables from their Egyptian masters. The Midrash explains that G-d wanted the peo-ple to ask for the valuables in order to allay Avraham's concern

• When the cup of wine is lifted, the matzos are covered. This is done just as we cover the challah during *kiddush* each

that G-d would not fulfill His promise about giving the people great wealth. But there is an obvious difficulty with this Midrash. Why would G-d be concerned only with appeasing Avraham? Why was He not simply concerned with fulfilling His own promise?

The Dubner Maggid answers with a parable. A man hired his neighbor's young son to do yard work over the summer. He promised to pay him two quarters an hour for the job. The young boy worked industriously and did a beautiful job keeping the lawn clean of litter and weeds. At the end of the summer, the man felt he would be taking advantage of the child if he paid him so little. He decided, instead, to give the child a check for a much greater sum than two quarters an hour would have totalled.

A little while later, the man received a call from the child's father. The father explained, apologetically, that he appreciated the man's generosity, but his son was devastated. His son had expected a pile of quarters, but now had only a piece of paper to show for all of his hard work. The father asked if his neighbor could pay at least part of the child's wages in shiny quarters.

When G-d promised Avraham

that his children would receive great wealth, He was referring to the great spiritual wealth of the Torah. But Avraham countered that although he could appreciate the riches of the Torah, the young nation emerging from slavery would not be able to appreciate it. Therefore, in order to allay Avraham's concerns for his children, G-d requested from Moshe that the Jews ask the Egyptians for material possessions and treasures. When the Egyptians would indeed show a sudden change of heart and shower the Jews with valuables, the Jews would then recognize G-d's kindness, even before they could appreciate the great value of His ultimate gift, the Torah.

However, we may find it difficult to make sense of the Dubner Maggid's interpretation. The Torah often promises material and physical benefits, such as abundant rains and bountiful crops, as a reward for the observance of mitzvos. These promises are understood to be literally fulfilled: They are not merely a token payment made to mollify those who fulfill the mitzvos but misunderstand the essence of the reward. Why is it assumed that the promise of wealth made to Avraham should be any different? Moreover, if the promise of great wealth indeed

week on Shabbos – to "spare the shame" of the bread. Generally, a *bracha* on bread precedes a *bracha* of wine. Accordingly, when the *bracha* on the wine is said first, as on Shabbos, the challah is covered to "spare it embarrassment." Similarly, during the Seder, when special attention is paid to the wine, the matzos are first covered.

refers to a spiritual reward, why should there be a concern that it may be misunderstood?

We may offer an explanation as follows. The Talmud (*Kiddushin* 39b) states that the real reward for mitzvos cannot be granted in this world. The reasoning is quite simple: A mitzvah is an action with eternal ramifications. It would not be fair to repay an eternal act with a finite physical reward.

An analogy can be made to paying an employee with the money from a board game such as Monopoly. The money has no intrinsic value, except during the game. Once the game board is shut, the money is totally worthless. This type of currency is obviously not accepted as payment for any debt outside the fantasy environment generated by playing the game.

Physical and material rewards maintain their value only during the fleeting years of life in this world. Once physical life has ended, money and physical pleasure have no value at all. One needs the physical world to provide a scale with which they can be measured. Accordingly, the real

reward for any mitzvah must be spiritual and infinite in nature, in order to correspond with the infinite nature of the mitzvah. The physical rewards described in the Torah must be understood as a fringe benefit, or as perhaps providing the opportunity through which one can fulfill other mitzvos – but not as the actual reward for the mitzvah itself (see Rambam *Teshuva* 9:1).

G-d's promise of wealth to Avraham, however, was not meant as a reward for mitzvos. Rather, it was meant as compensation for the years of slavery and persecution that the nation would endure. It is not farfetched to assume that the physical reward promised Avraham was meant to be understood literally: It was, after all, compensation for physical activity, something which is also finite in nature.

G-d's intention for granting great wealth, however, *had* been the gift of the Torah. That was the whole reason for the exile and the suffering. He had the Children of Israel request the Egyptian silver and gold as a consolation prize, because they were not yet mature enough to appreciate the value of the Torah.

וְהִיא שֶׁעָמְדָה לַאֲבוֹתֵינוּ וְלָנוּ. שֶׁלֹא אֶחָד בִּלְבָד עָמַד עָלֵינוּ לְכַלּוֹתֵינוּ. אֶלָּא שֶׁבְּכָל דוֹר

❖ Divine Calculations

והיא שעמדה לאבותינו

This is what has stood up for our fathers and for us....

Many of the commentaries infer that this paragraph refers to the promise that G-d made to Avraham (*Abudraham* and *Shibolei Haleket*). The same promise of redemption and retribution that was made concerning Egypt would also apply to the other exiles (*Bereishis Rabba* 42:22). This promise would serve as a source of hope for the Jews in every exile (Maharal and *Shibolei Haleket*).

However, the simplest understanding of the paragraph is that it is a reference to G-d's *recalculation* of the exile. The Haggadah thus comments that it is the awareness of the recalculation, that has kept the Jewish nation alive through all the exiles. The decree that the nation would be enslaved for 400 years was made – and was known – long before the Jewish people entered Egypt. During all the painful suffering of their slavery, many Jews must have despaired, knowing that it would not end for another 200 years. When G-d released the people 190 years earlier than He had decreed, the Jews saw that, although G-d's decrees would always be fulfilled,

there was some latitude in the way they would be fulfilled.

During the exile between the two Temples, the people knew of Yirmiyah's prophecy (*Yirmiyahu* 29:10): After seventy years, they would return to Jerusalem. However, no one knew exactly when the seventy years had begun. Belshazzar, the king of Persia, calculated the years from Nebuchadnezzar's ascent to the throne. When nothing happened at the "appointed" time, he thought that G-d had retracted His promise. He celebrated what he perceived to be G-d's forsaking of the Jews. Belshazzar's calculation, however, was mistaken.

Achashveirosh, too, made his own calculations, counting seventy years from the exile of King Yehoyachin. In celebration, he planned the great party that is described at the beginning of Megillas Esther. His calculation likewise proved to be incorrect. The exile would not end for another fourteen years, thereby marking seventy years from the destruction of the Temple.

The Jewish people could easily have despaired. The time passed that they might have assumed should have marked the end of the exile, with no change in their cir-

This is what has stood up for our fathers and for us! For not one alone has stood up against

cumstances. However, they had learned from their Egyptian experience, that G-d has many ways of computing His appointed times. Regardless how these periods had been calculated, the Jews knew that the redemption would still come. [8]

Concerning the present exile, we see a similar idea. The Talmud (*Sanhedrin* 98a) is bothered by a passage in *Yeshaya* (60:22) regarding the Redemption: "I, G-d, will hasten it in its time." Hastening the Redemption implies that the Redemption will occur before its destined time: "In its time," however, implies that the Redemption will not happen until its destined time. Will the Redemption be hastened or will it happen in its destined time?

The Talmud resolves this question in the following way: *If* the people are meritorious, the time for Redemption will be hastened. However, if they are *not* meritorious, it will come to pass just as preordained. In other words, although there may be a preordained time for the ultimate

Redemption, G-d has already shown that if the circumstances so require, He can calculate the time differently. The knowledge that there is flexibility regarding the arrival of redemption, even today, prevents the Jewish nation from becoming disillusioned and giving up hope.

❖ Egypt as a Model for Exile

שלא אחד בלבד עמד עלינו לכלותנו

For not one alone has stood up against us, but in every generation they rise up to finish us – and the Holy One Blessed is He saves us from their hand

The Egyptian exile served as a model for future exiles. As such, it must be examined carefully, in order that we may learn how to best prepare ourselves for other exiles.

The Egyptian exile began very subtly. When Yaakov and his sons came to Egypt, they established clear guidelines to prevent their children's assimilating into Egyptian culture. The Jews lived in separate cities, ate different foods

---

8. Pri Tzaddik ("Purim," p.196) asserts that the calculations of Belshazzar and Achashveirosh were not incorrect. Had the Jews been deserving, either of these earlier calculations could have been the right one. Unfortunately, this was not the case.

וָדוֹר עוֹמְדִים עָלֵינוּ לְכַלּוֹתֵינוּ. וְהַקָדוֹשׁ בָּרוּךְ
הוּא מַצִּילֵנוּ מִיָּדָם.

צֵא וּלְמַד, מַה בִּקֵשׁ לָבָן הָאֲרַמִּי לַעֲשׂוֹת
לְיַעֲקֹב אָבִינוּ, שֶׁפַּרְעֹה לֹא גָזַר אֶלָּא עַל

from those common to the Egyptian diet (*Beraishis* 43:32), and worked at occupations not customary for Egyptians. (For example, the Jews were shepherds, a vocation considered an abomination in Egyptian culture. See *Beraishis* 46:34.) However, with the passage of time, starting with the second generation of Jews, many of these differences began to blur.

The Jews began to emerge from their ghettos and become more involved in Egyptian society. Over time, the Egyptians became increasingly antagonized by the growing Jewish presence, and began to exploit the Jewish involvement in community. The Egyptians asked members of the Jewish community to help them build new cities. Over time, Jews were asked to perform other types of labor— at first with compensation and later without any pay. Eventually, the Jews realized that they had become enslaved to the Egyptians, and that they could not turn back, even if they wanted to. Later they suffered persecution and the murder of their children.

This scenario has repeated itself throughout Jewish history. Unfortunately, we do not learn the lessons of history, perhaps because our strong faith is mistakenly placed. Jews enter new countries and, at first, keep themselves separate from the larger culture. As time goes by, either the adults or their children (or both) yield to the desire to assimilate into the host culture. At first, we are oblivious to the new culture's reluctance to welcome the "intrusion" of outsiders and newcomers. Nonetheless, we soon become so entrenched in the pursuit of the host society's goals and dreams, that even when hostility towards us is obvious, we have great difficulty changing our ways. The ensuing pogroms, Inquisitions, and Holocausts are proof of our terrible misjudgment.

The Haggadah informs us that in every generation, the Jew must confront enmity: Attempts will always be made to destroy the Jewish people. Yet we realize, too, that even when we do not behave as befits the Chosen People, and we must suffer the consequences accordingly, G-d still does not desert us.

*us, but in every generation they rise up to fin-
ish us – and the Holy One Blessed is He saves
us from their hand!*

*Go out and learn what Lavan the Aramean
wanted to do to our father Ya'akov. Pharaoh
only wanted to kill the young boys, but Lavan*

Imagine somebody standing at the ruins of the Second Temple in Jerusalem and witnessing the small remnant of the broken Jewish nation: Captives – chained at the feet of the great Roman conquerors. Could anyone have envisioned that almost two thousand years later this same small nation would return to the land of its origins, whereas the great conquerors would be great only in the ash heaps of history? That the Jewish people have survived so long, against all odds, is proof that the Holy One, Blessed is He, will always rescue us from our enemies and not allow us to disappear.

❖ The Challenge of Recognizing Danger

צא ולמד מה בקש לבן
Go out and learn what Lavan the Aramean wanted to do to our father Yaakov....

It is not uncommon to hear about, or to see, a situation similar to one's own, yet fail to discern a connection. We have little perspective on our own circumstances.

A story is told about the *Shach*, Rav Shabsie Cohen, one of the great Halachic authorities of the seventeenth century. He was once involved in a monetary dispute with a Jew who lived in another city. The two of them decided to ask the local Rav, who did not know the *Shach* personally, to adjudicate the dispute. The *Shach* presented his position, and then tried to marshal support from an impressive array of sources. The Rav refuted the *Shach's* arguments, and explained that he had found this exact case discussed in the responsa of a contemporary authority named *Shach!* The *Shach* had not even realized that he, himself, had addressed this very same situation. It is indeed difficult to be an objective observer, when one is deeply involved.

The Egyptian exile and the redemption that followed are supposed to serve as models for other exiles. However, it is easy for a person to feel that the present exile cannot be compared with the Egyptian exile. Today, after all, we have no taskmasters forcing us to do slave labor. We are fortunate to have the opportunity to practice Torah as we see fit. In general,

הַזְּכָרִים וְלָבָן בִּקֵּשׁ לַעֲקוֹר אֶת הַכֹּל, שֶׁנֶּאֱמַר:
אֲרַמִּי אֹבֵד אָבִי, וַיֵּרֶד מִצְרַיְמָה וַיָּגָר שָׁם בִּמְתֵי
מְעָט, וַיְהִי שָׁם לְגוֹי גָּדוֹל, עָצוּם וָרָב.

then, it is easy for us to be lulled into a false sense of security, and think that our exile is not all that bad – if we are even aware of being in exile.

The Haggadah therefore states, "Go out and discover." We must take ourselves outside of our present mindset, in order to draw the parallels from the Egyptian experience to our own, and recognize the pitfalls we may stumble upon today. The experience of exile may not always be as obvious as it was in Egypt. Sometimes the danger may be insidious and harm unsuspecting victims, by subtly spreading its negative influence.

Yaakov's exile in the house of Lavan is such an example. Although the relationship between Yaakov and his uncle and father-in-law may have been strained at times, nowhere do we see that Lavan actually tried to destroy Yaakov. Yet this is exactly what the Torah reveals, long after Yaakov and Lavan had passed on from the world.

Lavan *did* try to destroy Yaakov. Lavan's tricking Yaakov into first marrying Leah, and then requiring him to work another seven years for Rachel; his efforts to cheat Yaakov out of his wages;

and his trying to prevent Yaakov from leaving – all were part of a surreptitious, campaign to "uproot everything." Undermining Yaakov's mission was the equivalent of undermining the foundation of the Jewish people. In fact, Yaakov's children would *be* the Jewish people. Lavan, then, was more dangerous than Pharaoh whose intentions to kill the male babies were more obvious and immediate.

Lavan serves as an example of the threat many individuals present in other periods of exiles. That Lavan's name is not even explicitly mentioned in the Torah passage is suggestive of this. The passage says only that "an Aramean tries [in the present tense] to destroy my father." The word "Aramean" is related to the word "ramai," a deceitful person; note, also, that the verb, "tries," is in the present tense. In other exiles, as well, up into the present day, there are deceitful people who try, in some manner, to destroy the Jewish people.

Only after people have been extricated from situations of jeopardy, can they appreciate the danger that faced them. Although we may not fully comprehend the inherent dangers of the present exile, we must take our cue from

wanted to uproot the whole [Jewish nation, by killing Ya'akov]. It is thus written, "An Aramean [tried to] destroy my father, but he went down to Egypt, and lived there as a stranger, few in number. There he became a nation, great, mighty, and many."

earlier exiles and learn from them how best to deal with our situation.

❖ Analyzing the Exile and its Lessons

ארמי אובד אבי וירד מצרימה

An Aramean [wanted to] destroy my father, but he went down to Egypt,

The next part of the Haggadah examines those passages in the Torah that are read by a person who brings the Bikkurim – the first fruits grown each year in Israel that are given to the kohen in Jerusalem. The passage in *Devarim* (26:5-9) reads as follows:

An Aramean [tried to] destroy my father but he went down to Egypt to live, with but a few people. There he became a great and powerful nation of many. The Egyptians treated us badly, oppressed us, and made us work very hard. We cried out to G-d, the G-d of our fathers, and He heard our voice and saw our oppression, difficulty, and suffering. G-d took us out of Egypt with a strong hand and an out-stretched arm, with great awe, with signs, and with wonders. He brought us to this place and gave us this land flowing with milk and honey....

These passages actually present a short synopsis of Jewish history, beginning with Lavan's efforts to destroy Yaakov, through the bondage and oppression in Egypt, and finally to the redemption from Egypt. The person bringing the Bikkurim reads these passages as a means of developing feelings of joy and appreciation for all that G-d has given. The Torah encourages this with the subsequent recitation of the words, "You shall rejoice in all the good that your G-d has given you."

Contemplation of these passages brings a powerful realization of the Divine plan: How one detail leads to another, ultimately resulting in the people's inheriting the Promised Land with all its blessings. This recognition of purpose, in all that transpires, allows one to truly appreciate and enjoy what one has acquired. There is no joy like that of a person who finds meaning in every facet of his life.

וַיֵּרֶד מִצְרַיְמָה, אָנוּס עַל פִּי הַדִּבּוּר.

וַיָּגָר שָׁם, מְלַמֵּד שֶׁלֹּא יָרַד יַעֲקֹב אָבִינוּ לְהִשְׁתַּקֵּעַ בְּמִצְרַיִם, אֶלָּא לָגוּר שָׁם. שֶׁנֶּאֱמַר, וַיֹּאמְרוּ אֶל פַּרְעֹה, לָגוּר בָּאָרֶץ בָּאנוּ, כִּי אֵין מִרְעֶה לַצֹּאן אֲשֶׁר לַעֲבָדֶיךָ, כִּי כָבֵד הָרָעָב

וירד מצרימה אנוס על פי הדבוד

. . . but he went down to Egypt – forced by the Word

The simplest understanding of this statement is this: Although ostensibly Yaakov chose to go down to Egypt with his family to be with his son Yosef, he was really only carrying out a Divine decree that would have been fulfilled in any case, regardless of his decision.

People often delude themselves by thinking that they can decide their own destiny. In truth, the areas over which man has complete control are extremely limited.[9] Most of what we decide is only the actualization of G-d's preordained will.

An example of this can be seen in the Talmud (*Succah* 53a). An incident is related, in which

King Shlomo noticed that the Angel of Death appeared to be worried. King Shlomo asked the Angel what was bothering him. The angel replied that he was supposed to take two of the King's servants, yet he could not find them. King Shlomo quickly sent the two servants to the distant city of Luz, a place where the Angel of Death had no jurisdiction.

As soon as the servants reached the gates of Luz, however, they both expired. When the king confronted the angel, he found him smiling. The angel explained that he was authorized to take these two servants *only* at the gates of Luz. Unwittingly, King Shlomo had sent the two servants to their death. The Talmud concludes that a person's feet carry him to the very place needed.

From this interpretation, then,

---

9. See Michtav M'Eliyahu (vol.1 Kuntres Habechirah) for an elaboration of this idea. Ultimately, only the choice between good and evil is in the hands of man.

"But he went down to Egypt" – forced by the Word.

"And lived there as a stranger" – This teaches that our father Ya'akov did not come to settle in Egypt, but only to remain there a short time,

G-d had preordained that the Jewish people had to be in Egypt, and Yaakov was the tool that led them there.

However, we may offer another interpretation of this statement. The Talmud (*Nedarim* 32a) suggests that Avraham's question to G-d, "And how will I know that my children will inherit the land?" implied an incomplete trust. This insufficiency of faith was one of the reasons for the exile.

The Maharal (*Gevuros Hashem* 9) explains that Avraham was a root of the Jewish people. And a minor problem in the root will be revealed, magnified, in the branches. The exile was necessary to extirpate this lack of faith. Moreover, it may be that "the word," in the phrase "forced by the word," refers to *Avraham's* words: The exile resulted from Avraham's words of concern that G-d's promise would not be fulfilled.

This may be an additional reason for discussing the Exodus at the Seder. The discussion of the Exodus strengthens our faith in G-d, as we have cited from the *Sefer Hachinuch*. On Pesach night, when we recall the exile in Egypt,

and that it resulted from a lack of faith, it is fitting to talk about the Exodus, in order to *strengthen* our faith.

❖ Preparing for Exile

ויגר שם מלמד שלא ירד יעקב

And he lived there as a stranger – This teaches that our father Yaakov did not come to settle in Egypt, but only to remain there for a short time, as it says, "They said to Pharaoh, 'We have come to live in your land a while, for there is no pasture for your servants' flocks. . .' "

Yaakov and his sons wanted Pharaoh to understand, right from the start, that they had no plans for making Egypt their permanent residence.

As soon as the brothers came down to Egypt, the Torah relates (*Beraishis* 46:31),

Yosef told his brothers, "I will go up and tell Pharaoh that my brothers have come to me. The men are shepherds, and they have brought their flocks and cattle with them. And when Pharaoh summons you and asks what is your occupation, you should say, 'Your servants

בְּאֶרֶץ כְּנַעַן, וְעַתָּה יֵשְׁבוּ נָא עֲבָדֶיךָ בְּאֶרֶץ
גֹּשֶׁן.

בִּמְתֵי מְעָט, כְּמָה שֶׁנֶּאֱמַר, בְּשִׁבְעִים נֶפֶשׁ יָרְדוּ
אֲבֹתֶיךָ מִצְרָיְמָה, וְעַתָּה שָׂמְךָ יְיָ אֱלֹהֶיךָ
כְּכוֹכְבֵי הַשָּׁמַיִם לָרֹב.

וַיְהִי שָׁם לְגוֹי מְלַמֵּד שֶׁהָיוּ יִשְׂרָאֵל מְצֻיָּנִים שָׁם.

have raised cattle since our youth etc.' in order that you will be able to live in Goshen, because shepherds are abhorrent to the Egyptians."

Yosef came to Pharaoh and said, "My father and brothers have come from Canaan with all their flocks and cattle, and they are now in Goshen." He brought five of his brothers before Pharaoh. Pharaoh asked them, "What is your occupation?" They said to Pharaoh, "We have come to live in the land, because there is no pasture land for our flocks."

Pharaoh said to Yosef, "Your father and brothers have come to you..."

Why was it necessary for Yosef and his brothers to say that they were shepherds repeatedly? The emphasis was intended to make them as unattractive to Pharaoh as possible. They knew that the Egyptians abhorred people who

raised sheep and cattle for food. They reasoned that the emphasis on their occupation would result in Pharaoh's not wanting Yosef's family to remain in Egypt for a lengthy period of time. This was a precautionary measure on the part of the Jews, to ensure that even if the future generations of Jews made themselves comfortable in Egypt, they still would not be welcome there.

For this reason, Pharaoh remarked to Yosef that "Your father and brothers have come to you..." Pharaoh meant "to Yosef alone" and not "to Egypt." That they had presented themselves to Pharaoh as shepherds was proof that they intended to remain "sons of Yaakov," even while dwelling among the Egyptians – and that they had no intention of making Egypt their home.

Yaakov also took precautionary measures to ensure that his children would not *want* to settle

as it says, "They said to Pharaoh, 'We have come to live in your land a while, for there is no pasture for your servants' flocks to eat, so great is the hunger in the land of Canaan. Now, if you please, let [us] your servants live in the land of Goshen.'" (Bereishis *47:4*).

"Few in number" – as it says, "With seventy souls your fathers went down to Egypt. Now G-d your Lord has made you as many as the stars of the sky." (Devarim *10:22*).

"There he became a nation" – This teaches that Israel was distinctive there.

permanently in Egypt. The *Meshech Chochma* (*Vayikra* 26:44) explains that Yaakov made Yosef take an oath that he would inter Yaakov's remains in Canaan. Yaakov did this to instill a desire in his children to return to Canaan. Had Yaakov been buried in Egypt, his children might have viewed Egypt as their home and forgotten about Canaan. However, if they saw how important it was to the patriarch that the family return to Canaan, they would realize that the Jewish nation could only thrive in their homeland.

❖ **The Markings of a Jew**

ויהי שם לגוי מלמד שהיו מצויינים

And he became a nation there – this teaches us that Israel was distinctive there

Some of the commentaries understand the Jews' distinctiveness as referring to their unique dress, language, and general conduct (Ritva, Abarbanel and *Kol Bo*). Although these may be primarily external features, the identity of a people or nation is established through its clothing and language.

My colleague, Rabbi Moshe Stoll, has shown me a source that also expresses this idea. After Aharon's death, the Torah relates that the Canaanites fought against the Children of Israel (*Bamidbar* 21:1). Rashi explains that the "Canaanite" warriors were actually Amalekites – but they spoke the language of Canaan to confuse the Jews. The hope of the enemy had been that the Israelites would mistakenly pray to G-d to save them from the Canaanites. However, when the enemy was seen in Amalekite dress, speaking the lan-

גָּדוֹל עָצוּם, כְּמָה שֶׁנֶּאֱמַר, וּבְנֵי יִשְׂרָאֵל פָּרוּ
וַיִּשְׁרְצוּ וַיִּרְבּוּ וַיַּעַצְמוּ בִּמְאֹד מְאֹד, וַתִּמָּלֵא
הָאָרֶץ אֹתָם.

וָרָב, כְּמָה שֶׁנֶּאֱמַר, רְבָבָה כְּצֶמַח הַשָּׂדֶה

guage of Canaan, the Jews prayed that G-d save them from the hands of their enemies – whoever they might be.

Rav Yitzchok of Vorka (cited in *Itturei Torah*) asks an obvious question: If the Amalekites wanted to fool the Jews, why didn't they change their clothing, as well? He answers that had they changed *both* their language and clothing to that of Canaan, they would have *become* Canaanites – because language and clothing create the identity of a people.

Another understanding of what constituted the Jews' distinctiveness in Egypt can be postulated.

What distinguishes one nation from another is its "character." In fact, one of the reasons for the Egyptian exile, was to afford the Jews the opportunity to develop a national "personality." G-d placed the Jewish people in a culture characterized by features and conduct that were the diametric opposite of Jewish standards – in order for the Jews to "own," practice, and strengthen behaviors that were intrinsic to Jewishness and that would set them apart.

The Talmud (*Yevamos* 79a) cites three traits that are inherent in the Jewish people: compassion, modesty, and lovingkindness. It may be that these characteristics were first developed in Egypt, a place that was known for its immorality and cruelty. Thus, the Haggadah says, the Jewish people first became a nation in Egypt through their distinctiveness.

We may now explain a seeming contradiction from the following paragraph. The Haggadah continues, **Great and mighty – as it is written, "The Children of Israel were fruitful, multiplied, and became very mighty and the land was filled with them."**

The Midrash (*Tanchuma* [Buber] *Shemos* 6) explains that as the Jewish population grew, they became more mighty and daring. They left the walls of Goshen and tried to assimilate into Egyptian culture. They frequented the Egyptian theatres and markets. This passage, therefore, states that, ". . . the land was filled with them," meaning that the Jews had become integrated into every area of Egyptian life.

"Great, mighty" – as it says, "The Children of Israel were fruitful and multiplied. They became very great in number and mighty, and the land became filled with them." (Shemos 1:74).

"Numerous" – as it says, "I made you as

Now, if the distinctiveness of the Jews was measured by their external appearance, how could they be praised, on the one hand, for maintaining a distinctive Jewish appearance, and be chastised, on the other hand, for assimilating into the Egyptian culture – all in the same breath, so to speak?

If, however, as we have just explained, the distinctiveness refers to the nation's innate character, the question can be easily answered. The distinctive Jewish character may have developed as a *result* of the nation's experiences in Egypt. The people's efforts to assimilate allowed them to witness the depraved Egyptian culture first-hand. Eventually, this experience served as an impetus to their developing a distinct Jewish character, as will be explained shortly.[10]

ובני ישראל פרו וישרצו
The Children of Israel were fruitful and multiplied. They became very great in number, and very mighty

Six times there are expressions of increasing. The Midrash derives from the repetitive terminology, that the Jewish women bore six children at a time. These multiple births were necessary to prove a point to the Egyptians.

The Egyptians had tried to disrupt Jewish family life by keeping Jewish husbands and wives apart. (See the section below, **"He saw our affliction"**). The Egyptians did this to prevent the Jewish population from increasing. To counter their efforts, G-d caused the Jewish women to have multiple births when they *did* conceive. Moreover, as the Abarbanel points out, although in multiple births babies are usually sickly and weak, these babies, as the Torah notes, grew into strong and mighty people.

רב כמה שנאמר רבבה
Numerous- as it says, "I made you as numerous as the plants of the field. You became many and grew, and became mature.... but you were naked and bare"

---

10. Although the Midrash does say that the Jews maintained their unique dress and tongue, it may be that these were not the same Jews who tried to assimilate.

נְתַתִּיךְ, וַתִּרְבִּי וַתִּגְדְּלִי וַתָּבוֹאִי בַּעֲדִי עֲדָיִים,
שָׁדַיִם נָכֹנוּ וּשְׂעָרֵךְ צִמֵּחַ, וְאַתְּ עֵרֹם וְעֶרְיָה.
וָאֶעֱבֹר עָלַיִךְ וָאֶרְאֵךְ מִתְבּוֹסֶסֶת בְּדָמָיִךְ,
וָאֹמַר לָךְ בְּדָמַיִךְ חֲיִי וָאֹמַר לָךְ בְּדָמַיִךְ חֲיִי.

The commentators are bothered by the Haggadah's restatement of the nation's proliferation through the inclusion of this passage from *Yechezkel*. The point has already been clearly stated in the previous passage: "The nation was fruitful and multiplied." (See *Shibolei Haleket*.) It also seems strange that proof of the nation's greatness is drawn from a passage in which the Jews are faulted for being "naked" of merit and thus undeserving of redemption.

An insight heard from Rav Simcha Wasserman may be helpful. He once posed the following question, "Which would be considered a greater asset: a library of 1,000 volumes, or one of 10,000 volumes?" He went on to explain, "Although most people would automatically assume that the bigger library would be the greater asset, that is not necessarily so. It would really depend upon how well the library was organized. If the books were arranged in an orderly fashion, the larger library would indeed prove to be a better resource. However, if the books were in a state of disarray, it would be much more difficult to find a specific title in the larger

library. In that case, the smaller library might very well be the greater asset."

In a similar vein, the Haggadah may cite this passage to show that although the nation was truly numerous, it may not have been to their advantage. It may even have worked against them. For despite their great numbers, they were still bereft of merit, and therefore not deserving of redemption.

ואעבור עליך ואראך מתבוססת

"And I passed over you and saw you wallowing in your blood, and I said to you: 'By your blood shall you live!' and I said to you: 'By your blood shall you live!'"

Pirkei d'Reb Eliezer (29) understands this passage to mean that in the merit of two different bloods, the nation was redeemed: the blood of circumcision and the blood of the Pesach offering.

The Torah prohibits any uncircumcised male from eating the Pesach offering. On the day of the Exodus, before they were able to bring their offerings, the Jewish males all had to be circumcised. (In Egypt, the males were no

numerous *as the plants of the field. You became many and grew, and became mature. Your breasts were full, your hair was grown, but you were naked and bare." I passed over you and saw you wallowing in your blood, and I said to you, 'By your blood shall you live!' – and I said to you, 'By your blood shall you live!'* (Yechezkel 16:7,6).

longer circumcised at the time of the Exodus.[11]) The blood from this mass circumcision, together with the blood from the sacrifices, was smeared on the doorposts, protecting the Children of Israel from the Plague of the Firstborn.

Interestingly, it was specifically *in the merit* of the mitzvah of circumcision that the nation was redeemed. Circumcision was the first mitzvah commanded to Avraham. It was to serve as an eternal sign of the covenant between G-d and the Children of Avraham. Until the Exodus, this was the only commandment that could differentiate the Children of Israel from all the other nations.

That the mitzvah of circumcision was no longer being observed by Jews during the Egyptian exile is the source for the nation's being described as "naked of merits."

Since this was the salient feature of Jewishness at the time, as well as the testimony to the Jews' commitment to G-d and G-d's commitment to them, it was incumbent upon them to resume practice of the mitzvah, if they were to be redeemed.

❖ Finding inspiration in despair

ואעבור עליך ואראך מתבוססת

"And I passed over you and saw you wallowing in your blood, and I said to you: 'By your blood shall you live!'"

Rav Avraham Chaim Levin, Rosh Yeshiva of Telshe-Chicago, once described the unique ability of the Jew to find inspiration in places where others find only reasons to despair. He cited his Rebbe, Rav Elya Meir Bloch, as an

---

11. There seem to be conflicting Midrashim as to whether circumcision had been prohibited by the Egyptians, or whether the people slacked off on their own. See Radal (31) on Pirkei d'Rav Eliezer (Ibid).

וַיָּרֵעוּ אֹתָנוּ הַמִּצְרִים וַיְעַנּוּנוּ, וַיִּתְּנוּ עָלֵינוּ עֲבֹדָה קָשָׁה.

וַיָּרֵעוּ אֹתָנוּ הַמִּצְרִים, כְּמָה שֶׁנֶּאֱמַר הָבָה נִתְחַכְּמָה לוֹ, פֶּן יִרְבֶּה וְהָיָה כִּי תִקְרֶאנָה

example. Rav Elya Meir was in the United States during the years of World War II, unsure of the whereabouts or the fate of his family. Although the situation would have torn apart the strongest of men, Rav Elya Meir held himself in check, and channeled all of his efforts into founding the Telshe Yeshiva in Cleveland.

In an insightful comment that could have been applied to his own circumstances, Rav Elya Meir once explained the above passage from the Haggadah in the following way. The Jews had been enthralled by the Egyptian culture and tried to become a part of it. The Midrash relates that the Jews frequented the Egyptian theaters, malls, and other places of entertainment (*Tanchuma,* ed.Buber, *Shemos* 6). Then came Pharaoh's "Final Solution." Pharaoh had the Jewish babies slaughtered, so that he could bathe in their blood. Human beings were literally used as bricks to fill the daily construction quotas. The brutal nature of this refined society was suddenly laid bare, and lost all of its appeal for the Jews. The glorious culture

became repulsive to them. Yet from that which should have disillusioned them, they were actually inspired to return to G-d. Where others might have felt only hopelessness and desolation, the Jews were able to derive inspiration: "Through your blood shall you live!"

Rav Elya Meir's sentiment is echoed in a story about Rabbi Akiva. The Talmud (*Makkos* 24b) relates that Rabbi Akiva and his colleagues passed by the ruins of the Temple in Jerusalem shortly after its destruction by the Romans. There they witnessed animals scurrying about the site of the *Kodesh Kodoshim,* the Holy of Holies. His colleagues began to weep, yet Rabbi Akiva smiled. His colleagues asked, "Akiva, why do you smile?" Rabbi Akiva asked in return, "And why do you cry?"

Taken aback by the question, Rabbi Akiva's colleagues responded, "We are witnessing the holiest spot in the Universe, the place that no man may enter except for one [the High Priest], and then only on one day of the year [Yom Kippur]. Now we see it overrun by animals

The Egyptians were bad to us. They made us suffer and gave us hard work.

"The Egyptians were bad to us" – as it says, "Come let us act wisely against them, lest they become so many that if there is a war, they

– Is that not reason enough to grieve?"

"It is for that very reason that I smile," Rabbi Akiva said. "The total destruction of Jerusalem was already prophesied— along with the promise of its rebuilding. Now that I have seen the fulfillment of the first part of the prophecy, I have no doubt that the second part will be fulfilled, as well."

Where others saw only destruction and despair, Rabbi Akiva drew inspiration and trust: "Through your blood shall you live!"

❖ Free Will and Destiny

וירעו אותנו המצרים

The Egyptians were bad to us – as it says, "Come, let us act wisely against them, lest they become so many that if there is a war, they will join our enemies, fight against us ..."

The commentators are bothered by the proof from this passage. All the passage tells us is that the Egyptians planned to take measures against the Jewish people, but not that the Egyptians

actually did anything wrong. (See *Malbim* and Abarbanel.)

An answer may be offered based on a statement of the Ra'avad (*Rambam, Hilchos Teshuva* 6:5). Rambam asks why the Egyptians should have been punished for enslaving the Jews, since G-d had informed Avraham, long before, that the Children of Israel would be enslaved and persecuted in a strange land. If that were the case, then the Egyptians were just G-d's tools in the fulfillment of Israel's destiny and should not have been punished. Ra'avad answers that G-d does not decree that a specific individual or nation will serve as His tool for negative acts, until that person or nation establishes a pattern of evil actions. Only after a person has decided to engage in bad behavior, is it decreed that he or she will serve as G-d's tool in the punishment of others.

Once the Egyptians decided to do evil – even before they put their plans into action – it was destined that they fill the role of enslaving and persecuting the Jews. The Haggadah therefore

מִלְחָמָה וְנוֹסַף גַּם הוּא עַל שֹׂנְאֵינוּ וְנִלְחַם בָּנוּ
וְעָלָה מִן הָאָרֶץ.

וַיְעַנּוּנוּ כְּמָה שֶׁנֶּאֱמַר, וַיָּשִׂימוּ עָלָיו שָׂרֵי מִסִּים
לְמַעַן עַנֹּתוֹ בְּסִבְלֹתָם, וַיִּבֶן עָרֵי מִסְכְּנוֹת
לְפַרְעֹה אֶת פִּתֹם וְאֶת רַעַמְסֵס

וַיִּתְּנוּ עָלֵינוּ עֲבֹדָה קָשָׁה, כְּמָה שֶׁנֶּאֱמַר,
וַיַּעֲבִדוּ מִצְרַיִם אֶת בְּנֵי יִשְׂרָאֵל בְּפָרֶךְ:

states that from the time of their planning, it was already considered, as if they had, in fact, committed the evil.

Another possible interpretation of the passage is that the Egyptians viewed us with an "*ayin ra'ah*," an evil eye: They begrudged the Jews their success and growth. Instead of allowing the Jewish people to multiply and live peacefully, they created an atmosphere of fear among the Egyptians. The Jews were then perceived as the enemy – an enemy that would fight against the Egyptians.

❖ The Definition of Work

ויתנו עלנו עבודה קשה

They gave us hard work – as it says: "The Egyptians made the Children of Israel do backbreaking work"

The Hebrew word "be'forech,"

or "avodas perech," is usually understood to mean "hard, crushing work." However, Tosafos (*Pesachim* 117b) cites a Midrash that implies otherwise. The Torah cites the commemoration of the Exodus as a reason for not doing "melacha," or prohibited work, on Shabbos (*Devarim* 5:15). The Midrash finds an allusion to the thirty-nine prohibited categories of work on Shabbos in the word "perech," used to denote the hard labor in Egypt.

In the Hebrew language, each letter is assigned a numerical value. א equals 1, ב equals 2, ג equals 3, and so forth. There are a few different numerical systems, in which the letters can take on different values. In the numerical system of א״ת ב״ש, the numerical value of the first letter, א(1), is interchangeable with that of the last letter, ת (400), and the value of

will join our enemies, fight against us, and leave the land." (Shemos 1:10).

"They afflicted us" – as it says, "They appointed slave drivers over them to make them suffer with hard work, and they built storage cities for Pharaoh, Pithom and Raamses." (Shemos 1:11).

"And they gave us hard work" – as it says, "The Egyptians made the children of Israel do backbreaking work." (Shemos 1:13).

the second letter, ב (2), is interchangeable with that of the next-to-last letter, ש (300), and so forth.

With this system of numerical equivalents, the Hebrew letters assigned to perech, פרך, total 39. It is considered significant that 39 categories of work are proscribed on Shabbos, and that the word for "work" used in the passage has the value of 39. After the Exodus from Egypt, the Torah proscribed on Shabbos those types of labor the Jews had to perform in Egypt.

Now, this might imply that it is only hard, crushing labor that is prohibited on Shabbos. However, Rav Samson Raphael Hirsch proves quite clearly that the Torah does not prohibit work, per se, on Shabbos. Little effort is exerted, when picking a flower, or when flicking on a light switch, yet both activities are prohibited on Shabbos. Rather, it is "creative labor" that is prohibited on Shabbos. The Torah designates Shabbos as a day when the Jew must recognize G-d's mastery over the world. He, therefore, may not engage in any labor that demonstrates human mastery over creation.

Now, if "avodas perech" meant just "hard work", it would have nothing to do with Shabbos, since hard work is not what the Torah prohibits on Shabbos. Clearly, there must be another understanding of "avodas perech."

The Midrash relates that the Egyptians forced the Jews to build cities on sinking, soft earth. No sooner would they finish erecting buildings, than the buildings would sink, and the Jews would have to start over again (*Shemos Rabba* 1). The intent was to break the spirit of the Jewish people, by quickly dashing their feelings of accom-

וַנִּצְעַק אֶל יְיָ אֱלֹהֵי אֲבֹתֵינוּ, וַיִּשְׁמַע יְיָ אֶת קֹלֵנוּ, וַיַּרְא אֶת עָנְיֵנוּ וְאֶת עֲמָלֵנוּ וְאֶת לַחֲצֵנוּ:

וַנִּצְעַק אֶל יְיָ אֱלֹהֵי אֲבֹתֵינוּ כְּמָה שֶׁנֶּאֱמַר, וַיְהִי בַיָּמִים הָרַבִּים הָהֵם וַיָּמָת מֶלֶךְ מִצְרַיִם וַיֵּאָנְחוּ בְנֵי יִשְׂרָאֵל מִן הָעֲבֹדָה וַיִּזְעָקוּ, וַתַּעַל שַׁוְעָתָם אֶל הָאֱלֹהִים מִן הָעֲבֹדָה:

וַיִּשְׁמַע יְיָ אֶת קֹלֵנוּ, כְּמָה שֶׁנֶּאֱמַר, וַיִּשְׁמַע

plishment. Thus it may be that "avodas perech" means constructive work that offers a false sense of accomplishment – in other words, work that is ultimately disillusioning and demoralizing.

The relationship between Shabbos-prohibited work and "avodas perech" may now be better understood. The Jews who had been in Egypt could appreciate the feelings of mastery that come with working constructively towards a goal. Repeatedly, they had seen the products of their creativity and labor destroyed. They had been degraded by the foreknowledge that, under the circumstances, their toil was pointless. The "avodas perech" of Egypt was the catalyst for the Shabbos-prohibited work, which only included constructive and creative labor. Pointless work, such as what had been experienced in Egypt, is not even restricted by Torah law on Shabbos, since it does not bring any feelings of accomplishment or mastery to the worker.

This definition of "avodas perech" allows us to understand something else, as well. The Midrash offers another interpretation of "perech": as a contraction of the two words "peh rach," which means "a soft mouth." "Soft mouth" refers to Pharaoh's sweet-talking the Jews into a work relationship with the Egyptians that would lead to slavery. First Pharaoh encouraged them to join the Egyptians in building up the country, as a sign of their loyalty. The Jews were more than happy to oblige. But gradually, the Egyptians ceased to do any of the work, and the Jews found themselves working alone for Pharaoh.

We cried out to G-d, Lord of our fathers. G-d heard our voice, and He saw our suffering, our labor, and our oppression.

"We cried out to G-d, Lord of our fathers" – as it says, "During that long period, the king of Egypt died. The children of Israel groaned because of the hard work, and they cried out. Their moaning from the labor came up before G-d." (Shemos 2:23).

"G-d heard our voice" – as it says, "G-d

Before they knew it, they were ensnared and enslaved.

It seems odd that the Midrash would interpret the word "perech" to mean something so contrary to its normal definition of "hard, crushing work." However, according to our understanding, the harshness of "perech" may be psychological, and not necessarily physical. This, then, may be the connection between the two interpretations.

Sometimes a person is trapped in a difficult situation, one over which he has no control. Other times, however, had the person been sufficiently cautious, the ensuing problems would never have developed. In the latter instance,the person may feel more guilty, feeling partially responsible for the situation that has evolved. That the Jews permitted themselves

to be sweet-talked into slavery intensified their misery and made their suffering harder to bear. Thus, the "soft mouth" of "perech" actually *resulted* in the "demoralizing work" of "perech."

❖ Prayers without Words

ונצעק אל ה' אלקי אבותנו

We cried out to G-d, Lord of our fathers – as it says, "During that long period, . . . the Children of Israel groaned because of the hard work, and they cried out. Their moaning from the labor came up before G-d. "

"G-d heard our voice" – as it says, "G-d heard their groaning, and G-d remembered His promise to Avraham, Yitzchak, and Yaakov."

The first statement implies that they prayed to G-d, but the

אֱלֹהִים אֶת נַאֲקָתָם, וַיִּזְכֹּר אֱלֹהִים אֶת בְּרִיתוֹ
אֶת אַבְרָהָם אֶת יִצְחָק וְאֶת יַעֲקֹב:

וַיַּרְא אֶת עָנְיֵנוּ, זוֹ פְּרִישׁוּת דֶּרֶךְ אֶרֶץ, כְּמָה
שֶׁנֶּאֱמַר, וַיַּרְא אֱלֹהִים אֶת בְּנֵי יִשְׂרָאֵל, וַיֵּדַע
אֱלֹהִים:

Scriptural evidence is only that they groaned from the hard work – not that they actually prayed. Similarly, in the second statement, the Haggadah does not say that G-d heard the prayers of the Jews, but rather that He heard their voice. This expression also implies that the "prayers" were not composed of words, but rather were merely sounds from their throats.

There are prayers without words, and there are words without prayers. We find two intriguing passages in *Tehillim*: "G-d is close to the broken-hearted" (34:19), and "G-d is close to all who call Him with truth" (145:18). The implication is that G-d is close to two types of people: (1) those who are broken-hearted, even if they do not call out to G-d, and (2) those who call Him with sincerity. No mention is made of the necessity

for any specific wording to be used by either of these people.

The groans of the broken Children of Israel in Egypt were the equivalent of "We cried out to G-d." Their sincere cries to G-d were heard as a "voice" – regardless of the form of expression. The conditions for accepting this communication as "prayer" had been met –a broken heart and sincerity – and, as such, G-d would be more attentive to their cries than He would have been to mere words, even formulated as a prayer, but uttered without sincerity.[12]

וירא את ענינו זו פרישות דרך ארץ
And He saw our affliction – This is the separation of husband and wife, as it says 'G-d saw the Children of Israel, and G-d knew'

The Midrash cited in Rashi

12. We do not refer here to the obligatory prayers said each day. These prayers do indeed require a specific format and a sincere heart. The discussion, above, refers only to the sort of informal prayer that spontaneously occurs when an individual needs to communicate with G-d.

heard their groaning, and G-d remembered His promise to Avraham, Yitzchak, and Ya'akov." (Shemos 2:24).

"And He saw our affliction" – This is the separation of husband and wife, as it says, "G-d saw the children of Israel, and knew". (Shemos 2:25)

(*Shemos* 37:8) relates that the Jews were worked so hard, that when they came home in the evenings, they had lost all desire to be with their wives. This was essential to Pharaoh's plan to prevent the Jews from overpopulating the country. The righteous women, however, used copper mirrors to beautify themselves, and thereby enticed their husbands to live normal family lives. This infused the people with hope for redemption.

For this reason, these very same copper mirrors were later used in the Tabernacle to make the *kiyor*, or basin. Although mirrors are often used to beautify oneself for immoral purposes, the righteous Jewish women in Egypt used them properly, to encourage their husbands to procreate. A mirror that is used appropriately is worthy of use in the Tabernacle.

It is fitting, too, that these mirrors were used to rectify disrupted family life both during the Egyptian exile and in the time of the Tabernacle. The copper basin in the Tabernacle played a role in a procedure, in which the *Sotah*, a suspected adulteress, was tested with a special drink. To prove her innocence, she drank a mixture that included water from the basin. If the drink did not affect her, she could return to her husband with G-d's blessing. Just as the copper mirrors restored Jewish family life during the time in Egypt, so, too, the drink from the copper basin restored the relationship between a husband and wife so that they could share family life once again.

Furthermore, the mirrors in the Tabernacle, through their reflection, may have been reminiscent of G-d's watching –His careful observation of His people and His concern for their suffering. The mirrors may have been a metaphor for the words of our passage, "G-d saw our affliction." In the mirrors, the Jews could see themselves as G-d saw them.

וְאֶת **עֲמָלֵנוּ**, אֵלּוּ הַבָּנִים, כְּמָה שֶׁנֶּאֱמַר, כָּל
הַבֵּן הַיִּלּוֹד הַיְאֹרָה תַּשְׁלִיכֻהוּ, וְכָל הַבַּת
תְּחַיּוּן.

וְאֶת **לַחֲצֵנוּ**, זוֹ הַדְּחַק כְּמָה שֶׁנֶּאֱמַר, וְגַם
רָאִיתִי אֶת הַלַּחַץ אֲשֶׁר מִצְרַיִם לֹחֲצִים אֹתָם:

וַיּוֹצִאֵנוּ יְיָ מִמִּצְרַיִם בְּיָד חֲזָקָה וּבִזְרֹעַ
נְטוּיָה וּבְמֹרָא גָּדֹל, וּבְאֹתוֹת וּבְמֹפְתִים:

ואת עמלנו אלו הבנים

**Our labor – These are the chil-
dren, as it says, "Every boy that
is born, you shall throw into
the river. . ."**

The commentaries are bothered by the use of this strange
expression to denote children.
Why should the beautiful gift of
children be referred to as
"amoleinu," "our difficult labor"?
(See Ritva and *Kol Bo*.)

We can perhaps better understand this with an insight from the
Chafetz Chaim (*Al HaTorah* p.178).
He discusses the prayer that an
individual says after completing a
tractate of the Talmud, "Modeh
Ani." In this prayer, in which we
thank G-d for granting us the
unique opportunity to study Torah,
we say, ". . . .for we toil ['ameilim']
and they toil; yet we toil and
receive compensation, and they
toil but do not receive compensation."

The Chafetz Chaim asks, "Why
does it say the others toil without
receiving reward? What type of
person works without receiving
compensation?"

He explains with a parable. A
man once ordered a suit from a
tailor. When he went to pick up
the suit, he found that it was a
very poor fit. The man protested,
and would not pay for the suit,
since he could not wear it. The tailor, however, objected that even
though the suit did not fit, he
should be compensated for all the
work he had done to make the
suit. The man laughed at the tailor's foolishness, and explained
that the payment was for the suit,
not merely for the labor. If the
work did not produce the desired
result, there could be no compensation.

This is what the prayer means,
explains the Chafetz Chaim,
Although others may be compen-

"Our labor" – These are the children, as it says, "Every boy that is born, you shall throw into the river, but every daughter you shall let live". (Shemos 1:22)

"And our oppression" – This is the pressure, as it says, "I have seen the oppression, how Egypt is pressing them". (Devarim 26:8)

G-d brought us out of Egypt with a strong hand and an outstretched arm, with great fear, signs and wonders.

---

sated, it is not for the toil, but for the results. The study of Torah is different, however, because a person is rewarded for his toil and effort, even if it does not produce any concrete results.

According to this interpretation, "ameilus" refers to toil that produces no fruit. We may understand the Haggadah's usage of the term "ameilus" in reference to children in a similar vein. Although ordinarily, a tremendous amount of effort is invested in the rearing of children, parents are nevertheless usually happy to expend the energy. They expect to reap the rewards of their efforts through the success of their children and the joy their children give them. However, in Egypt such was not the case. Parents knew from the very beginning that it was only a matter of time before their son would be taken away from them and drowned in the river. The

toil of bringing a child into the world, knowing of the loss to come, never realizing the fruit of their efforts – that was truly "ameilus," a difficult labor.

ואת לחצנו זו הדחק

Our oppression – this is the pressure, as it says: "I have also seen the oppression with which the Egyptians oppress them"

The *Mesilas Yesharim* (Chapt. 2) explains that one of Pharaoh's tactics was to keep the Children of Israel working so busily and under such great pressure, that they would not have time to think about escape. In this way, he could ensure that the Jews would remain completely under his control. Every person requires some time and privacy to be able to pause for reflection and establish goals. By precluding such opportunities through his policies, Pharaoh oppressed the

וַיּוֹצִאֵנוּ יְיָ מִמִּצְרַיִם, לֹא עַל יְדֵי מַלְאָךְ, וְלֹא
עַל יְדֵי שָׂרָף, וְלֹא עַל יְדֵי שָׁלִיחַ, אֶלָּא הַקָּדוֹשׁ
בָּרוּךְ הוּא בִּכְבוֹדוֹ וּבְעַצְמוֹ, שֶׁנֶּאֱמַר, וְעָבַרְתִּי
בְאֶרֶץ מִצְרַיִם בַּלַּיְלָה הַזֶּה, וְהִכֵּיתִי כָל בְּכוֹר
בְּאֶרֶץ מִצְרַיִם מֵאָדָם וְעַד בְּהֵמָה, וּבְכָל אֱלֹהֵי
מִצְרַיִם אֶעֱשֶׂה שְׁפָטִים אֲנִי יְיָ.

וְעָבַרְתִּי בְאֶרֶץ מִצְרַיִם בַּלַּיְלָה הַזֶּה – אֲנִי
וְלֹא מַלְאָךְ;

וְהִכֵּיתִי כָל בְּכוֹר בְּאֶרֶץ מִצְרַיִם – אֲנִי וְלֹא
שָׂרָף;

Jews spiritually, psychologically, and physically. Through this oppression, Pharaoh kept the Jews from functioning normally.

❖ G-d's Love for Israel

ויוציאנו ה׳ ממצרים
לא על ידי מלאך

G-d brought us out of Egypt — not by an angel, not by a seraf, and not by a messenger. It was G-d alone, in His glory. . .

The Haggadah explains that at every point in the Exodus G-d's will was carried out through His personal involvement, as it were. No tasks were delegated to His Divine messengers. Why is this reiterated so many times?

The Talmud (*Kiddushin* 41a) states that it is preferable for a person to perform a mitzvah by himself rather than delegating it to another party. The reason is quite simple: If one really enjoys and loves engaging in an activity, one should do it himself. By not delegating the mitzvah to others, the person demonstrates true appreciation.

Ramban (*Vayikra* 18:25) expresses a similar idea regarding G-d's relationship with the Land of Israel. To some extent, G-d places the destiny of nations under the dominion of Divine messengers, or forces of nature. However, the fate of the Land of Israel He reserves for Himself, because of His intense love for the land. The Ramban

"G-d brought us out of Egypt" – not by an angel, not by a seraf, and not by a messenger. It was G-d alone, in His glory, and by Himself. It is thus written, "On that night I will pass through the land of Egypt, and I will strike down all the first- born of Egypt, man and beast". (Shemos 12:12)

"On that night I will pass through the land of Egypt"– I, not an angel!

"And I will strike down all the first- born of Egypt" – I, not an archangel!

goes on to explain that the same intensity is reserved for the Jewish people. Whereas the fates of other peoples are delegated to Divine messengers, G-d, alone, controls the destiny of the Jews.

Thus, the Exodus from Egypt was directed and carried out by G-d Himself, from the slaying of the Egyptian firstborn to the destruction of the Egyptian idols. This was *not* because the Egyptians deserved harsh punishment meted out by G-d – this could have been implemented by a messenger. But the slaying of the Egyptian firstborn was essential to the Jews' gaining freedom and becoming G-d's Chosen People. Moreover, G-d's singular involvement enabled the Jews to recognize and perceive G-d and His wonders, in a more concrete way.

Another interpretation may be drawn from the Midrash (*Bamidbar Rabba* 19) that cites the following passage in *Iyov* (14:3): "Who can bring the pure out of the impure? Not one." The Midrash explains it as saying, "Who could have extracted a righteous person from a wicked person: an Avraham from a Terach; a Chizkiah from an Achaz; a Yoshiahu from an Ammon; or a Jewish nation from an idolatrous nation? It could have been only the Unique One of the world.... "

The Midrash is teaching that to extract something pure from something impure is so difficult a task, so hard to comprehend, that it could only be done by G-d. Only G-d, alone, without the assistance of any messengers, could have extracted the Jews from Egypt without their having been contaminated by Egyptian impurities.

וּבְכָל אֱלֹהֵי מִצְרַיִם אֶעֱשֶׂה שְׁפָטִים – אֲנִי וְלֹא הַשָּׁלִיחַ;

אֲנִי יְיָ – אֲנִי הוּא וְלֹא אַחֵר.

בְּיָד חֲזָקָה, זוֹ הַדֶּבֶר, כְּמָה שֶׁנֶּאֱמַר, הִנֵּה יַד יְיָ הוֹיָה בְּמִקְנְךָ אֲשֶׁר בַּשָּׂדֶה, בַּסּוּסִים בַּחֲמֹרִים בַּגְּמַלִּים בַּבָּקָר וּבַצֹּאן, דֶּבֶר כָּבֵד מְאֹד:

וּבִזְרֹעַ נְטוּיָה, זוֹ הַחֶרֶב, כְּמָה שֶׁנֶּאֱמַר, וְחַרְבּוֹ שְׁלוּפָה בְּיָדוֹ נְטוּיָה עַל יְרוּשָׁלָיִם:

וּבְמֹרָא גָּדֹל, זוֹ גִּלּוּי שְׁכִינָה, כְּמָה שֶׁנֶּאֱמַר, אוֹ

ביד חזקה זו הדבר
ובזרוע נטויה זו החרב

With a strong hand – This is the pestilence, as it says "Behold, G-d's hand will be against your livestock in the fields. . . a very severe pestilence"

With an outstretched arm – This is the sword, as it says, "His sword was drawn in His hand, outstretched over Jerusalem"

These two references seem strange. Why does the Haggadah explain the first passage as referring to the plague of pestilence more than any of the other plagues? And where does the sword brandished by G-d fit into the Exodus? Perhaps, these state-

ments may be understood better within the context of the preceding passage: "G-d took us out of Egypt."

The Haggadah explains that "G-d took us out of Egypt" refers to the slaying of the Egyptian firstborn and other occurrences of that night, but *not* to the Exodus in its entirety. It is logical to assume that the description in the rest of the sentence – "with a strong hand," "with an outstretched arm," and "with great awe" – refer as well to events of the same night. Accordingly, the Haggadah explains that "with a strong hand" represents the pestilence that killed the firstborn animals that night; the next words,

"I will judge all the gods of Egypt" – I, not a messenger!

"I am G-d"– It is I and none other!

"With a strong hand" – This is the pestilence, as it says, "Behold, G-d's hand will be against your livestock in the field, against the horses, donkeys, camels, cattle and sheep – a very severe pestilence". (Shemos 9:3)

"And with an outstretched arm" – This is the sword, as it says, "His sword was drawn in his hand, outstretched over Jerusalem". (Divrei HaYamim I 21:16)

"With great awe" – This is the revelation of the

"with an outstretched arm," indicate the sword that killed the firstborn humans; and the last words, "with great awe," are understood to mean the revelation of G-d's Presence that night, when He passed over the houses of the Children of Israel.

This interpretation fits in well with the passage cited earlier in the Haggadah: "I will pass through the land of Egypt that night, I will slay all the firstborn in Egypt, from man to beast, and I will bring judgment upon all the gods in Egypt, I am G-d." This is a clear reference to the aforementioned occurrences, that G-d will slay the human beings and the animals, and that His Presence will be revealed.

ובמורא גדול זו גלוי השכינה

With great awe – This is the revelation of the Divine Presence, as it says, "Has any god ever tried to take for himself a nation out from another nation ...and with great awesome acts , like all that G-d your Lord did for you ..."

The Haggadah describes, first, a single revelation, but then cites a passage that speaks of *revelations*, suggesting, in fact, that there was *more* than one revelation.

Rav Shlomo Wolbe (*Alei Shur,* vol. 2, p. 391) explains that the revelation that was made manifest the night of the slaying of the firstborn in Egypt was actually the cul-

הֲנִסָּה אֱלֹהִים לָבוֹא לָקַחַת לוֹ גוֹי מִקֶּרֶב גּוֹי,
בְּמַסֹּת בְּאֹתֹת וּבְמוֹפְתִים וּבְמִלְחָמָה וּבְיָד חֲזָקָה
וּבִזְרוֹעַ נְטוּיָה וּבְמוֹרָאִים גְּדֹלִים, כְּכֹל אֲשֶׁר
עָשָׂה לָכֶם יְיָ אֱלֹהֵיכֶם בְּמִצְרַיִם לְעֵינֶיךָ:

וּבְאֹתֹת, זֶה הַמַּטֶּה, כְּמָה שֶׁנֶּאֱמַר, וְאֶת
הַמַּטֶּה הַזֶּה תִּקַּח בְּיָדֶךָ, אֲשֶׁר תַּעֲשֶׂה בּוֹ אֶת
הָאֹתֹת.

וּבְמוֹפְתִים, זֶה הַדָּם, כְּמָה שֶׁנֶּאֱמַר, וְנָתַתִּי
מוֹפְתִים בַּשָּׁמַיִם וּבָאָרֶץ.

mination of the Exodus. At the moment of this revelation, at midnight, the full potential of every Jew's individual relationship with G-d was exposed in its pristine glory. This was the moment of redemption that would serve as a watershed for every spiritual accomplishment that the Jewish people would ever achieve. All the holidays and mitzvos that in any way commemorate the Exodus from Egypt, in fact, commemorate this moment of revelation.

Yet this moment of revelation was also the moment that the Egyptians' firstborn died. The blinding truth of G-d's glory, the intensity of this revelation, was too powerful for those who had not shared the Jewish experience, and they perished. The revelation is thus spoken of in the plural, because although it occurred during a single moment in time, it was perceived differently by different people – as if there had been more than one revelation.

The Talmud (*Nedarim* 8b) likewise says that in the Messianic Era G-d will remove the sun from its sheath. The righteous will be healed by its intensity, but the wicked will find its intensity punishing. *Michtav M'Eliyahu* (vol. 1, p. 301) explains that neither the healing nor the punishment should be understood as a physical experience. Rather, these will occur on a metaphysical plane: There will be a great revelation of clarity and truth that will be tremendously

Divine Presence, as it says, "Has any G-d ever tried to take for himself one nation out from another nation, with trials, signs, wonders, and war, with a strong hand and an outstretched arm, and with great awesome acts, *like all that G-d your Lord did for you in Egypt,* before your very eyes?" (Devarim 4:34)*

"Signs" – This is the staff, as it says, "Take this staff in your hand, and with it perform the signs". (Shemos 4:17)

"And wonders" – This is the blood, as it says, "I will display wonders *in heaven and earth:*

uplifting to some and destructive to others.

❖ The Potential of a People

ובאותות זה המטה
ובמופתים זה הדם

With signs – This is the staff, as it says, "Take this staff in your hand, and with it perform the signs"

With wonders – This is the blood, as it says, " I will display wonders in heaven and on earth"

Why is it that the Haggadah emphasizes the miracles of the staff and the blood more than the other miracles?

The Ramban (*Devarim* 13:2)

differentiates between אות, "os" meaning "a sign," and מופת, "mofais," which means "a wonder." The purpose of a sign is to foretell, whereas the purpose of a wonder is to prove a point "supernaturally."

Moshe's staff, Ramban explains, is described as "a sign," when it is used directly for the benefit of the Children of Israel; it is called "a wonder," when it's capabilities are displayed before Pharaoh. Each of these functions served a purpose. For the Jewish people, who did not need proof of G-d's existence, the transformation of the stick relayed a message of hope; the event was not meant to impress them with miracles. However, for Pharaoh, who did

• Using the index finger, a little wine is spilled from the cup, when each of the words דָם וָאֵשׁ וְתִימְרוֹת עָשָׁן is said, and when each of the plagues is mentioned. A drop of wine is also spilled when Rabbi Yehudah's abbreviations (דְּצַ"ךְ עֲדַ"שׁ) are said for a total of sixteen drops (ibid.). After the recitation of the plagues has been completed, the cups are refilled.

דָּם וָאֵשׁ וְתִימְרוֹת עָשָׁן:

דָּבָר אַחֵר, בְּיָד חֲזָקָה שְׁתַּיִם. וּבִזְרֹעַ נְטוּיָה שְׁתַּיִם. וּבְמֹרָא גָדֹל שְׁתַּיִם, וּבְאֹתוֹת שְׁתַּיִם. וּבְמֹפְתִים שְׁתַּיִם:

not believe in the existence of a G-d Who controls nature, the changing of the stick into a snake was needed to convince him of G-d's existence.

The Midrash relates that G-d's ineffable Name was engraved on the staff, and thus it is sometimes referred to as the "Holy Stick." The *Tiferes Shlomo* explains that the transformation of the Holy Stick symbolizes the transformation of the Jewish people at their nadir. When the stick was thrust to the ground, it became a snake: Similarly, the Children of Israel – however great their potential – when thrust into the bowels of exile, became lowly, despicable creatures. Yet when Moshe grabbed the snake by its tail, once again it became the stick of G-d. Likewise, when the Jewish leaders assumed proper leadership of the Jewish nation – grabbing the

nation by its tail, as it were – the Jews were restored to their former glory. The message of the staff for the Jews was encouragement – a sign not to despair. It is for this reason that the stick is used as an example of "signs."

The use of "wonders," to impress the Egyptians with G-d's dominion over nature, is most powerfully demonstrated by the first plague: Blood. Whereas the other plagues were all manifestations of nature gone awry—for example, the unnatural proliferation of frogs and locust – the plague of Blood revealed G-d's ability to change one object into another, to change matter.

Incidentally, the commentators are bothered by the need for the stick in the implementation of some of the other plagues. Why couldn't Moshe perform miracles without

Blood, fire, and pillars of smoke. (Yoel 3:3)"
Another explanation in this:
"A strong hand" – makes two plagues,
"An outstretched arm" – another two.
"Great fear" – two more,
"Signs" – another two,
"And wonders" – the last two.

the staff? Perhaps the staff was used to remind the Jews of G-d's sustained presence. The stick had been used for the transformation of stick into snake. This was G-d's work. The use of the staff in the plagues would have reminded the Jews that G-d had not deserted them: With the proper leadership, they could still maintain their status as a holy nation.

דם ואש ותמרות עשן
...blood, fire and pillars of smoke

It is customary to spill a few drops of wine when mentioning each of the plagues. The Abarbanel explains that the source for this custom is based on a passage in *Mishlei* (24:17): "When your enemy falls, do not rejoice." Wine is drunk as a symbol of joy. In *Tehillim* (104:15), we read: "Wine gladdens the heart of man." It is therefore fitting to spill some of the wine when each plague is named, to show a minimizing of joy for the suffering of the Egyptians.

It is quite interesting to note that the suffering of the Egyptians is marked, not by overt sadness, but by diminished joy. On the one hand, the Egyptians received their just deserts, and we should rejoice that they could no longer persecute the Children of Israel. Thus we drink wine, because our salvation from their hands is cause for celebration. On the other hand, the knowledge that the victory came at the cost of human lives appropriately diminishes our joy. We bear witness to the suffering of the Egyptians by spilling our wine.

This, however, does not explain why the wine is also spilled at the words "blood, fire, and pillars of smoke." These words refer not to the Egyptian experience, but rather to the Messianic era. Why should we minimize our joy today, for something that has not yet happened?

The spilling of the wine, at this point, may be an allusion to the prayer we say, later in the Seder: *"Sh'foch chamoscho"*: "Pour Your wrath upon the nations that do not

אֵלּוּ עֶשֶׂר מַכּוֹת שֶׁהֵבִיא הַקָּדוֹשׁ בָּרוּךְ הוּא
עַל הַמִּצְרִים בְּמִצְרַיִם וְאֵלּוּ הֵן:

דָּם. צְפַרְדֵּעַ. כִּנִּים. עָרוֹב. דֶּבֶר. שְׁחִין.
בָּרָד. אַרְבֶּה. חֹשֶׁךְ. מַכַּת בְּכוֹרוֹת.

recognize You . . . " The pouring of a little wine reminds us that G-d poured His wrath upon the Egyptians. We hope He will do the same, in the future, to all His enemies.

❖ The Lessons of the Plagues

אלו עשר מכות שהביא הקב״ה

These are the ten plagues that G-d brought upon the Egyptians in Egypt

The *Mishna Berura* (473:64) states that this is one of the most important parts of the Haggadah, because it describes the great miracles G-d performed for the sake of the Jews. Therefore, even if some of the women are preparing the festive meal in the kitchen, they should come to the Seder table to recite this section of the Haggadah.

Accordingly, we should not simply name the plagues, but rather discuss their underlying purpose and the miracles associated with them.

The Steipler Rav (*Chayei Olam,* Chapter 15) offers clarification. From the plague of Blood, the Jews saw that G-d controls the water.

From the plague of Frogs, they understood that G-d has dominion over marine creatures. The plague of Wild Animals demonstrated His control over the land animals. The plague of Locusts showed G-d's control of insects and flying creatures, and the winds, as well; He caused a western wind to blow away the locusts. The plague of Pestilence made it clear that G-d controls animal life; the plague of the Firstborn, human life. The plague of Lice demonstrated G-d's mastery over the earth: He caused the land to turn into vermin. The plague of Boils showed G-d control over human health. The plague of Darkness made clear that G-d controls the heavenly lights; the plague of Hail – in which ice and fire were fused together – the weather, and that mutually exclusive conditions can coexist, when G-d sees fit.

❖ Divine Fairness

The Midrash (*Lekach Tov*) perceives the lesson of "measure for measure" in the plagues. For each plague, there had been corresponding acts of cruelty on the part of the Egyptians.

These are the Ten Plagues that G-d brought upon the Egyptians in Egypt.

"And these are [The Ten Plagues]:

1. *Blood* ***2.*** *Frogs* ***3.*** *Lice* ***4.*** *Wild Beasts*
5. *Pestilence* ***6.*** *Boils* ***7.*** *Hail* ***8.*** *Locusts*
9. *Darkness* ***10.*** *Death of the First-born*

• In the first plague, Blood, the water turned to blood, to punish the Egyptians for spilling Jewish blood – especially the drowning of Jewish baby boys in the Nile River.

• The plague of Frogs brought sleepless nights to the Egyptians. This was punishment for their arousing the Jews from their sleep to go to work in the fields.

• The plague of Lice punished the Egyptians for preventing the Children of Israel from bathing and maintaining proper hygiene.

• Wild Animals were brought for forcing the Jews to capture animals as sport for the Egyptians.

• Pestilence was a response to isolating the Jewish shepherds, forcing them to tend their flocks in far-flung areas, such as the mountains and the wilderness.

• The plague of Boils precluded the afflicted Egyptians from bathing in either hot or cold water. This was punishment for forcing Jewish slaves to heat or cool the Egyptian bath water.

• Hail came as punishment for forcing the Jewish slaves to plant trees and gardens. The hail destroyed all of these trees.

• The plague of Locusts came for a similar reason: The locusts devoured the grain that the Children of Israel had been forced to plant.

• Darkness came to obscure the death of those Jews who did not want to leave Egypt. Had their bodies been visible, the Egyptians would have thought that the plague of Darkness had also affected the Jewish population. This would have given the Egyptians solace, as well as provided them a reason to dismiss this plague as proving nothing.

• The Plague of the Firstborn was punishment for killing Jews.

❖ **Mocking the Wicked**

Each plague, and many of the miracles that were performed in Egypt, served as a source of mockery or derision of the Egyptians and their beliefs. Although the Talmud generally prohibits all forms of mockery, the single exception is our contempt for idolatry (*Megillah* 25b).

To digress a bit, the explanation of this Talmudic dictum is that certain types of mistaken ideas may be intellectually attractive to those who cannot discern that these ideas, and the reasoning behind them, are specious. As a rule, in such a situation, all that is needed to diffuse any harm is to expose the inaccuracies of the idea. However, there are erroneous philosophies whose appeal is emotional rather than intellectual. Idolatry, for example, though it may be illogical, exerts a magnetic attraction.[13]

Among its other enchantments, idolatry allows the individual "worshiper" to experience a sense of purpose, and provides the individual with a battery of justifications for a range of unacceptable behaviors. With idolatry, intellectual rebuttal is insufficient, since the appeal is not itself intellectual. Therefore, the only suitable response to such philosophical ideas is mockery and insult: Only through derision is the powerful emotional appeal of false gods neutralized and destroyed. For this reason, the Torah says that one should destroy the names of idols (*Devarim* 12:3). The Talmud relates that it was customary to call the various idols by derogatory names, to diffuse their "power" and render the entire idolatrous belief system a farce (*Avodah Zara* 46a).

Be'er Yosef and *Eved HaMelech* (quoted in *Yalkut Lekach Tov*) both cite the following passage in the Torah:

> "That you may relate in the ears of your son and your son's son how I made a mockery of Egypt, and my signs that I placed among them, and you will know that I am G-d" (*Shemos* 10:2).

This statement means that there is an obligation upon parents *not only* to relate to their children the events that occurred in Egypt, but *more specifically* to relate the ways in which G-d exposed the Egyptians to ridicule.

❖ Mockery in Egypt

The Egyptian idols and culture held an emotional appeal for the Jewish people. G-d therefore felt it necessary to punish the Egyptians in such a way that would prove to the Jews His complete mastery over Creation. By doing this, G-d both exacted retribution from the Egyptians and obviated the need the Jews had felt to participate in Egyptian culture.

The first example of this mockery is seen in Moshe's upbringing. Pharaoh had received word from his astrologers that the Jewish savior would be born and would suffer his downfall through water. Pharaoh immediately decreed that all Jewish boys born subsequent to this "revelation" were to be thrown

---

13. See Talmud, Avodah Zara (27b)

into the Nile River. Because of this decree, Moshe's parents were forced to place him in a basket and put him in the reeds near the riverbank. Pharaoh's own daughter found the baby, had compassion on him, and raised him in Pharaoh's own home, among great affluence. What a mockery this must have made of Pharaoh! Pharaoh, alone, was responsible for the royal upbringing of the Jewish savior!

We see a similar example in Moshe's appearance before Pharaoh, eighty years later. G-d told Moshe to perform a few miracles before Pharaoh to prove that he had been sent by G-d. Thus, Aharon threw down his staff, and it was transformed into a snake. When Aharon retrieved the snake, it was transformed once again into a staff.

Pharaoh laughed at their trick. The Egyptians were well-known for their sorcery, and this trick did not impress Pharaoh. His magicians all transformed their sticks into snakes, as part of their repertoire of magic, and they were also able to turn them back into sticks again. However, Aharon's staff swallowed all the sticks of the Egyptian magicians.

We can only imagine how this must have embarrassed Pharaoh. Although Pharaoh had assured himself that his magicians were as powerful as Moshe and Aharon, Moshe proved him wrong. Not only did Aharon's staff consume the other staffs, but it did so *after*

it had changed back from a snake into a staff – thereby magnifying the irony.

❖ Mockery and the Plagues

Along the same lines, the Talmud and Midrash describe the ways in which mockery was manifest throughout the plagues.

1) Before the plague of Blood, G-d told Moshe to go to Pharaoh in the morning, when Pharaoh was accustomed to going down to the Nile River, and inform him that the water was going to turn into blood. The Midrash explains that Pharaoh, who proclaimed himself a god, claimed to have no need for normal bodily functions. Each morning, however, he went to the river to relieve himself in secrecy. Moshe deliberately went to Pharaoh at that time when it would be most humiliating to him. The "great deity," who had successfully fooled the entire Egyptian nation, was now exposed as a charlatan by his enemy. At the same time, the Egyptian populace were shown to be gullible fools, easily tricked by their leader's chicanery.

2) The first plague primarily affected the Nile River, turning the water into blood. This was a mockery of Egyptian religious beliefs. The Nile River was worshipped as a life-giving god by the Egyptians, since it was their main source of water and created the fertile Delta. By turning the water to blood, G-d showed that their

source of life could become a source of death for them.

3) The Midrash relates that all of the water in Egypt turned to blood, except for the water of the Jews. Thus it came to pass that when an Egyptian wanted to drink water, he would try to take the water from a Jew. However, as soon as he had it, it would turn into blood. The Egyptian would try to drink out of a vessel shared with a Jew. Yet even then, the Egyptian would drink blood, but the Jew would drink water. The only way the Egyptians were able to drink water was if they paid the Jews large sums of money.

The Egyptians were thus ridiculed. They had done what they could to outwit G-d, but to no avail.

4) The Talmud (*Sanhedrin* 67b) says that when G-d first brought the plague of Frogs, a single frog emerged from the river. However, when the Egyptians hit the frog, it became two frogs. As they continued to strike the frogs, the frogs multiplied again and again, until the entire land was swarming with them.

In essence, the Egyptians brought the plague upon themselves. Had they exercised self-control and refrained from striking the frogs, they would not have suffered their overwhelming presence. Thus the Egyptians' lack of self-discipline was exposed in a most ridiculous manner.

5) When Pharaoh pleaded with Moshe to remove the frogs, Moshe asked Pharaoh *when* he would like them removed. Pharaoh answered, "Tomorrow." Ibn Ezra and Rabbenu Bachya explain that Pharaoh gave this answer, because he thought it would expose Moshe as a charlatan. Pharaoh suspected Moshe of possessing knowledge of the occult. Consequently, he assumed that Moshe knew just when the plague was to end – and that Moshe had asked Pharaoh when he wanted the frogs removed at that very time when the plague was going to end in any case. Pharaoh anticipated that Moshe expected him to answer, "Immediately!," and Moshe would be unable to fulfill his request that the plague last yet another day. Of course, Moshe agreed to Pharaoh's request, and the frogs died the following day. Pharaoh thus had thought that he could outwit Moshe, but just ended up making things more difficult for himself, and appearing absurd.

6) The Torah states, that when the second plague ended, all of the frogs that had died throughout the land were piled up in heaps. Their decomposition created a strong stench, which lay like a cloud across the nation. This, also, was a mockery, because even after the Egyptians had relief from the actual plague of the frogs, they still suffered greatly from its repercussions. Their failed expectations of relief from the frogs further exposed how little control the Egyptians really had over the situation.

The pattern of events, in the plague of Frogs, led the Egyptians to experience yet another set of false expectations, during the plague of Wild Animals that occurred later. The Egyptians figured that just as the bodies of the frogs had remained at the conclusion of that plague, so would those of the Wild Animals. Had that been the case, the Egyptians could have used their skins for clothing. However, neither the animals nor their skins materialized: When the plague of Wild Animals ended, the animals escaped from the land, with none remaining behind. Once again, mockery took the form of thwarted hopes.

7) During the first two plagues of Blood and Frogs, the Egyptian magicians were partially able to save face by producing results similar to those created by Moshe and Ahron. The commentaries explain that although the magicians could not really *change nature* as Moshe had done, they were able to create the *appearance* of blood and frogs, thereby minimizing the effect of the miracles wrought by Moshe and Aharon. (See *Midrash Lekach Tov, Sechel Tov* and *Rabbenu Sa'adia Gaon* cited in *Sha'arei Ahron, Shemos* 7:11.)

With the coming of the plague of Lice, however, the Egyptian magicians were unable to duplicate their earlier successes. The *Da'as Zekeinim* states that Egyptian magic required the magician to have his feet touching the floor, if he were going to work a spell. But in the plague of Lice, the lice were so numerous, they created a barrier between the magicians' feet and the floor on which they were standing. This prevented their magic from being actualized, and no lice appeared. The well-respected sorcerers must have been greatly shamed before the Egyptians, when they realized that the lice were so thick, they had been prevented from standing directly on the floor. They could not save face, and were forced to admit that this was the "finger of G-d." Thus their fraudulence was exposed before their own people.

8) Some of the commentaries express the opinion that the plague of Lice also infested the area where the Jews resided. Miraculously, the lice did not bother the Jews. (See Ritva and Rambam's commentary on *Avos* 5:4.) This phenomenon – the infestation of the Jewish area – may have been intentional: The Egyptians would have been fooled into believing that they were not the sole victims of the plague; they would have then mistakenly concluded that this plague was not a form of Divine Retribution. The plagues that followed, though, would have mocked their wishful thinking.

9) Rav Meir Lehmann, in his commentary on the Haggadah, explains Rabbi Yehuda's mnemonic for the plagues – *Detzach, Adash,* and *BeAchav* – as follows: In all three groups of three plagues, there was a spiral of affliction:

Each of the three plagues, in turn, affected the Egyptians more directly. This progression, or cycle, was repeated in each triad. In the first group of plagues, Blood, Frogs, and Lice, (a) Blood affected the Nile River, but, technically speaking, this did not have the physical proximity of the second and third plagues; (b) As the frogs proliferated, they came nearer to human beings and could not be avoided; and (c) the lice came even closer, infesting the Egyptians' hair and clothing.

The Egyptians had assumed that the fourth plague would affect them more seriously than did the lice. But, this was not to be the case, as the plague of Wild Animals started the cycle over again, at the bottom of the spiral. (This may be another example of mockery, as the cycles would have resulted in the sort of confusion that makes expectation impossible. The very arrangement and sequence of the plagues meant that the Egyptians could not know when the worst blow would fall!) Thus the fourth plague was more distanced from human beings, affecting wild animals of the wilderness. The fifth plague, Pestilence, moved closer, and affected the domestic animals of the Egyptians. Boils, the sixth plague, was parallel to the lice, as it affected their bodies – a worse affliction than either Wild Animals or Pestilence, and worse, yet, than Lice.

The cycle began a third time

with Hail, the seventh plague, which destroyed the fields and animals. The Locusts of the eighth plague ate all of the Egyptians' remaining food, affecting them more intimately than Hail. But, the plague of Darkness came closest of all, as it totally immobilized the Egyptians.

The Egyptians were thus repeatedly taunted. Twice, after their growing fear of the plagues that were to come, they were given a brief, surprise reprieve. However, each time the surprise was short-lived, because with each cycle, there was a spiral of intensity, as the plagues once again began to affect them more directly.

After the Egyptians had endured this cycle three times, they thought they perceived a pattern. But once again, they were surprised. Instead of the tenth plague's bringing an affliction of diminished intensity, it was the most destructive plague of all – the Killing of the Firstborn in each house.

10) Rashi comments that during the plague of Pestilence only the domestic animals that remained outside, in the fields, were killed. Those that were kept indoors were untouched. Although the Egyptians had *not* been cautioned beforehand to keep their animals indoors, those who had nevertheless done so were fortunate and their animals were spared.

Before the Plague of Hail, however, the Egyptians were

explicitly told to gather their animals and bring them indoors, so that they would be protected from the hail. The Egyptians had seen, earlier, during the plague of Pestilence, that those animals that had been kept indoors had survived. Nonetheless, many of them disregarded the warning. In fact, even some of those that had kept their animals inside during the Pestilence when there had been no warning, did not heed Moshe's advice, and left their animals in the fields, to be victims of the Hail.

Two questions are in order. First, why did the Egyptians ignore the warning, once given. Second, why did Moshe forewarn the Egyptians regarding the Hail, but not with the earlier plague of Pestilence? The answers to these questions suggest that both *warning* and *not warning* may have been strategically intended, contributing to the element of mockery.

Regarding the first question, we may point to the nature of human beings, which is to resent authority.[14] The very fact of the Egyptians' being ordered to bring their animals indoors during the hail resulted in their choosing not to do so. Even those Egyptians who had kept their animals inside during the plague of Pestilence

would not do so during the hail, just to flout the authority of G-d. As to the second question, the Egyptians were not forewarned before the Pestilence, because G-d wanted them to see that there *was* a possible escape from that plague, and, perhaps, from future ones. This laid the foundation for their trusting the truth of Moshe's suggestion of protecting the animals during the plague of Hail. However, given the resistance to authority, juxtaposed against the precedent of the indoor animals' being spared the Pestilence, it was as though Moshe had dared the Egyptians *not* to take advantage of the chance to save their animals. In the end, however, the Egyptians opted to try and save face, rather than animals, and were thus mocked.

11) No mention is made of the magicians in the Torah after they were forced to admit defeat during the plague of Lice – with a single exception: their absence during the plague of Boils. Apparently, following their humiliation with the lice, the magicians still claimed that they could duplicate Moshe's feats. However, the plague of Boils silenced them for good. During that time, they were embarrassed to appear before Moshe, because they, themselves, were covered

---

14. For this reason we find that the reward for keeping an obligatory mitzvah is greater than that of observing an optional mitzvah, because the resistance to observing an obligatory mitzvah is much stronger. (See Talmud, Avodah Zara 3a and Tosafos).

with boils. They could not bear to appear afflicted in public, admitting that they were powerless to do anything about it. Once again, the magicians' powers were being mocked!

12) During the plague of Hail, the Torah relates, only the early-ripened crops were destroyed. The wheat and spelt crops, which ripen later, were spared. Rashi cites sources who say that this was a natural occurrence, because unripened crops would be soft and pliable, bending easily in the hail. He cites other sources, however, who claim that the survival of these crops was miraculous. If the latter claim is correct that there was indeed a miracle, we may well ask, why did G-d spare these crops destruction? And if the former assessment is accurate, and no miracle was necessary, why did the Torah report this seemingly insignificant piece of information?

The hail destroyed nearly all the vegetation in Egypt. When the Egyptians saw that some crops had survived the destruction, they felt a sense of relief. At least something had been left for them to eat. However, their relief was short-lived. In the plague that followed, the locusts ate everything that had survived the hail. That these two plagues allowed the Egyptians to experience some small illusion of comfort, only to have it dashed before their eyes, was another example of mockery.

13) Before the Locusts of the eighth plague, Pharaoh had finally agreed to allow the Jewish men to go serve G-d, as long as the women and children remained behind. When Moshe refused his offer, Pharaoh banished him from his presence. Subsequently, when the Locusts struck, Pharaoh wanted Moshe to pray for their removal. He had to recant his earlier dismissal of Moshe, in order to summon him to come quickly before him. This public reversal must have been a source of great shame to Pharaoh.

After the plague of Darkness, Pharaoh behaved similarly. He offered Moshe to let the nation go, but without their animals. Moshe refused this offer, as well. Pharaoh angrily told Moshe that he never wanted to see his face again.

But when the plague of the Firstborn struck, Pharaoh ran madly through the streets of Egypt, calling out wildly, "Where does Moshe live? Where does Aharon live? Go out from my people and you may serve G-d, as you have spoken! Bless me too, that I not die!" Could there have been a greater embarrassment for Pharaoh? The great and feared monarch was reduced to running through the streets, seeking a man he said he never wanted to see again, begging for his own life.

14) During the plague of Locusts, the Egyptians caught many locusts and pickled them in jars, to be used for food. When the plague ended, a strong West wind blew all the locusts into the sea. Even those that had been pickled,

were swept away in the wind. Not one locust remained in all of Egypt. The resourceful Egyptians, who thought that they would try to salvage something from the plague, were thwarted at every turn and could be held up to ridicule.

15) Rashi cites the Midrash that during the plague of Darkness, the Jews were able to search the houses of the Egyptians to see where they kept their valuables. They took nothing for themselves, however. Later, when the Jews were ready to leave Egypt, they asked the Egyptians for their valuables. When an Egyptian denied possessing any treasures, the Jew would mock him, and identify exactly where each valuable was hidden. The Egyptian was forced to admit his own lie, and acknowledge that the Jews had the integrity not to have taken the valuables on their own.

16) Finally, the Mechilta (*Beshalach* 14:5) states that *all* the plagues, in general, brought derision to the Egyptians. The Torah says, "Pharaoh and his servants had a change of heart and they said, 'What is this that we have done that we sent away this people from serving us?'" The Mechilta describes how the Egyptians complained that had they been punished, but not been forced to send away their slaves, they could have accepted their lot. Likewise, had they been punished and been forced to send away their slaves, but had not lost their valuables,

they would not have complained. Now that they were punished, forced to send away their slaves, and deprived of their valuables as well, they had become a laughing-stock.

The Mechilta illustrates the absurdity of the situation with a parable. A man ordered his servant to buy a fish in the marketplace. The servant brought back a fish that had spoiled. The master was angry and told the servant that as punishment for his actions he had to choose one of three possible consequences: He could eat the rotten fish; or receive one hundred lashes; or pay a fine of one hundred coins. The servant decided to eat the spoiled fish. However, after tasting it, he decided that he could not tolerate the rotten stench, so he chose to receive the whipping instead. After a few lashes, though, the servant could not bear the pain, and he finally agreed to pay the money. People then laughed at the servant, who, through his own choice, received all three punishments instead of only one.

The Egyptians, too, could have been spared a great deal of pain had they freed the Jews earlier. By not doing so, they had to endure greater suffering, physically, emotionally, and financially.

מכת בכורות
Plague of the Firstborn

The commentators are puzzled as to why the tenth plague is called "makas bechoros," which means "the plague of the

רַבִּי יְהוּדָה הָיָה נוֹתֵן בָּהֶם סִמָנִים:
דְּצַ"ךְ. עֲדַ"שׁ. בְּאַחַ"ב.

רַבִּי יוֹסֵי הַגְּלִילִי אוֹמֵר, מִנַּיִן אַתָּה אוֹמֵר
שֶׁלָּקוּ הַמִּצְרִים בְּמִצְרַיִם עֶשֶׂר מַכּוֹת, וְעַל הַיָּם
לָקוּ חֲמִשִּׁים מַכּוֹת. בְּמִצְרַיִם מָה הוּא אוֹמֵר,

Firstborn," rather than just "bechoros," or "firstborn." Each of the other nine plagues is referred to by just *one* word, without the prefatory "makas," which means "the plague of." (See *Malbim Haggadah*.)

The Midrash (*Shochar Tov* 136) relates that when the Egyptian firstborn heard that they were going to die and that Pharaoh *still* would not let the Jews go, they started an uprising, and themselves killed many of their fellow Egyptians. There were, therefore, two causes of death in the tenth plague – as alluded to in the words "plague of the Firstborn" – the plague, itself, and the revolt of the firstborn.

An additional reason may be given for calling the tenth plague "makas bechoros," based on an interpretation I once heard from Rabbi Yosef Meisels, of the Hebrew Academy of Cleveland. He explained that the tenth plague was actually a disease that struck only those who were firstborn in their families – a "firstborn-itis," if you will. The actual name of the disease was "Firstborn-Plague." For this reason, only firstborn children were at risk during this plague. But that part of the plague that was air-borne, the disease affecting firstborn males, was only one component. The Angel of Death posed an independent danger to *everyone*, both Egyptian and Jew, firstborn and otherwise.[15]

This interpretation helps us understand an additional oddity about the name of the plague. Note that the expression "makas bechoros" takes the Hebrew plural feminine form. This is rather surprising. Why would the male firstborn be called "bechoros," rather than the masculine "bechorim"?

---

15. Ramban (Shemos 12:23) explains that the Jews were all prohibited from stepping out of their houses the whole night of the plague of the Firstborn, to protect them from the danger of the Angel of Death.

Rabbi Yehuda used to express them with an abbreviation:
Detzach, Adash, BeAchav

Rabbi Yosi the Gallilean said: How do we know that the Egyptians were smitten with ten plagues in Egypt, and with fifty plagues at the Sea? In Egypt we find the statement, "The

Perhaps the expression should not be translated "the plague of the firstborn," but rather the *firstborn plague*. If the word "plague" is a noun in the feminine gender, and "firstborn" is an adjective rather than a noun in the genitive case, it would have to take the feminine form, as well – not because the victims were female, but because it is an adjective describing the type of plague.

רבי יהודה היה נותן בהם סימנים
Rabbi Yehuda made a mnemonic of their Hebrew initials

See the discussion above (p. 19), regarding the necessity for a mnemonic.

❖ The Art of Appreciation

רבי יוסי הגלילי אומר
Rabbi Yosi of Galillee says: "How do we know that the Egyptians were smitten with ten plagues in Egypt and with fifty plagues at the Sea? . . . "

Rabbi Eliezer says: "How do we know that each plague that G-d

brought upon the Egyptians in Egypt was really made up of four plagues? . . . "

The ten plagues listed in the Haggadah are very specific about the sort of punishment each one entailed. Yet, what elements and events characterized the fifty, or 150, or 200 additional plagues that were visited upon the Egyptians? Why is there no mention of these other plagues in the Torah?

Perhaps the lessons being taught in this section of the Haggadah and in the sections that follow it – Rabbi Eliezer, Rabbi Akiva, *Dayenu,* and Rabban Gamliel – derive *not* from the information they provide us, but rather from the examples they set of a rigorous intellectual, analytical, and spiritual pursuit of meaning, and of an unceasing struggle to appreciate what we are given by G-d.

We tend to be quite lazy intellectually. Often we find ourselves using vague expressions such as "everything," "a thing," or "you

וַיֹּאמְרוּ הַחַרְטֻמִּם אֶל פַּרְעֹה אֶצְבַּע אֱלֹהִים
הוּא. וְעַל הַיָּם מָה הוּא אוֹמֵר, וַיַּרְא יִשְׂרָאֵל
אֶת הַיָּד הַגְּדֹלָה אֲשֶׁר עָשָׂה יְיָ בְּמִצְרַיִם, וַיִּירְאוּ
הָעָם אֶת יְיָ, וַיַּאֲמִינוּ בַּיְיָ וּבְמֹשֶׁה עַבְדּוֹ. כַּמָּה
לָקוּ בְּאֶצְבַּע, עֶשֶׂר מַכּוֹת, אֱמוֹר מֵעַתָּה,
בְּמִצְרַיִם לָקוּ עֶשֶׂר מַכּוֹת, וְעַל הַיָּם לָקוּ
חֲמִשִּׁים מַכּוֹת:

רַבִּי אֱלִיעֶזֶר אוֹמֵר, מִנַּיִן שֶׁכָּל מַכָּה וּמַכָּה,
שֶׁהֵבִיא הַקָּדוֹשׁ בָּרוּךְ הוּא עַל הַמִּצְרִים
בְּמִצְרַיִם, הָיְתָה שֶׁל אַרְבַּע מַכּוֹת. שֶׁנֶּאֱמַר,

know what I mean." Our conversations are punctuated by cliches, platitudes, and content-free statements because we are too lazy to clarify what it is, exactly, that we mean. On the other hand, when we take the time to reflect, we are capable of deep appreciation and a range of perceptions, even regarding a single dynamic or object. When we glance at a diamond, for example, one person may appreciate its shape, another its brilliance. But to truly appreciate the diamond, one must examine every facet of the stone. Its overall beauty results from the precision and clarity of every aspect of the diamond.

Rabbi Yosi, Rabbi Eliezer and Rabbi Akiva were not satisfied with the simple account of the plagues given in the Torah. They understood that the Torah only touched on the general miracles. They knew that to gain a deeper appreciation of what G-d had done, they had to analyze all facets of the miracles and their possible ramifications.

Rav Meir Lehmann cites the first plague, Blood, as an example. The general plague involved the waters of the Nile River turning to blood. This was accompanied by the death of the fish, and by the poisoning of the air. However, the Midrash relates, the stored containers of water also turned into blood, as well as the Egyptians'

magicians said to Pharaoh, 'It is G-d's finger.'"
At the Sea of Reeds, it is written, "Israel saw
the great hand that G-d had directed against
Egypt. The people believed in G-d and in His
servant Moshe."

Now if one finger brought ten plagues, [an
entire hand would bring fifty]. From this we
see that if there were ten plagues in Egypt,
there were fifty at the Sea of Reeds.

Rabbi Eliezer said: How do we know that each
plague that G-d brought on the Egyptians in
Egypt was really made up of four plagues?
[When the Psalms speak of the ten plagues] it

saliva. A further consequence of the plague was the financial gain for the Jews, because the Egyptians were forced to pay large sums of money to the Jews in order to obtain drinking water. Thus, we see several different dimensions of a single plague.

Rabbi Yosi marshaled support from Scripture that in fact there were fifty dimensions to the plagues in Egypt and at the Sea. Rabbi Eliezer and Rabbi Akiva found sources for even more than fifty. As they endeavored to gain a fuller understanding of all of the facets of G-d's acts of retribution, they looked deeper and deeper to make certain they missed nothing.

The exact nature of the plagues is not mentioned in the Haggadah because it is not relevant. Each person must gain his own appreciation of the different dimensions of the plagues, by trying to analyze the plagues to the best of his ability.

Looked at this way, the discussion that took place all night in B'nei Brak among Rabbi Akiva and his colleagues, not only makes greater sense to us, but provides us as well with an analytical model. They tried to analyze and appreciate the different dimensions of each of the plagues and miracles, each sage according to his ability.

יְשַׁלַּח בָּם חֲרוֹן אַפּוֹ עֶבְרָה וָזַעַם וְצָרָה מִשְׁלַחַת מַלְאֲכֵי רָעִים.

עֶבְרָה אַחַת.

וָזַעַם שְׁתַּיִם.

וְצָרָה שָׁלֹשׁ.

מִשְׁלַחַת מַלְאֲכֵי רָעִים אַרְבַּע.

אֱמֹר מֵעַתָּה, בְּמִצְרַיִם לָקוּ אַרְבָּעִים מַכּוֹת. וְעַל הַיָּם לָקוּ מָאתַיִם מַכּוֹת:

רַבִּי עֲקִיבָא אוֹמֵר, מִנַּיִן שֶׁכָּל מַכָּה וּמַכָּה, שֶׁהֵבִיא הַקָּדוֹשׁ בָּרוּךְ הוּא עַל הַמִּצְרִים בְּמִצְרַיִם, הָיְתָה שֶׁל חָמֵשׁ מַכּוֹת. שֶׁנֶּאֱמַר, יְשַׁלַּח בָּם חֲרוֹן אַפּוֹ, עֶבְרָה וָזַעַם וְצָרָה, מִשְׁלַחַת מַלְאֲכֵי רָעִים.

חֲרוֹן אַפּוֹ אַחַת.

עֶבְרָה שְׁתַּיִם.

וָזַעַם שָׁלֹשׁ.

וְצָרָה אַרְבַּע.

מִשְׁלַחַת מַלְאֲכֵי רָעִים

חָמֵשׁ. אֱמֹר מֵעַתָּה, בְּמִצְרַיִם לָקוּ חֲמִשִּׁים מַכּוֹת. וְעַל הַיָּם לָקוּ חֲמִשִּׁים וּמָאתַיִם מַכּוֹת:

says, "[G-d] sent against them His fierce anger, fury, rage, trouble, [and] a mission of evil angels." (Tehillim 78:49)

"Fury"- makes one.

"Rage"- makes two.

"Trouble"- makes three.

"A mission of evil angels" – makes four.

From this we see that in Egypt they were struck with a total of forty plagues. Therefore, at the Sea, they were struck with two hundred plagues.

"Rabbi Akiva said: How do we know that each plague that G-d brought upon the Egyptians was made up of five different plagues. Take the same verse: "He sent against them His fierce anger, fury, rage, trouble,[and] a mission of evil angels." (Tehillim 78:49)

"His fierce anger" – makes one.

"Fury" – makes two.

"Rage" – makes three.

"Trouble" – makes four.

"A mission of evil angels" – makes five.

From here we see that in Egypt they were struck with fifty plagues. Therefore, at the Sea, they were struck with 250 plagues.

כַּמָּה מַעֲלוֹת טוֹבוֹת לַמָּקוֹם עָלֵינוּ.

אִלּוּ הוֹצִיאָנוּ מִמִּצְרַיִם, וְלֹא עָשָׂה בָהֶם שְׁפָטִים דַּיֵּנוּ:

אִלּוּ עָשָׂה בָהֶם שְׁפָטִים, וְלֹא עָשָׂה בֵאלֹהֵיהֶם, דַּיֵּנוּ:

אִלּוּ עָשָׂה בֵאלֹהֵיהֶם, וְלֹא הָרַג אֶת בְּכוֹרֵיהֶם, דַּיֵּנוּ:

אִלּוּ הָרַג אֶת בְּכוֹרֵיהֶם, וְלֹא נָתַן לָנוּ אֶת מָמוֹנָם, דַּיֵּנוּ:

אִלּוּ נָתַן לָנוּ אֶת מָמוֹנָם, וְלֹא קָרַע לָנוּ אֶת הַיָּם, דַּיֵּנוּ:

אִלּוּ קָרַע לָנוּ אֶת הַיָּם, וְלֹא הֶעֱבִירָנוּ בְּתוֹכוֹ בֶּחָרָבָה, דַּיֵּנוּ:

How many good things has G-d done for us!

אלו הוציאנו ממצרים
לא עשה בהם שפטים

If He had brought us out from Egypt, but had not judged against them, it would have been enough.

Here we have an exercise that helps us develop our awareness and appreciation of G-d's miracles. Often, when we express our appreciation to a benefactor, we lump everything together and say, for example, "Thanks for everything!" This inability to properly express words of gratitude does little to help us truly appreciate kindness that is shown us.

When we want to say thank-you, we must analyze all the separate aspects of a single action. We must also distinguish between separate acts of kindness and recognize each on its own merits.

The *Dayenu* poem isolates each stage of the Exodus. It then gives us pause for reflection, regarding each individual stage, and how each one is worthy of appreciation. Many of these stages would have been insufficient in

How many good things has G-d done for us!

If He had brought us out of Egypt,
But had not judged against them,
It would have been enough   *(Dayenu).*

If He had judged against them,
But had not destroyed their idols,
It would have been enough   *(Dayenu).*

IF He had destroyed their idols,
But had not killed their first-born,
It would have been enough   *(Dayenu).*

If He had killed their first-born
But had not given us their treasure,
It would have been enough   *(Dayenu).*

If He had given us all their treasure,
But had not split the Sea for us,
It would have been enough   *(Dayenu).*

If He had split the Sea for us,

---

the absence of the others, and some were merely steps to reach the final goal – for example, the splitting of the Sea and the receiving of the Egyptian wealth. However, each step deserves celebration in its own time.

When parents raise a child, they take great pleasure in the child's first smile, his first tooth, the good grade he has achieved on a spelling test, and so forth. However, if the child only had these minor achievements for the rest of his life, it would surely not be a reason for joy. Nonetheless, each step in the child's development deserves appreciation at that stage of his life.

Dayenu helps us appreciate the overall Exodus much more, by helping us concentrate on the progress of its individual stages.

אלו קרע לנו את הים
ולא העבירנו בתוכו בחרבה

If He had split the Sea for us, but had not brought us through it on dry land, it would have been enough.

אִלוּ הֶעֱבִירָנוּ בְתוֹכוֹ בֶּחָרָבָה, וְלֹא שִׁקַע צָרֵינוּ

בְּתוֹכוֹ,   דַּיֵּנוּ:

אִלוּ שִׁקַע צָרֵינוּ בְּתוֹכוֹ, וְלֹא סִפֵּק צָרְכֵּנוּ

בַּמִּדְבָּר אַרְבָּעִים שָׁנָה,   דַּיֵּנוּ:

אִלוּ סִפֵּק צָרְכֵּנוּ בַּמִּדְבָּר אַרְבָּעִים שָׁנָה, וְלֹא

הֶאֱכִילָנוּ אֶת הַמָּן,   דַּיֵּנוּ:

אִלוּ הֶאֱכִילָנוּ אֶת הַמָּן, וְלֹא נָתַן לָנוּ אֶת

הַשַּׁבָּת,   דַּיֵּנוּ:

אִלוּ נָתַן לָנוּ אֶת הַשַּׁבָּת, וְלֹא קֵרְבָנוּ לִפְנֵי הַר

סִינַי,   דַּיֵּנוּ:

Although the purpose of splitting the Sea was to allow the Children of Israel to walk through it, G-d, in His munificence, performed other miracles during the crossing that were not really necessary, but were an expression of His love and concern.

The Jews surely could have crossed, even if the seabed had been muddy and the walking difficult. Since their primary objective was to escape from the Egyptians, a muddy passage would have been only a minor hindrance. Yet G-d wanted to make the journey as comfortable as possible. He made the seabed dry and firm, which made it easier for the Jews to travel.

❖ The Complete Exodus

אלו ספק צרכנו במדבר
ארבעים שנה

If He had provided our needs in the desert for forty years, but had not fed us the manna, it would have been enough.

The last six verses of the *Dayenu* do not seem to fit in the Haggadah, since they describe events that occurred during the forty-year period that followed the Exodus. Why are these verses recited at the Seder?

The Torah recounts the journeys of the Jews through the desert and states, "These are the journeys of the Children of Israel when they left Egypt ...." The

But had not brought us through it on dry land,
It would have been enough   (Dayenu).

If He had brought us through it on dry land,
But had not drowned our foes in it,
It would have been enough   (Dayenu).

If He had drowned our foes in it,
But had not provided our needs in the desert
for forty years,
It would have been enough   (Dayenu).

If He had provided our needs in the desert for
forty years,
But had not fed us the Manna,
It would have been enough   (Dayenu).

If He had fed us the Manna,
But had not given us the Sabbath,
It would have been enough   (Dayenu).

If He had given us the Sabbath,
But had not brought us to Mt. Sinai,
It would have been enough   (Dayenu).

Lubavitcher Rebbe (*Likutei Sichos, Massei*) notes that, in truth, only the first journey can be said to have occurred "when they left Egypt." The ensuing journeys were made during the next forty years in the desert. They did not occur when the Jews left Egypt, but rather, when they had left the previous campsite.

The Rebbe asks, what is meant by "these are the journeys when they left Egypt"? He answers that each journey pulled the nation farther away from their bondage to Egypt, and was, in fact, another Exodus of sorts.

The Vilna Gaon (*Aderes Eliyahu, Balak*) states, in a similar vein, that the Exodus from Egypt is mentioned fifty times throughout the Torah. Each mention represents yet another Exodus through which the Jews were able to elevate themselves, one level at a time, from the forty-ninth level of impu-

אִלוּ קֵרְבָנוּ לִפְנֵי הַר סִינַי, וְלֹא נָתַן לָנוּ אֶת
הַתּוֹרָה, דַּיֵּנוּ:

אִלוּ נָתַן לָנוּ אֶת הַתּוֹרָה, וְלֹא הִכְנִיסָנוּ לְאֶרֶץ
יִשְׂרָאֵל, דַּיֵּנוּ:

אִלוּ הִכְנִיסָנוּ לְאֶרֶץ יִשְׂרָאֵל, וְלֹא בָנָה לָנוּ אֶת
בֵּית הַבְּחִירָה, דַּיֵּנוּ:

rity to which they had sunk in Egypt.

Ibn Ezra (*Shemos* 14:13) states, similarly, that the Jews had to wander in the desert for forty years, in order to rid themselves of the residual influence of the Egyptian bondage. Only then could they establish a model society in their own land.

The reasoning of the Lubavitcher Rebbe, the Vilna Gaon, and Ibn Ezra suggests that the Exodus was not really complete until the Children of Israel entered the Promised Land. Therefore, we may say that the entire forty-year period that preceded settlement in Israel was part of the Exodus from Egypt. It is completely appropriate, then, to discuss highlights of the journey through the desert on the night of the Seder.

We may ask, however, why G-d's building the Holy Temple, which did not occur until many years after the Jews entered the Land of Israel, is the subject of *Dayenu's* final verse. Two explana-

tions come to mind. First, it may be that the Exodus was not finished until the Temple was built. Only then could the nation have achieved the ultimate goal of its freedom: complete service to G-d in His house. A second explanation is that the Haggadah may not be referring to the earthly Temple, but rather to the Heavenly Temple that exists parallel to the earthly one. (See *Midrash Tanchuma Vayakhel* 7.) This latter explanation fits well with the words, " He built us the Temple," since G-d did not build the earthly Temple – the Jewish people built it themselves.

אלו קרבנו לפני הר סיני ולא נתן לנו את התורה

If He had brought us to Mount Sinai, but had not given us the Torah, it would have been enough.

The commentaries ask, "What would have been the significance of the Children of Israel's standing at Mount Sinai, had they not received the Torah?" (See

If He had brought us to Mt. Sinai,
But had not given us the Torah,
It would have been enough   (Dayenu).

If He had given us the Torah,
But had not brought us to the Land of Israel,
It would have been enough   (Dayenu).

IF He had brought us to the Land of Israel,
But had not built us the Holy Temple,
It would have been enough   (Dayenu).

Abudraham, Baruch She'amar and others).

In the Torah, it is written that the Jewish people encamped at Mount Sinai: "ויחן שם ישראל נגד ההר" "Yisroel camped there, opposite the mountain." The Hebrew for the word, "camped," "vayichan," is rendered in the third-person, singular form of the verb. The Midrash comments on this odd use of the singular, as meaning that when the Israelites encamped before the mountain, they were "כאיש אחד בלב אחד": "like one man with one heart." Rashi points out that this is the only time we find the nation achieving such a level of unity.

Unity is a prerequisite for the giving and receiving of the Torah. The Torah could only be given to a single entity, not to various separate individuals. The Haggadah is therefore telling us that had we achieved this degree of unity, but not received the Torah, that, alone, would have been a great accomplishment.

❖ Reliving Sinai

Rav Shlomo Wolbe offers another interpretation for the importance of being at Mount Sinai, and why that experience would have sufficed, even without the giving of the Torah. It is based on an idea suggested by his own Rebbe, Rav Yerucham Levovitz, Mashgiach of the Mirrer Yeshiva.

The Talmud (*Yevamos* 79a) discusses three character traits inherent in the Jewish people: compassion, shame, and lovingkindness. The Talmud proceeds to cite a source from the Torah for each of these traits. The source for shame is a passage that follows the Divine Revelation at Mount Sinai.

According to the passage, after the people saw the thunder and the smoking mountain, they trembled and told Moshe that they were too frightened to hear the words directly from G-d, lest they die. Moshe answered them, "Do not fear, for G-d has come to elevate you, so that

עַל אַחַת כַּמָּה וְכַמָּה,
טוֹבָה כְפוּלָה וּמְכֻפֶּלֶת לַמָּקוֹם עָלֵינוּ.
שֶׁהוֹצִיאָנוּ מִמִּצְרַיִם, וְעָשָׂה בָהֶם שְׁפָטִים.
וְעָשָׂה בֵאלֹהֵיהֶם. וְהָרַג אֶת בְּכוֹרֵיהֶם. וְנָתַן
לָנוּ אֶת מָמוֹנָם, וְקָרַע לָנוּ אֶת הַיָּם. וְהֶעֱבִירָנוּ
בְתוֹכוֹ בֶּחָרָבָה. וְשִׁקַּע צָרֵינוּ בְּתוֹכוֹ. וְסִפֵּק
צָרְכֵּנוּ בַּמִּדְבָּר אַרְבָּעִים שָׁנָה. וְהֶאֱכִילָנוּ אֶת
הַמָּן. וְנָתַן לָנוּ אֶת הַשַּׁבָּת. וְקֵרְבָנוּ לִפְנֵי הַר
סִינַי. וְנָתַן לָנוּ אֶת הַתּוֹרָה. וְהִכְנִיסָנוּ לְאֶרֶץ
יִשְׂרָאֵל. וּבָנָה לָנוּ אֶת בֵּית הַבְּחִירָה לְכַפֵּר עַל
כָּל עֲוֹנוֹתֵינוּ:

the awe of Him shall be seen upon your faces, and you will not sin" (*Shemos* 20:17). The "awe upon their faces" is understood to be shame before G-d.

Rav Yerucham asked, How could the Talmud cite a proof for the inherent characteristic of shame, to be applied to generations of Jews thousands of years later, from the generation that experienced the Divine Revelation? Perhaps that generation had this shame because of their own experiences. What proof exists that future generations of Jews, who did not experience the Revelation at Sinai, also have a share in this inherent shame?

Rav Yerucham explained that

the awesome revelation at Sinai must remain an eternal experience. The Torah, itself, may be compared to a thermos that maintains the heat of its contents, long after it has been filled. Every time a Jew opens up a book of the Torah in order to study it, he can relive Sinai all over again. Thus, the Sinai experience leaves its impact on every Jew at all times. An innate sense of shame becomes a part of that person's very fiber. It is for this reason, that Judaism assigns Torah study such high priority.

This, explains Rav Wolbe, is the explanation of the words in *Dayenu*, "Had He brought us to Mount Sinai and not given us the

Therefore, how much good, doubled and doubled again, has G-d done for us!

1. *He brought us out of Egypt,*

2. *Judged against them,*

3. *Destroyed their idols,*

4. *Killed their first-born,*

5. *Gave us their treasure,*

6. *Split the Sea of Reeds,*

7. *Brought us through it dry,*

8. *Drowned our foes in it,*

9. *Helped us 40 years in the desert,*

10. *Fed us the Manna,*

11. *Gave us the Sabbath,*

12. *Brought us to Mt. Sinai,*

13. *Gave us the Torah,*

14. *Brought us to the Land of Israel,*

15. *And built us the Holy Temple, to atone for all our sins.*

Torah." Even had G-d only brought us to Sinai and allowed us to experience its awesome effect, but not given us the Torah – the means through which we are able to re-experience Sinai – *Dayenu*. That, too, would have been a great accomplishment.

רַבָּן גַּמְלִיאֵל הָיָה אוֹמֵר. כָּל שֶׁלֹּא אָמַר
שְׁלֹשָׁה דְבָרִים אֵלּוּ בַּפֶּסַח, לֹא יָצָא יְדֵי חוֹבָתוֹ,
וְאֵלּוּ הֵן. פֶּסַח. מַצָּה. וּמָרוֹר:

❖ The Benefits of Exile

רבן גמליאל היה אומר כל
שלא אמר שלשה דברים אלו בפסח

Rabban Gamliel used to say: "Whoever does not discuss the following three things on Pesach has not fulfilled his obligation: Pesach, Matza, and Marror.

Rabban Gamliel's statement seems to be somewhat out of place. If, indeed, this is such an important part of the Haggadah, why does he wait until most of the discussion has concluded to say so? Furthermore, the ideas he highlights – the persecution and the Exodus – have already been talked about during the course of the evening. What does Rabban Gamliel add now, that was not known before?

There is another glaring question that must be asked. Why does the expression, "Pesach, Matza, and Marror," not follow a meaningful chronological order? Marror is mentioned last. But marror represents the suffering in Egypt. Its mention should precede that of Pesach and matza, which represent elements of the later redemption.

Before answering these questions, we must first answer another, more elementary, question: Why is it necessary for us to show so much appreciation to G-d for having taken us out of Egypt, when it was He who decreed that we be there in the first place?!

This can be answered with an analogy. Reuben has an argument with Simon. In a fit of temper, he breaks Simon's arm. Reuben then tells Simon that he is an orthopedic surgeon, and will fix Simon's arm at no charge. Under these circumstances, there is little reason for Simon to feel gratitude for Reuben's providing professional services at no charge. Had Reuben not caused the damage in the first place, his services would not have been needed, and Simon would have been spared the pain of a broken bone.

In quite a different set of circumstances, Simon has a problem with a bone in his arm and is unable to use his arm as a result. To fix Simon's arm, Reuben, the orthopedic surgeon, breaks the arm, in order to reset the bone. In this story, Simon would surely be an ingrate if he did not express his appreciation to Reuben.

In each if these incidents, the

Rabban Gamaliel used to say: Whoever does not discuss three things on Passover has not kept [the Seder] properly. they are:

The Passover Lamb,

the matza,

and the marror.

same action of breaking someone's arm, occurs, but with very different meanings. In the first case, Reuben lost control, acted violently, and broke another person's arm. In the second instance, Reuben broke the arm in his role as a physician, in order to heal another person. Because the breaking of the arm is therapeutic, Reuben deserves proper expressions of thanks.

This same thought can be applied to the Exodus from Egypt. If G-d had simply enslaved the Jewish people without purpose, and then redeemed them, He would hardly be deserving of thanks. However, this was not the case. The slavery itself was not inflicted out of G-d's anger, or for punishment. Rather, the experience of bondage was necessary for the development of the nation, for the Jews to have matured sufficiently to be worthy of receiving the Torah. Therefore, we must show G-d appreciation not only for the redemption, *but for the slavery as well.* We actually celebrate our slavery on Pesach. We do not merely recall a series of events.

We can now return to our earlier question: Why does Rabban Gamliel not list marror first, when the suffering that it represents occurred before the Pesach and matza of the redemption?

A person might be able to appreciate the importance of a period of suffering – in the way that the bondage of the Jews in Egypt was important for our development – *after* some time has elapsed. But it would be too much to ask that the person appreciate suffering, *while* enduring it.

HaRav Elazar Shach *Shlit"a*, the great Rosh Yeshiva of Ponovezh, once wrote a letter of encouragement to a young American Rosh Yeshiva who was suffering from cancer. He told him that every ounce of suffering he endured was extremely valuable, for it served as an atonement for any misdeeds he might have done. Then he added that, although it might be too much to ask of him to appreciate his pains while suffering them, he should at least not regret the pain that he had already endured.

• During the discussion of the Pesach offering, the zeroa (shankbone) should not be lifted, lest it appear one is sanctifying the meat for the Korbon Pesach (ibid.,[72]).

פֶּסַח שֶׁהָיוּ אֲבוֹתֵינוּ אוֹכְלִים בִּזְמַן שֶׁבֵּית הַמִּקְדָּשׁ הָיָה קַיָּם, עַל שׁוּם מָה, עַל שׁוּם שֶׁפָּסַח הַקָּדוֹשׁ בָּרוּךְ הוּא עַל בָּתֵּי אֲבוֹתֵינוּ בְּמִצְרַיִם. שֶׁנֶּאֱמַר, וַאֲמַרְתֶּם זֶבַח פֶּסַח הוּא לַיְיָ, אֲשֶׁר פָּסַח עַל בָּתֵּי בְנֵי יִשְׂרָאֵל בְּמִצְרַיִם, בְּנָגְפּוֹ אֶת מִצְרַיִם וְאֶת בָּתֵּינוּ הִצִּיל, וַיִּקֹּד הָעָם וַיִּשְׁתַּחֲווּ:

• The smaller, broken middle piece of matza should be lifted and displayed to the participants while discussing the matza (ibid.).

מַצָּה זוּ שֶׁאָנוּ אוֹכְלִים, עַל שׁוּם מָה. עַל שׁוּם

Similarly, Rabban Gamliel discusses the Pesach and matza, symbols of redemption, first. Only then does he mention the marror – because only after we have experienced the Exodus, can we appreciate the exile.

We now have the answer to our question, why does Rabban Gamliel wait until most of the Seder discussion has already occurred, to make his remarks? *Slavery* can be appreciated only after a thorough understanding of the whole story. It is this appreciation that Rabban Gamliel wants us to experience.

We now have a new understanding of the paragraphs of praise that begin with, "Therefore, we are obligated to thank and praise,...." (page 123). The commentaries are bothered by the adverb, "therefore" (see *Kol Bo* and *Abudraham*). But from our discussion, we understand that the Haggadah has led us , through the placement and meaning of Rabban Gamliel's statement, to a deeper understanding of the exile. *Therefore,* we now know, more than we did previously, that we owe a debt of gratitude and praise to G-d for everything He did in Egypt.

*Our fathers ate the Passover Lamb long ago
when the Holy Temple [In Jerusalem] stood.
What was the reason for it? It was because G-d
passed over our fathers' houses in Egypt. It is
thus written, "You shall say, 'It is the Passover
offering to G-d, because He passed over the
houses of the children of Israel in Egypt. He
struck the Egyptians with a plague, but He
spared our houses and the people kneeled and
bowed down'". (Shemos 12:27)*

We eat this matza, but what is the reason for

**פסח שהיו אבותינו אוכלים
בזמן שבית המקדש היה קים**

**Our fathers ate the Pesach Lamb
when the Holy Temple stood.
What was the reason for it? It
was because G-d passed over
our fathers' houses in Egypt, ...**

As we explained earlier (see
page 27, **Kadesh U'Rchatz**), G-d's
skipping over the houses is the
most significant of all the miracles.
Passing over the houses represented G-d's willingness to overlook
the nation's shortcomings and
redeem the Jews, despite their not
deserving redemption.

Another allusion may lie in the
skipping over the houses. The
Children of Israel had been destined to stay in Egypt for 400
years. But the exile lasted only
210, because G-d saw that the
Jews would not survive four cen-
turies in Egypt. It may be that

"skipped over" also refers to the
190 years of suffering that G-d
"skipped," in order to save the
Jews from oblivion.

Rabban Gamliel may have considered the shortening of the exile
as the common denominator
between Pesach, matza, and marror. The matza, which traditionally
represents the haste with which
the Jews left Egypt, also signifies
G-d's hastening of the redemption,
by ending the exile 190 years earlier than He had ordained. The
marror represents the bitter persecution in Egypt, which was G-d's
justification for condensing the 400
years of bondage into 210 years.
Thus, Pesach, matza, and marror
all allude to the shortening of the
exile.

מצה זו שאנו אוכלים

**We eat this matza, but what is
the reason for it? ...**

שֶׁלֹּא הִסְפִּיק בְּצֵקָם שֶׁל אֲבוֹתֵינוּ לְהַחֲמִיץ. עַד
שֶׁנִּגְלָה עֲלֵיהֶם מֶלֶךְ מַלְכֵי הַמְּלָכִים הַקָּדוֹשׁ
בָּרוּךְ הוּא וּגְאָלָם. שֶׁנֶּאֱמַר, וַיֹּאפוּ אֶת הַבָּצֵק
אֲשֶׁר הוֹצִיאוּ מִמִּצְרַיִם עֻגֹת מַצּוֹת כִּי לֹא
חָמֵץ, כִּי גֹרְשׁוּ מִמִּצְרַיִם וְלֹא יָכְלוּ לְהִתְמַהְמֵהַּ
וְגַם צֵדָה לֹא עָשׂוּ לָהֶם:

מרור זו שאנו אוכלים

**We eat this marror, but what is
the reason for it? ...**

Rabban Gamliel directs the discussion of matza and marror rather
dramatically. The Seder leader is
directed to lift up the matza and
the marror for all the participants
to see, as he involves them in
examining the reasons for the
mitzvos. This is meant to serve as
an example of how to command
attention and imbue the participants with a deeper sense of
appreciation.

Dale Carnegie, author of *How
to Win Friends and Influence
People*, writes of the importance
and power of visual aids, and of
acting things out. He relates that a
salesman had been trying to meet
with the manager of a grocery
store, in order to persuade him to
buy a new cash register. After
months of persevering, the salesman was finally granted a five-
minute meeting with the store
manager. He realized that with so
short a meeting, he had to do

something dramatic to make a
favorable impression in the few
minutes allotted to him.

As the salesman entered the
office, he reached into his pocket,
pulled out a handful of change,
and threw it on the floor. The
manager looked at him as if he
were crazy. The salesman said,
"That, dear sir, is what you are
doing every time a customer goes
through your check-out counter.
You are literally throwing money
away!"

Needless to say, this got the
manager's ear for longer than five
minutes, and he received an order
to replace all of the store's old
machines.

Punctuating our words with
actions, gestures, and concrete
demonstrations generates interest
and intensifies their impact.
Rabban Gamliel adds a new
dimension to our appreciation of
the Exodus by lifting the foods for
everyone to see, as a prelude to
the discussion.

The source of Rabban

it? It is because the dough prepared by our fathers did not have time to rise before G-d revealed Himself to them and immediately delivered them. It is thus written, "They baked the dough that they had brought out of Egypt into matza cakes, because it did not rise. They had been driven out of Egypt, and could not wait; they had also not prepared any other food". (Shemos 21:39)

Gamliel's innovation is in the Torah, itself. The Torah says, "It is because of *this,* that G-d did for me when I went out of Egypt." The word "this" always implies something visual, as if the speaker was pointing to something that can be seen (see Rashi on *Shemos* 12:2 and on *Vayikra* 11:2). The Torah, by its own example, is teaching that the discussion must be reinforced through the actual display of the concrete objects being discussed.

❖ **The Dual Message of Matza**

מצה זו שאנו אוכלים ...
על שום שלא הספיק
בצקם של אבותינו להחמיץ

. . .**this matza, what is the reason for it? It is because the dough prepared by our fathers did not have time to rise before the King of kings, the Holy One, Blessed be He, revealed Himself . . .**

Rabban Gamliel's statement regarding the matza is puzzling. G-d had commanded the Children of Israel to eat matza with the Pesach offering before they even left Egypt (*Shemos* 12:8). How can Rabban Gamliel say that the matza commemorates the redemption – an event that had not yet occurred?

Abarbanel explains that matza, in fact, has a double meaning: slavery and redemption. He cites Ibn Ezra, who relates that in many countries it was common practice for slaves to be fed matza, because it was both cheap and convenient. Matza takes a long time to digest, which meant less frequent feeding of the slaves. Therefore, it can be reasonably assumed that the Jews in Egypt ate matza, as well. Seforno (*Devarim* 16:3) also mentions that the Egyptians fed their Jewish slaves matza, because it took less time to bake. This, then, is what the Haggadah is referring to, earlier, when it states, "This is

• The *marror* is lifted and displayed while discussing the *marror* (ibid.).

מָרוֹר זֶה שֶׁאָנוּ אוֹכְלִים, עַל שׁוּם מָה. עַל שׁוּם שֶׁמֵּרְרוּ הַמִּצְרִים אֶת חַיֵּי אֲבוֹתֵינוּ בְּמִצְרַיִם, שֶׁנֶּאֱמַר, וַיְמָרְרוּ אֶת חַיֵּיהֶם בַּעֲבֹדָה קָשָׁה,

the bread of affliction that our fathers ate in Egypt."[16]

Once the Jews were freed, it should no longer have been necessary for them to eat matza. However, because they had to leave Egypt in haste, the dough that they had prepared for baking bread did not have time to rise. Thus, the Torah obligates us to eat matza, to commemorate the Exodus.

The double meaning of the matza may explain the obligation to eat matza twice at the Seder: once before the meal and once, as the Afikoman, after the meal. The first matza, eaten before the meal, commemorates the haste of the Exodus. The Afikoman matza, eaten after the meal, commemorates the matza eaten with the Pesach offering while the Jews were still in Egypt, and is therefore a reminder of slavery.

❖ **The Reasons for Mitzvos**

Another interpretation of Rabban Gamliel's statement regarding the matza may derive from the underlying reason for performing mitzvos. A fundamental insight of the Brisker Rav may be helpful in understanding this correlation.

The Brisker Rav explains that it is a mistake to assume that there is a logical, cause-and-effect relationship between the object of a mitzvah and the mitzvah itself.

It is generally assumed, for example, that the mitzvah of honoring one's parents is a moral imperative. In other words, because the father and mother have brought their children into the world and have nurtured them, their sons and daughters should behave with decency and respect towards them.

The Brisker Rav, however, explains that this is not the case.

---

16. Maharal (Gevuros Hashem, ch.50), however, strongly takes issue with this opinion and claims that there is no source from which it is reasonable to infer that Jews ate matzo in Egypt.

We eat this marror, but what is the reason for it? It is because the Egyptians made our fathers' lives bitter in Egypt. It is thus written, "They made their lives bitter with hard work,

The mitzvah of honoring one's parents was not created for the parents. Rather, it is the other way around. Think for a moment, that G-d could just as easily have created a world in which there were no parents. Human beings could have been generated through an entirely different form of reproduction: for example, by fission, as with amoebas.

So why did G-d create parents? He created them *for* the mitzvah. Because there is a mitzvah in the Torah to honor one's parents, G-d created parents to honor.

G-d used the Torah as a blueprint for Creation. He created the world, in accordance with the mitzvos.

Similarly, G-d prevented the rising of the dough, in order to generate circumstances that required commemoration, *because there already existed a mitzvah of matza.* The mitzvah of matza preceded the actual Exodus. G-d took the Jews out of Egypt in great haste, specifically so that they could fulfill the mitzvah of matza with the commemoration of the Exodus!

In fact, this understanding is stated quite clearly in Rashi. Regarding the passage, "It is because of *this,* that G-d did for me when I left Egypt" (*Shemos* 13:8), Rashi renders the following meaning: "Because of *this* – in order that I should fulfill His mitzvos, such as matza and marror." In other words, Rashi is saying that G-d took us out of Egypt, specifically so that we would fulfill the mitzvos of matza and marror.[17]

_____

17. Similarly, Rav Shlomo Wolbe once discussed the verse that describes the experience at Mount Sinai: "All the mountain of Sinai was smoking because G-d had descended upon it in fire, and the smoke rose like a smoking furnace" (Shemos 19:18). He asked several questions. What was the purpose of the smoke? And why was the simile of a smoking furnace used in the Torah? Is it not well known what smoke looks like? Rav Wolbe explained that G-d wanted to create an experience that could be easily recollected. The Torah was given in such a way, that whenever a Jew would see a smoking chimney, he would be reminded of the Sinai experience.

בְּחֹמֶר וּבִלְבֵנִים וּבְכָל עֲבֹדָה בַּשָּׂדֶה, אֵת כָּל
עֲבֹדָתָם אֲשֶׁר עָבְדוּ בָהֶם בְּפָרֶךְ:

בְּכָל דּוֹר וָדוֹר חַיָּב אָדָם לִרְאוֹת אֶת עַצְמוֹ
כְּאִלּוּ הוּא יָצָא מִמִּצְרַיִם, שֶׁנֶּאֱמַר, וְהִגַּדְתָּ
לְבִנְךָ בַּיּוֹם הַהוּא לֵאמֹר, בַּעֲבוּר זֶה עָשָׂה יְיָ
לִי בְּצֵאתִי מִמִּצְרָיִם:

לֹא אֶת אֲבוֹתֵינוּ בִּלְבָד גָּאַל הַקָּדוֹשׁ בָּרוּךְ
הוּא, אֶלָּא אַף אוֹתָנוּ גָּאַל עִמָּהֶם. שֶׁנֶּאֱמַר,
וְאוֹתָנוּ הוֹצִיא מִשָּׁם, לְמַעַן הָבִיא אֹתָנוּ לָתֶת
לָנוּ אֶת הָאָרֶץ אֲשֶׁר נִשְׁבַּע לַאֲבֹתֵינוּ:

❖ An Eternal Nation

בכל דור ודור חייב אדם לראות
את עצמו כאלו הוא יצא ממצרים

In every generation one must look upon himself as if he had personally left Egypt.

This is a most difficult obligation to fulfill. In our own times, second and third generations of Jews born since the Holocaust, have difficulty relating to the atrocities of the concentration camps, the relief of the liberation, and the exhilaration of the survivors at the founding of the State of Israel. The Holocaust occurred only half a century ago. If the horrifying events of the Holocaust seem far removed and difficult to grasp –

despite eyewitness accounts, photographs, and newsreel – how can we, ourselves, possibly feel that we were the very people who left Egypt more than 3,300 years ago?

Rav Shimon Schwab answered this question with a personal anecdote. As a young child, fifty years earlier, he had once burned his arm badly. It took a long time for his arm to fully heal. Recounting this incident, he pointed to the arm and said, "If I were to tell you that this is the arm that I burned fifty years ago, it would be true. This, despite the fact that there is probably not a single cell in the arm that was there fifty years ago, since the cells are constantly regenerating themselves. The arm

with mortar and bricks, and all kinds of work in the field. All the work that they made them do was backbreaking". (Shemos 1:14)

In every generation one must look upon himself as if he had personally left Egypt. It is thus written, "You shall tell your child on that day, 'Because of this, G-d did [things] for me when I was in Egypt'". (Shemos 13:8)

For not only our fathers did G-d save from Egypt, but He also saved us with them. It is thus written [in the answer that we give our children on Passover], "It was ourselves that He brought out of there, so that He might lead us, and give us the land that He swore to our fathers". (Devarim 6:23)

is also much bigger today, than it was when I was a young child. So why is it the same arm? Because the original arm regenerated itself piece by piece, growing little by little, day after day. Every cell, every part of the arm that is there today is a continuation of that original arm and, thus, it is considered the same arm."

The same is true of the nation that left Egypt. The original nation regenerated slowly, person by person, one person being born and another passing away, but the heart and soul of that nation has been retained, and every Jew is a part of that heart and soul. Although thousands of years have passed and no one is alive today who lived then, it is still the same nation that left Egypt 3,300 years ago.(See Rabbi M. Lieber, *The Living Exodus* p. 142 and *Ma'ayan Beis Hashoeivah* p.155)

When we reflect on this, it is easier for us to feel a part of the Exodus. Although we have not lived through it ourselves, we retain the essence of those Jews who actually lived in, were enslaved in, and departed from Egypt. We thus may well feel it, personally.

• The matzos are covered, and the cup of wine is lifted and held until it is drunk, because G-d's praise should be said over a cup of wine (ibid., [77]).

לְפִיכָךְ אֲנַחְנוּ חַיָּבִים לְהוֹדוֹת, לְהַלֵּל, לְשַׁבֵּחַ, לְפָאֵר, לְרוֹמֵם, לְהַדֵּר, לְבָרֵךְ, לְעַלֵּה, וּלְקַלֵּס. לְמִי שֶׁעָשָׂה לַאֲבוֹתֵינוּ וְלָנוּ אֶת כָּל הַנִּסִּים הָאֵלּוּ. הוֹצִיאָנוּ מֵעַבְדוּת לְחֵרוּת. מִיָּגוֹן לְשִׂמְחָה. וּמֵאֵבֶל לְיוֹם טוֹב. וּמֵאֲפֵלָה לְאוֹר גָּדוֹל. וּמִשִּׁעְבּוּד לִגְאֻלָּה. וְנֹאמַר לְפָנָיו שִׁירָה חֲדָשָׁה הַלְלוּיָהּ:

הַלְלוּיָהּ, הַלְלוּ עַבְדֵי יְיָ, הַלְלוּ אֶת שֵׁם יְיָ: יְהִי שֵׁם יְיָ מְבֹרָךְ, מֵעַתָּה וְעַד עוֹלָם: מִמִּזְרַח שֶׁמֶשׁ

לפיכך אנחנו חייבים להודות
Therefore, we are obligated to thank, to praise, to exalt, . . .

We have explained how some of the previous paragraphs in the Haggadah have functioned as exercises in developing a greater appreciation of what G-d has done for us. We have shown that Rabbi Yosi, Rabbi Akiva and Rabbi Eliezer delved more deeply into each of the miracles and revealed some of their hidden facets. For each of these new dimensions, we are obligated to make a separate expression of gratitude. The Haggadah therefore employs several different expressions of praise,

each one corresponding to a different dimension of the miracles.

הללוקה הללו עבדי ה'
Halleluyah! Let G-d's servants praise, let them praise G-d's Name

The commentaries question the *Hallel's* division into two parts on the Seder night. If the major part of the *Hallel* is said after the meal, why is it necessary to recite the first two paragraphs during Maggid? (See Abudraham, and Maharal, *Gevuros Hashem*, ch. 62.)

Perhaps these paragraphs of *Hallel* are actually part of the discussion of the Exodus. The Ritva

Therefore, we are obligated to thank, to praise, to be grateful, to glorify, to exalt, to acclaim, to bless, to hold high, and to sing out to the One who did all these miracles for our fathers and for us. He led us from slavery to freedom, from misery to joy, from mourning to a holiday, from deep darkness to great light, and from bondage to redemption. Let us therefore sing before Him a new song: Halleluyah– Praise G-d!

Halleluyah – praise G-d! Let G-d's servants praise, let them praise G-d's name; May G-d's name be praised now and forever! From when the sun rises until it sets, let G-d's name be

(in *Hilchos Seder HaHaggadah*) says that a person is obligated to recite the Haggadah "b'ne'imus u'vkol rom" – sweetly and loudly. The *Shibolei Haleket* also states that the Haggadah should be said "be'hallel b'shir u've'nachas" – with praise, song, and joy.

Part of the purpose of discussing the Exodus is to be able to feel the joy of the redemption. It is therefore proper that some of the discussion itself be in the form of song and *Hallel*. The first two paragraphs of the *Hallel* – which, in fact, discuss the Exodus – are therefore appropriately included in Maggid, to fulfill the obligation of discussing the Exodus in "*Hallel* form."

הללו עבדי ה׳

Let G-d's servants praise

We have talked earlier about freedom: Freedom, without any direction, has no real value, because it will ultimately become anarchy and chaos. G-d therefore said, "For the Children of Israel are my servants whom I have taken out of the land of Egypt" (*Vayikra* 25:55). The meaning of this passage is that the purpose of their being taken out was their acceptance of G-d's mastery. Only then, would the Exodus take on meaning.

The Psalmist therefore opens his praise with the words, "Praise G-d, you servants of G-d," for only

עַד מְבוֹאוֹ, מְהֻלָּל שֵׁם יְיָ: רָם עַל כָּל גּוֹיִם, יְיָ,
עַל הַשָּׁמַיִם כְּבוֹדוֹ: מִי כַּיְיָ אֱלֹהֵינוּ, הַמַּגְבִּיהִי
לָשָׁבֶת: הַמַּשְׁפִּילִי לִרְאוֹת, בַּשָּׁמַיִם וּבָאָרֶץ:
מְקִימִי מֵעָפָר דָּל, מֵאַשְׁפֹּת יָרִים אֶבְיוֹן:
לְהוֹשִׁיבִי עִם נְדִיבִים, עִם נְדִיבֵי עַמּוֹ: מוֹשִׁיבִי
עֲקֶרֶת הַבַּיִת, אֵם הַבָּנִים שְׂמֵחָה, הַלְלוּיָהּ:

after the Jews realize that they *are* servants of G-d, can they properly thank Him for taking them out of Egypt.

מי כה׳ אלקינו המגביהי לשבת

Who is like G-d our Lord, Who sits on high, yet lowers Himself to look upon heaven and earth? He raises the poor man from the dust ... to make him sit with the princes

The terminology may seem strange. If G-d's seat is upon high, why must He lower Himself, as it were, to look upon heaven? Furthermore, what exactly *is* it, that He views in the heaven?

The Torah (*Shemos* 24:10) describes the vision of G-d that Moshe, Aharon, and the seventy elders saw at Mount Sinai: "Under His feet was the likeness of a sapphire brick." The *Me'am Loez* cites a passage from the Zohar (vol. II, 66b), that explains the nature of this brick. During the harsh slave labor in Egypt, there was a pregnant woman who helped her husband meet his quota of work by

kneading the mud that was used to make bricks. The work proved too strenuous for her, and she miscarried into the mixture. The fetus-mixture was subsequently formed into a brick. The angel Gabriel brought this brick up to heaven and placed it at the foot of the Throne of Glory, in order to arouse G-d's compassion for His children. Perhaps, when the Psalmist says that G-d lowers Himself to look upon heaven, the meaning is that G-d looks at the brick at the foot of His throne, and remembers the suffering of the Children of Israel on earth.

The second sentence, "G-d raises the impoverished from the dust," is now beautifully juxtaposed with the first. The quotation refers to G-d's raising up the Children of Israel from their back-breaking labor in Egypt, where they worked with dirt to make bricks and mortar. Once G-d decided it was time to take the Jews out of Egypt, they were elevated – in just a few weeks – from their lowly status to noblemen, as

praised. High above all nations is G-d, His glory is above the heavens. Who is like G-d our Lord, whose throne is so high, Yet lowers Himself to look upon heaven and earth? He raises the poor from the dust, From the trash heap, He lifts the beggar, To make him sit with princes, with the princes of his people. He turns the barren woman of the house into a joyful mother of children, Halleluyah – praise G-d!

it says in the Torah, "You will be to Me a kingdom of priests" (*Shemos* 19:6).

❖ The Divine Mission

מושיבי עקרת הבית
אם הבנים שמחה

He turns the barren woman of the house into a joyful mother of children.

A childless woman feels the intense pain of her unfulfilled desire to be a mother. Her need to give herself to her own children is an integral part of her nature. The Psalmist uses the barren woman as a metaphor for the Jewish nation unfulfilled. The Children of Israel are barren, if the Divine directive that they should be "a light unto the nations" (*Yeshaya* 49:6) – that they should influence and educate the nations regarding the Divinity of the One G-d [18] –is frustrated.

The Exodus from Egypt, and the ensuing Sinai experience, afforded the Jewish people the opportunity to fulfill their essential mission. As their own belief in, understanding of, and love of G-d crystallized, they were able to communicate these ideals to others. Thus, the barren woman was transformed, through her fulfillment, into a joyous mother of children.

---

18. See Rambam in Sefer Hamitzvos, Positive commandment 3. He cites the Sifri that this directive is part of the commandment to love G-d, because the commandment requires a Jew to influence all mankind to recognize and to worship G-d.

בְּצֵאת יִשְׂרָאֵל מִמִּצְרָיִם, בֵּית יַעֲקֹב מֵעַם לֹעֵז:
הָיְתָה יְהוּדָה לְקָדְשׁוֹ, יִשְׂרָאֵל מַמְשְׁלוֹתָיו: הַיָּם
רָאָה וַיָּנֹס, הַיַּרְדֵּן יִסֹּב לְאָחוֹר: הֶהָרִים רָקְדוּ
כְאֵילִים, גְּבָעוֹת כִּבְנֵי צֹאן: מַה לְּךָ הַיָּם כִּי

❖ A Jew's Speech

בצאת ישראל ממצרים
בית יעקב מעם לעז

When Israel went out from Egypt, Yaakov's family from a foreign-speaking people;

The Haggadah emphasizes that the Jews were freed from a land with a foreign tongue. Why is this so important that it deserves mention? Doesn't it go without saying that the Egyptians spoke a language that was not native to the Jewish nation?

Some commentaries interpret this as referring to the Midrash that says that one of the merits through which the Jews earned their freedom was their use of their Hebrew names and the Holy Tongue throughout the Exile. (See *Chasam Sofer.*) This explanation, however, requires understanding. Why were these specific merits so creditable? After all, throughout the ages, many great Jews have used foreign names and spoken foreign languages. Yosef, himself, adopted an Egyptian name, *Tzofnas Pane'ach.* Moshe, too, is referred to by the name he was given by Pharaoh's daughter – presumably an Egyptian name – not by the name that his parents gave him.

Perhaps the Holy Tongue does not refer to a specific language, but rather to a way of communicating. The Jew is supposed to speak in a soft, refined manner. His demeanor should be modest and gentle. His speech must reflect an inner holiness of spirit. This is the "Kol kol Yaakov" – meaning "the voice is the voice of Yaakov." (*Bereishis* 27:22) And this is what is referred to as the "Holy Tongue." The Jewish name also reflects the same characteristics. According to the Torah, the purpose of a name is to define the essence of the object named.

In Egypt, the Jews were careful not to allow the gruff, coarse

---

19. See Malbim. Ibn Ezra, however, suggests that "Moshe" is the Hebrew translation of the Egyptian name given to him by the daughter of Pharaoh. Abarbanel takes strong issue with this opinion. He believes that "Moshe" was actually the name given to him by his mother, Yocheved, not by Pharaoh's daughter.

When Israel went out of Egypt, Ya'akov's family from a foreign-speaking people; Yehuda became his holy one, Israel his own kingdom. The sea looked and fled, the Jordan turned backwards; The mountains danced like rams,

nature of Egyptian culture to penetrate or compromise them. Even if they adopted Egyptian names, they took pains to preserve their inner nature – as it was represented by their true names. It was through this merit that they deserved to be redeemed.

The Talmud (*Sotah* 36b) relates that after Yosef successfully interpreted Pharaoh's dream, Pharaoh wanted to appoint him viceroy of Egypt (*Breishis* 4:40). Pharaoh's advisors, however, objected that Yosef was unfamiliar with the seventy known languages, and as such, was unfit for the position.

That night, the angel Gabriel taught Yosef all the other languages. The next day, Pharaoh tested Yosef's knowledge of the languages and found him to be proficient in them all. Then, Yosef began to speak the Holy Tongue, but Pharaoh could not understand what he was saying. Yosef tried to teach Pharaoh the Holy Tongue but found him incapable of learning it. Pharaoh made Yosef take an oath that he would not reveal his ineptitude to anyone.

It is odd that Pharaoh, who had mastered so many languages,

could not learn the Holy Tongue. His incapacity may be explained by the Holy Tongue's not being merely a language, but the expression of an inner holiness that Pharaoh did not possess. This language had no place in Egyptian society.

Thus, the Haggadah states that the Children of Israel left a people with "a foreign tongue," because this encapsulates the essence of the Egyptian nation.

הים ראה וינס הירדן יסב לאחור

The Sea looked and fled, the Jordan turned backward. The mountains danced like rams...

Why does the Psalmist describe the splitting of the Sea as though it were fleeing – as if the Sea, itself, were trying to escape from danger?

Earlier, we discussed the passage, "And with great awe' – this is the revelation of the Divine Presence. . . " (see p. 83). Quoting Rav Wolbe, we said that at the moment of redemption, there was a clear revelation of the full potential of every Jew's relationship with G-d. This same revelation, however, was too intense for the

תָנוּס, הַיַּרְדֵּן תִּסֹּב לְאָחוֹר: הֶהָרִים תִּרְקְדוּ
כְאֵילִים, גְּבָעוֹת כִּבְנֵי צֹאן: מִלְּפְנֵי אָדוֹן חוּלִי
אָרֶץ, מִלִּפְנֵי אֱלוֹהַ יַעֲקֹב: הַהֹפְכִי הַצּוּר אֲגַם
מָיִם, חַלָּמִישׁ לְמַעְיְנוֹ מָיִם:

בָּרוּךְ אַתָּה יְיָ, אֱלֹהֵינוּ מֶלֶךְ הָעוֹלָם, אֲשֶׁר
גְּאָלָנוּ וְגָאַל אֶת אֲבוֹתֵינוּ מִמִּצְרַיִם, וְהִגִּיעָנוּ
הַלַּיְלָה הַזֶּה לֶאֱכָל בּוֹ מַצָּה וּמָרוֹר. כֵּן יְיָ

Egyptians to behold, and the first-born Egyptians subsequently perished.

The repercussions of the revelation may still have been evident at the Sea, with nature itself fleeing from the Divine Presence. This resulted in the splitting of the Sea.

Similarly, the dancing of the mountains – a reference to the experience at Sinai, where again the Divine Presence was revealed – may have resulted from an experience so intense, that all of nature was affected. Ramban (*Shemos* 20:15) emphasizes that "dancing mountains" is not meant to be understood metaphorically. The mountains are mentioned in the sentence immediately following the description of the Sea. Just as the splitting of the Sea is not used figuratively, so the skipping mountains are meant to be understood literally.

❖ The Nature of Miracles

ההפכי הצור אגם מים

He turns the rock into a pool of water....

This passage seems to be a reference to the miracle in which Moshe smote the rock, which gave forth water. It is unclear, however, what meaning the transformation of rock into water has in this paragraph, the general theme of which is the Exodus.

The Abarbanel and Meiri explain that this miracle brings our appreciation of G-d's mastery over nature full circle: When the need arose, G-d transformed liquid into solid, as with the splitting of the Sea; when the opposite was required, G-d changed solid into liquid.

A similar idea is conveyed during Moshe and Aharon's appearance before Pharaoh. Aharon throws down his staff, and it

the hills like lambs. What is with you, Sea, that you flee, Jordan that you turn backwards? Mountains, why do you dance like rams, you hills, like lambs? Before the Master, who formed the earth! Before the G-d of Ya'akov! He turns the rock into a pool of water, bedrock into a flowing spring!

Blessed are You, G-d our Lord, King of the world, who freed us and our fathers from Egypt, and let us be here this night to eat matza and bitters. So, G-d our Lord and Lord

becomes a snake. He then picks up the snake, and it is transformed into a staff. Why was it necessary for the snake to be returned to its original form, the staff? What did this add to the wonder? The implied message is that G-d exercises total control over nature, and He does with it as He sees fit.

מצה – מרור
MATZA – MARROR

The Talmud (*Pesachim*116b) draws a distinction between the mitzvah of matza and the mitzvah of marror. If a person swallows matza without chewing it first, the mitzvah of eating matza is still fulfilled. Marror, however, must first be chewed. One must be able to taste its bitterness. If the marror is swallowed without first being chewed, the mitzvah has not been fulfilled. What is the reason for this distinction?

The Haggadah states that there is an obligation upon the individual to feel as though the Exodus has been experienced personally. The various foods that are eaten at the Seder are meant to foster this feeling.

Matza is unique because of the way it is made. The dough is produced in great haste, so there is no opportunity for it to become leavened. This commemorates the hurried departure from Egypt. It is not the *taste* of matza that affects the way an individual feels. After all, the taste of a matza whose dough has had virtually no time to rise, is probably not very different from matza whose dough has risen for eighteen minutes. Therefore, since flavor is not such an important feature of matza, the mitzvah is fulfilled, even if the matza has not been chewed to bring out its taste.

אֱלֹהֵינוּ וֵאלֹהֵי אֲבוֹתֵינוּ: יַגִּיעֵנוּ לְמוֹעֲדִים
וְלִרְגָלִים אֲחֵרִים הַבָּאִים לִקְרָאתֵנוּ לְשָׁלוֹם.
שְׂמֵחִים בְּבִנְיַן עִירֶךָ וְשָׂשִׂים בַּעֲבוֹדָתֶךָ. וְנֹאכַל
שָׁם מִן הַזְּבָחִים וּמִן הַפְּסָחִים (במוצ״ש אומרים: מִן
הַפְּסָחִים וּמִן הַזְּבָחִים) אֲשֶׁר יַגִּיעַ דָּמָם עַל קִיר
מִזְבַּחֲךָ לְרָצוֹן. וְנוֹדֶה לְךָ שִׁיר חָדָשׁ עַל
גְאֻלָּתֵנוּ וְעַל פְּדוּת נַפְשֵׁנוּ: בָּרוּךְ אַתָּה יְיָ, גָּאַל
יִשְׂרָאֵל:

הֲרֵינִי רוֹצֶה לְקַיֵּים מִצְוַת כּוֹס שֵׁנִי שֶׁל אַרְבַּע כּוֹסוֹת לְשֵׁם
יְחוּד קוּדְשָׁא בְּרִיךְ הוּא וּשְׁכִינְתֵּיהּ עַל יְדֵי הַהוּא טָמִיר
וְנֶעְלָם בְּשֵׁם כָּל יִשְׂרָאֵל. וִיהִי נוֹעַם אֲדֹנָי אֱלֹהֵינוּ עָלֵינוּ
וּמַעֲשֵׂה יָדֵינוּ כּוֹנְנָה עָלֵינוּ, וּמַעֲשֵׂה יָדֵינוּ כּוֹנְנֵהוּ.

• The second cup of wine should also be drunk while
reclining to the left. If one forgets to recline, another cup of
wine should be drunk, but no *bracha* should be recited
(472:7, [21]).

בָּרוּךְ אַתָּה יְיָ, אֱלֹהֵינוּ מֶלֶךְ הָעוֹלָם, בּוֹרֵא פְּרִי
הַגָּפֶן.

The experience of eating marror, which is extremely pungent, is
just the opposite. Its bitter taste is
what reminds us of the bitterness
of enslavement. For this reason,
the marror must be tasted – in
order to feel this bitterness – or we
are not truly recalling the Exile.

Of course, this explanation
only makes sense, if the marror
has a truly bitter taste. Earlier, we
explained that the preferred vegetable for marror is Romaine lettuce, which does not have much
of a bitter taste to it. Romaine lettuce, however, commemorates the

of our fathers, may You bring us to [celebrate]
other holidays and festivals in peace. May we
rejoice in the building of Your city, and be
happy in serving You. There may we be able
to eat (weekday nights) of the offerings and
Passover Lambs (Saturday night) of the Passover
Lambs and offerings whose blood is placed on
the side of Your altar for acceptance. May we
thank you with a new song for our freedom,
and for saving our lives. Blessed are You G-d,
who freed Israel.

I am ready and prepared to keep the commandment of
drinking the second of the four cups of wine, for the
sake of the One G-d and His presence, may it be
counted as done in the name of all Israel.

Blessed are You G-d Our Lord, King of the
world, Creator of the fruit of the grape- vine.

Egyptian experience, because it
starts off with a sweet taste and a
soft texture, and only later, as it
remains in the ground, does it
harden and develop a more bitter
taste. How, then, does the *taste*
of this type of marror contribute
to our recollection of bitter servitude?

The *Aruch HaShulchan*
(275:15) admits that, in truth, it is
not the flavor of Romaine lettuce
that contributes to our feeling the
bitterness of Egypt. However, once
the Torah permits other vegetables
to be used for marror – vegetables
whose only association to the bitter exile is in their bitter taste – it
does not distinguish between the
different types of vegetables and
requires that they all be chewed
and not merely swallowed.

6. **Rachtza/** Wash for Bread

• Each participant should wash his hands, in the manner described above for *Karpas,* but at this point the *bracha* should be recited before drying the hands (158:11,[41]).

בָּרוּךְ אַתָּה יְיָ אֱלֹהֵינוּ מֶלֶךְ הָעוֹלָם, אֲשֶׁר קִדְּשָׁנוּ בְּמִצְוֹתָיו, וְצִוָּנוּ עַל נְטִילַת יָדַיִם.

Blessed are You, G-d our Lord, King of the world, who made us holy with His command-ments and instructed us regarding washing the hands.

7. **Motzi Matza/** Bless and Eat Matza

• The three matzos should be lifted with the broken one in the middle: the upper and lower matzos constitute the two whole loaves needed for המוציא, and the broken middle matza is utilized to fulfill the mitzvah of *lechem oni,* the poor man's bread (475:1).

• After the *bracha* of *Hamotzi* is made, the bottom matza is dropped, and the *bracha* of על אכילת מצה is made on the two upper matzos (ibid.).

• The two remaining upper matzos should be broken simultaneously, and a *kezayis* should be eaten from each matza (a *kezayis* is equal to approximately 1/4 of a hand-made matza or 1/3 of a machine-made matza) (475:1, [3]). Additional matzos should be distributed to all the partici-pants, in order that each person eat two *kezaisim.*

• The general custom is not to dip the matza in salt (475:1,[4]).

• A piece of both matzos should be placed in the mouth at the same time, and the two *kezaisim* should be swallowed within 3-4 minutes. One should not speak from the time that Hamotzi is said, until after eating the Korech sandwich (473:1). If one does interrupt, however, another *bracha* need not be made on the Korech (475, [24]).

• The matza must be eaten while reclining. If one forgets to recline, he should eat another *kezayis*, without a *bracha*, while reclining (472:7,[22]).

• The first *kezayis* of matza must be eaten before halachic midnight (the halfway point between sunset and sunrise). (If one is not able to eat the matza before midnight, the *bracha* of על אכילת מצה should not be recited.)

הֲרֵינִי מוּכָן וּמְזוּמָן לְקַיֵּם מִצְוַת אֲכִילַת מַצָּה. לְשֵׁם יִחוּד קוּדְשָׁא בְּרִיךְ הוּא וּשְׁכִינְתֵּיהּ עַל יְדֵי הַהוּא טָמִיר וְנֶעְלָם בְּשֵׁם כָּל יִשְׂרָאֵל. וִיהִי נֹעַם אֲדֹנָי אֱלֹהֵינוּ עָלֵינוּ וּמַעֲשֵׂה יָדֵינוּ כּוֹנְנָה עָלֵינוּ, וּמַעֲשֵׂה יָדֵינוּ כּוֹנְנֵהוּ.

בָּרוּךְ אַתָּה יְיָ, אֱלֹהֵינוּ מֶלֶךְ הָעוֹלָם, הַמּוֹצִיא לֶחֶם מִן הָאָרֶץ.

בָּרוּךְ אַתָּה יְיָ, אֱלֹהֵינוּ מֶלֶךְ הָעוֹלָם, אֲשֶׁר קִדְּשָׁנוּ בְּמִצְוֹתָיו, וְצִוָּנוּ עַל אֲכִילַת מַצָּה.

I am ready and prepared to keep the commandment to eat matza, for the sake of the One G-d and His presence, may it be counted as done in the name of all Israel.

Blessed are You, G-d our Lord, King of the world, who brings bread out of the earth.

Blessed are You, G-d our Lord, King of the world, who made us holy with His commandments and instructed us to eat matza.

8. **Marror/** The Bitter Herb

• A *kezayis* of *marror* should be dipped into the *charoses*. It should not be immersed so long that it loses its taste. For the same reason, one should shake off any excess *charoses* (475:1).

• One need not recline while eating the *marror*, because it commemorates slavery, not freedom (ibid.).

• The *marror* must be eaten before halachic midnight. If this is not possible, it should be eaten without the *bracha* על אכילת מרור (477, [6]).

• If one swallowed the *marror* without first chewing it, the mitzvah is not fulfilled, because its bitterness must be tasted (475:3).

❖ **Sweet Dreams in Bitter Nights**

מרור / **MARROR**

The bitter herb, representing the bitter exile, is dipped into the sweet *charoses* mixture. What does this symbolize?

The *charoses* is a thick mixture made of chopped apples, nuts, cinnamon, and wine. Its texture is supposed to represent the bricks and mortar that the Jews were forced to make, while building cities for the Egyptians. It is understandable why cinnamon sticks, representing straw, are used. Nuts and wine, too, combine to form a pasty consistency, representing the mortar. It is strange, however, that a sweet apple is used as an ingredient.

Tosafos (*Pesachim* 116a) finds a source for using apples. A narrative in the Talmud (*Sotah* 11b) tells us that the Jewish women in Egypt would go to the apple orchards to give birth. This enabled them to deliver their children in secrecy, and prevented the Egyptians' discovering them. Sometimes, however, they were not successful in hiding their children from the Egyptian police. These children

הֲרֵינִי מוּכָן וּמְזוּמָן לְקַיֵּם מִצְוַת אֲכִילַת מָרוֹר לְשֵׁם יִחוּד
קוּדְשָׁא בְּרִיךְ הוּא וּשְׁכִינְתֵּיה עַל יְדֵי הַהוּא טָמִיר וְנֶעֱלָם
בְּשֵׁם כָּל יִשְׂרָאֵל. וִיהִי נוֹעַם אֲדֹנָי אֱלֹהֵינוּ עָלֵינוּ וּמַעֲשֵׂה
יָדֵינוּ כּוֹנְנָה עָלֵינוּ וּמַעֲשֵׂה יָדֵינוּ כּוֹנְנֵהוּ:

בָּרוּךְ אַתָּה יְיָ, אֱלֹהֵינוּ מֶלֶךְ הָעוֹלָם, אֲשֶׁר
קִדְּשָׁנוּ בְּמִצְוֹתָיו, וְצִוָּנוּ עַל אֲכִילַת מָרוֹר.

*I am ready and prepared to keep the commandment to
eat the Bitter Herb, for the sake of the One G-d and
His presence, may it be counted as done in the name
of all Israel.*

*Blessed are You, G-d our Lord, King of the
world, who made us holy with His commandments, and instructed us to eat the bitter vegetable.*

would be brutally killed. The Midrash says that bodies of these murdered children were even used as a filler for building materials, when supplies fell short.(See Rashi, *Sanhedrin* 101b.) Thus, the apples may serve as a reminder of the Jewish children born in the apple orchards, who were placed in the walls with the mortar. This would complement the bitter marror quite well.

However, the apples also convey an uplifting message. The apple orchards represent the strong courage and faith which the righteous women showed in Egypt.

Although they understood the great risks they faced in bringing children into the world, they gladly fulfilled their roles as Jewish wives and mothers. Not only did they not despair, but they actually encouraged and inspired their husbands not to give up hope either.

The apple in the mortar-mixture thus symbolizes maintaining hope and faith in the future – in the midst of darkness and slavery. Dipping the marror into the *charoses* sends a message of trust in G-d's promise for the future to the Jew in exile.

9. **Korech/** Combine Matza and Bitters

• Hillel was of the opinion that the matza and marror must be eaten together (*Pesachim* 115a). For this reason, after the matza and marror are eaten separately, we eat them as a sandwich in order to satisfy Hillel's opinion.

• A *kezayis* of the bottom matza should be taken together with a *kezayis* of *marror*. Most authorities are of the opinion that the sandwich should be dipped in the *charoses*. The excess *charoses* should again be shaken off (475:1,[19]).

• The sandwich should be eaten while reclining (ibid.). If one forgets to recline, it need not be eaten a second time (*Kol Dodi*).

זֵכֶר לְמִקְדָּשׁ כְּהִלֵּל. כֵּן עָשָׂה הִלֵּל בִּזְמַן שֶׁבֵּית הַמִּקְדָּשׁ הָיָה קַיָּם. הָיָה כּוֹרֵךְ (פֶּסַח) מַצָּה וּמָרוֹר וְאוֹכֵל בְּיַחַד. לְקַיֵּם מַה שֶׁנֶּאֱמַר עַל מַצּוֹת וּמְרֹרִים יֹאכְלֻהוּ:

❖ **Suffering With Faith**

כורך / KORECH

During the times of the Temple in Jerusalem, Hillel would eat the Pesach offering together with the matza and marror, creating a kind of sandwich. Today, since the Temple no longer stands and the Pesach offering cannot be brought, the obligation to eat marror is only required by Rabbinic law, and the matza and marror may not be eaten together. This is because of the Halachic principle that states that the taste of a lesser obligation (marror) can over-whelm, and thereby cancel, that of a greater obligation (matza). Therefore, we first eat the matza and marror separately, in order to fulfill the mitzvos. Only *then* do we eat the two together, as a remembrance of what Hillel did in the days of the Temple.

Two questions are in order here. First, what is the significance of Hillel's eating the Pesach with the matza and marror? Why are they eaten together, rather than separately? Secondly, if we wanted to commemorate Hillel's opinion, would it not have made more sense to eat the marror after the

In memory of the Temple, according to Hillel. This is what Hillel would do [long ago] when the Temple stood: He would make a sandwich of the Passover Lamb, matza, and bitter herbs and eat them all together. This would be to keep what the Torah says, "They shall eat [the Passover Lamb] together with matza and bitter herbs".

meal with the Afikoman, since the Afikoman commemorates the Pesach offering?

We have explained that the Pesach offering represents the essence of the Pesach holiday: recognition of G-d's great kindness in "skipping over" the nation's inadequacies, and rescuing the Jews from total oblivion. (It is fitting that the *Targum Onkelos* emphasizes this by explaining the word "pesach" as "chos," "to show compassion," rather than with the usual translation, "to skip over.") As we have said many times previously, although the Children of Israel may not have thoroughly deserved G-d's compassion, they were nonetheless rescued. He saved them on two accounts: First, He had compassion for them, because of the terrible persecution they had had to endure at the hands of the Egyptians; second, the Jews showed great trust and devotion, when they followed G-d into the wilderness with no provisions. G-d's foreknowledge of their devotion led Him to free them.

This, then, may answer our questions. Hillel states that the Pesach must be eaten with matza and marror, because the Pesach, which represents G-d's compassion, should be eaten with the foods that represent the source of G-d's compassion. The marror represents the bitter persecution the Jews endured; the matza, the trust that they demonstrated, when they followed G-d in such haste they had no time to bake bread.

Accordingly, we can also understand why the sandwich is eaten now and not after the meal as part of the Afikoman. We have explained that the matza eaten before the meal, and the matza eaten after it, represent two different concepts: The first matza represents the haste of the redemption and the nation's departing Egypt without time to bake bread; the second matza, the Afikoman (the matza eaten with the Pesach offering in Egypt), commemorates the matza eaten during the enslavement in Egypt, long before the Jews' departure. (See the discussion of

10. **Shulchan Orech/** The Meal is Served

• It is preferable to recline during the entire meal (472:7).

• Some have the custom to eat eggs during the meal (476:2).

• One must be careful not to overeat during the meal in order to be able to eat the *Afikoman* with an appetite (476:2).

• It is customary not to eat roasted meat or poultry at the Seder. Accordingly, the *zeroa* from the Seder plate may not be eaten during the Seder. The reason for this is that we do not want to give the appearance that we are eating the *Korbon Pesach*, which was also roasted. Thus, only meat which has been cooked with liquid may be eaten (476:1,[1]).

Rabban Gamliel, above, p. 117.) The matza eaten in Hillel's sandwich was obviously the matza of redemption, and symbolized the nation's devotion to G-d. Thus, since it was not the matza of slavery, it is eaten *before* the meal, when the matza represents freedom.

Another question is raised by the commentators regarding the source for Hillel's opinion. As his source, Hillel cites *Bamidbar* (9:11), which describes the Pesach Sheni, the "make-up" Pesach sacrifice that may be brought a month after Pesach by those who could not bring it on time due to extenuating circumstances; he does *not* cite *Shemos* (12:8), which discusses the original Pesach sacrifice and the eating of matza and marror with it. Why? (See *Seder He'Aruch*, ch.151.)

According to our interpretation,

we can answer that the first Pesach sacrifice was eaten in Egypt, right before the Exodus. When the passage from *Shemos* describes eating matza and marror with the Pesach sacrifice, the matza was not the matza of redemption, since the Jews had not yet left Egypt. Hillel would not have explained the *Shemos* passage as obligating one to eat the matza and marror with the Pesach sacrifice. Rather, Hillel cites *Bamidbar,* which describes the Pesach Sheni, which occurred *after* the Exodus, as his source.

❖ Preventing Arrogance
שלחן עורך /
SHULCHAN ORECH

The *Rema* (476:2) cites the custom of serving hard-boiled eggs at the meal. He explains that the egg is a food eaten by mourners, and we mourn because we no

11. **Tzafun/** The Afikoman

• After the meal has been completed, the Afikoman is eaten as a reminder of the *Korbon Pesach,* which was also eaten after the meal (477:1).

• Again, each participant should preferably eat two *kezaisim* of matza, one corresponding to the *Korbon Pesach* and one corresponding to the matza that was eaten with the *Korbon Pesach* (ibid.)

• The *Afikoman* should be eaten before halachic midnight, if possible (ibid.)

• The *Afikoman* should be eaten while reclining; however, if one forgets to recline, it should not be eaten a second time (472, [22]).

---

longer have the Temple, and thus cannot bring the Pesach offering ourselves.

Perhaps another explanation may be offered. Many mitzvos are performed during the Seder, as a way of celebrating freedom. The festive meal also celebrates our freedom. For this reason, all our finest dinnerware is placed on our tables (*Orach Chaim* 472:2), and some people even recline throughout the meal (*Ibid.,*472:7). However, although the mitzvos regarding what must be eaten before and after the meal are clearly defined, the Seder meal, itself, has no such stipulations.

Eating all kinds of delicacies, with one's beautiful dishes and utensils, puts the individual at risk of becoming arrogant and complacent. *Pirkei Avos* teaches that to

avoid sin, one should always focus on three things: where we have come from, where we are going, and before Whom we must give a reckoning. We begin as but a tiny drop, our end is the grave, and we will be accountable for all our actions before the Holy One, Blessed is He (3:1). Rabbenu Yonah (ibid.) explains that contemplation of one's lowly beginnings prevents a person from becoming arrogant. Contemplation of one's end discourages the emphasis on amassing material wealth and honor. The recognition of one's final reckoning will stop a person from sinning.

The egg is a reminder of a person's humble beginnings, the tiny drop. Partaking of the egg during the festive meal reminds us that we should not allow our newfound freedom to lead us astray.

• One must eat the *Afikoman* in one place, just as was true for eating the *Korbon Pesach*. One should not even change places in the same room while eating the *Afikoman* (478:1, [4]).

• One may not eat anything after the *Afikoman,* in order to preserve the taste of the matza. If anything is eaten afterwards, the *Afikoman* should be eaten again (478:1, [2]). There are different opinions concerning drinking after the *Afikoman*. One should preferably not drink anything other than water, tea, or other mild-tasting beverages (ibid., [2]).

• If one forgets to eat the *Afikoman* and does not remember until after *Bircas Hamazon,* he should wash again and eat the *Afikoman* (477:2).

הֲרֵינִי מוּכָן וּמְזוּמָן לְקַיֵּים מִצְוַת אֲכִילַת אֲפִיקוֹמָן לְשֵׁם
יִחוּד קוּדְשָׁא בְּרִיךְ הוּא וּשְׁכִינְתֵּיה עַל יְדֵי הַהוּא טָמִיר
וְנֶעֱלָם בְּשֵׁם כָּל יִשְׂרָאֵל. וִיהִי נוֹעַם אֲדֹנָי אֱלֹהֵינוּ עָלֵינוּ
וּמַעֲשֵׂה יָדֵינוּ כּוֹנְנָה עָלֵינוּ, וּמַעֲשֵׂה יָדֵינוּ כּוֹנְנֵהוּ.

I am ready and prepared to keep the commandment to eat the Afikoman, for the sake of the One G-d and His presence, may it be counted as done in the name of all Israel.

12. **Barech** / Grace after the Meal

• The third cup should be filled before *Bircas Hamazon*.

ברך / BARECH

❖ **Eating to Bless and Blessing to Eat**

בורא פרי הגפן
. . . Creator of the fruit of the grape-vine.

The third of the Four Cups of wine is somewhat different from the others. The other three cups are said over blessings that are unique to Pesach night: Kiddush, Maggid, and the special *Hallel* that is said at the Seder. The third cup, however, is said over the Bircas

If the cup is not clean, it should be rinsed out before being filled (479:1, [1]).

• If there are three males over thirteen at the Seder, the head of the household should lead the *Bircas Hamazon* (ibid.).

Hamazon. This cup can be drunk after any meal, at any time of the year, and has no specific connection to Pesach, whatsoever. Why is this included among the Four Cups?

A story is told about a young Chasid who was present at the home of Rav Ahron Karliner. He saw the Rebbe take an apple, make the proper blessing, and eat the apple. The Rebbe noticed that the Chasid seemed perturbed. He asked what was bothering him.

"Rebbe," the young man replied, "I had always assumed that a Rebbe would conduct his life in a manner much holier than that of a common person, such as I myself. Yet I see that you also eat apples, just like I do! What is the difference between us?"

"Let me explain the difference," the Rebbe responded. "When you get hungry, you take an apple to eat. But knowing, of course, that an apple may not be eaten without first making the proper blessing, you make the blessing, in order to be able to eat the apple. A Rebbe, however, is different. He sometimes feels the need to just bless G-d, yet he realizes that Jewish Law does not

allow one to make a blessing in vain. So the Rebbe eats an apple, just so that he can make a blessing to G-d."

In both situations, the person makes the blessing, and then eats the apple. Yet, whereas one person makes the blessing in order to eat, the other eats, in order to make the blessing.

The Rabbis wanted us to offer four blessings to G-d at the Seder, to commemorate the four expressions of redemption. But blessings may not be said in vain. They therefore attached the blessings to four cups of wine, since wine also contributes to the joy of the celebration. The cups did not have to be unique to Pesach, as long as they provided the opportunity to make another blessing.

This idea is actually presented in the Talmud (*Pesachim* 108b). The Talmud discusses a situation in which a person had drunk all four cups at one time. The Halacha is that he has fulfilled the mitzvah of drinking wine, but not the mitzvah of drinking the Four Cups, since the cups must be drunk at their proper times.

Thus the mitzvah of the Four Cups is independent of the mitz-

שִׁיר הַמַּעֲלוֹת, בְּשׁוּב יְיָ אֶת שִׁיבַת צִיּוֹן,
הָיִינוּ כְּחֹלְמִים: אָז יִמָּלֵא שְׂחוֹק פִּינוּ וּלְשׁוֹנֵנוּ
רִנָּה, אָז יֹאמְרוּ בַגּוֹיִם, הִגְדִּיל יְיָ לַעֲשׂוֹת עִם
אֵלֶּה: הִגְדִּיל יְיָ לַעֲשׂוֹת עִמָּנוּ, הָיִינוּ שְׂמֵחִים:
שׁוּבָה יְיָ אֶת שְׁבִיתֵנוּ, כַּאֲפִיקִים בַּנֶּגֶב:
הַזֹּרְעִים בְּדִמְעָה בְּרִנָּה יִקְצֹרוּ: הָלוֹךְ יֵלֵךְ
וּבָכֹה נֹשֵׂא מֶשֶׁךְ הַזָּרַע, בֹּא יָבֹא בְרִנָּה, נֹשֵׂא
אֲלֻמֹּתָיו:

הֲרֵינִי מוּכָן וּמְזוּמָּן לְקַיֵּם מִצְוַת עֲשֵׂה שֶׁל בִּרְכַּת הַמָּזוֹן כְּמָה
שֶׁנֶּאֱמַר וְאָכַלְתָּ וְשָׂבָעְתָּ וּבֵרַכְתָּ אֶת ה׳ אֱלֹקֶיךָ עַל הָאָרֶץ הַטּוֹבָה
אֲשֶׁר נָתַן לָךְ. לְשֵׁם יִחוּד קוּדְשָׁא בְּרִיךְ הוּא וּשְׁכִינְתֵּיהּ עַל יְדֵי
הַהוּא טָמִיר וְנֶעֱלָם בְּשֵׁם כָּל יִשְׂרָאֵל. וִיהִי נֹעַם אֲדֹנָי אֱלֹהֵינוּ
עָלֵינוּ וּמַעֲשֵׂה יָדֵינוּ כּוֹנְנָה עָלֵינוּ, וּמַעֲשֵׂה יָדֵינוּ כּוֹנְנֵהוּ.

*If three or more males, aged thirteen years or older, are at the
table, the following sentences are added.*

*If there are more than ten men or boys over thirteen years of age
present, the words in parentheses are added.*

Host:

רַבּוֹתַי נְבָרֵךְ

Guests:

יְהִי שֵׁם יְיָ מְבוֹרָךְ מֵעַתָּה וְעַד עוֹלָם.

Host:

יְהִי שֵׁם יְיָ מְבוֹרָךְ מֵעַתָּה וְעַד עוֹלָם.
בִּרְשׁוּת מָרָנָן וְרַבָּנָן וְרַבּוֹתַי נְבָרֵךְ (אֱלֹהֵינוּ) שֶׁאָכַלְנוּ מִשֶּׁלּוֹ.

A song of steps: When G-d returns the captives of Zion, we will be like dreamers. Then our mouths will be full of laughter, and our tongues will be singing. Then it will be said among nations, "G-d has done great things with them!" G-d has done great things with us! We are very happy! Return our exiles G-d, like the flood streams in the Negev. Those who plant in tears, may they harvest in joy. He who went along crying, carrying his bag of seed, may he come back singing, carrying his bundle of grain.

I am ready and prepared to keep the commandment of Grace after Meals, as it is written, "And you shall eat and be filled, and you shall bless the Lord your G-d for the good land He gave you". For the sake of the One G-d and His presence, may it be counted as done in the name of all Israel.

If three or more males, aged thirteen years or older, are at the table, the following sentences are added.

If there are more than ten men or boys over thirteen years of age present, the words in parentheses are added.

Leader:
Gentlemen, let us say Grace!

Others:
May G-d's name be blessed now and forever.

Leader:
May G-d's name be blessed now and forever.
With permission of all those present let us bless Him
(our G-d) whose food we have eaten.

Guests:

בָּרוּךְ (אֱלֹהֵינוּ) שֶׁאָכַלְנוּ מִשֶּׁלּוֹ וּבְטוּבוֹ חָיִינוּ.

Host:

בָּרוּךְ (אֱלֹהֵינוּ) שֶׁאָכַלְנוּ מִשֶּׁלּוֹ וּבְטוּבוֹ חָיִינוּ.

Host:

בָּרוּךְ הוּא וּבָרוּךְ שְׁמוֹ:

בָּרוּךְ אַתָּה יְיָ, אֱלֹהֵינוּ מֶלֶךְ הָעוֹלָם, הַזָּן אֶת הָעוֹלָם כֻּלּוֹ, בְּטוּבוֹ בְּחֵן בְּחֶסֶד וּבְרַחֲמִים. הוּא נוֹתֵן לֶחֶם לְכָל בָּשָׂר, כִּי לְעוֹלָם חַסְדּוֹ. וּבְטוּבוֹ הַגָּדוֹל, תָּמִיד לֹא חָסַר לָנוּ, וְאַל יֶחְסַר לָנוּ מָזוֹן לְעוֹלָם וָעֶד, בַּעֲבוּר שְׁמוֹ הַגָּדוֹל, כִּי הוּא אֵל זָן וּמְפַרְנֵס לַכֹּל, וּמֵטִיב לַכֹּל, וּמֵכִין מָזוֹן לְכָל בְּרִיּוֹתָיו אֲשֶׁר בָּרָא. (כָּאָמוּר פּוֹתֵחַ אֶת יָדֶךָ, וּמַשְׂבִּיעַ לְכָל חַי רָצוֹן.) בָּרוּךְ אַתָּה יְיָ, הַזָּן אֶת הַכֹּל.

נוֹדֶה לְךָ יְיָ אֱלֹהֵינוּ, עַל שֶׁהִנְחַלְתָּ לַאֲבוֹתֵינוּ אֶרֶץ חֶמְדָּה טוֹבָה וּרְחָבָה, וְעַל שֶׁהוֹצֵאתָנוּ יְיָ

vah of drinking wine. The significance of the Four Cups is held in the four blessings that are made over them. This can only be accomplished, if the cups are drunk as directed in the Haggadah, at the appropriate moments.

וְעַל שֶׁהוֹצֵאתָנוּ מֵאֶרֶץ מִצְרַיִם וּפְדִיתָנוּ מִבֵּית עֲבָדִים

...for You brought us out, O G-d

our Lord, from the land of Egypt and You saved us from the house of bondage

The order of these phrases appears to be chronologically reversed, since redemption from servitude actually preceded the Exodus from Egypt by six months (Talmud *Rosh Hashana,* 11a). But, as we explained above in **Dayenu,**

Others:

*Blessed be He (our G-d) whose food we have eaten
and in whose goodness we live.*

Leader:

*Blessed be He (our G-d) whose food we have eaten
and in whose goodness we live.*

All:

Blessed be He and blessed be His name.

*Blessed are You, G-d our Lord, King of the
world, who feeds all the world with His goodness, with kindness, love and pity. He gives
bread to all flesh, for his love is endless. And in
His great goodness He has never failed us, and
He will never fail us with food, for ever and
ever. For the sake of His great name for He is
G-d who feeds and provides for all, He is good
to all and prepares food for all His creatures that
He created. (It is thus written, "You open Your
hand and satisfy the desire of all living things".)
Blessed are You G-d our Lord, who feeds all
things.*

*We thank you, G-d our Lord, for You granted
our fathers a lovely, good, and spacious land;
because You brought us out, G-d our Lord, from*

the redemption from slavery was not complete until the Jewish people received the Torah and were cleansed of the last vestiges of Egyptian influence. These events did not occur until some time after the Jews had left the physical boundaries of Egypt. Hence, the redemption is mentioned after the Exodus from the land of Egypt.

אֱלֹהֵינוּ מֵאֶרֶץ מִצְרַיִם, וּפְדִיתָנוּ מִבֵּית עֲבָדִים, וְעַל בְּרִיתְךָ שֶׁחָתַמְתָּ בִּבְשָׂרֵנוּ, וְעַל תּוֹרָתְךָ שֶׁלִּמַּדְתָּנוּ, וְעַל חֻקֶּיךָ שֶׁהוֹדַעְתָּנוּ, וְעַל חַיִּים חֵן וָחֶסֶד שֶׁחוֹנַנְתָּנוּ, וְעַל אֲכִילַת מָזוֹן שָׁאַתָּה זָן וּמְפַרְנֵס אוֹתָנוּ תָּמִיד, בְּכָל יוֹם וּבְכָל עֵת וּבְכָל שָׁעָה.

וְעַל הַכֹּל יְיָ אֱלֹהֵינוּ, אֲנַחְנוּ מוֹדִים לָךְ, וּמְבָרְכִים אוֹתָךְ, יִתְבָּרַךְ שִׁמְךָ בְּפִי כָּל חַי תָּמִיד לְעוֹלָם וָעֶד. כַּכָּתוּב, וְאָכַלְתָּ וְשָׂבָעְתָּ, וּבֵרַכְתָּ אֶת יְיָ אֱלֹהֶיךָ עַל הָאָרֶץ הַטֹּבָה אֲשֶׁר נָתַן לָךְ. בָּרוּךְ אַתָּה יְיָ, עַל הָאָרֶץ וְעַל הַמָּזוֹן.

רַחֶם נָא יְיָ אֱלֹהֵינוּ, עַל יִשְׂרָאֵל עַמֶּךָ, וְעַל יְרוּשָׁלַיִם עִירֶךָ, וְעַל צִיּוֹן מִשְׁכַּן כְּבוֹדֶךָ, וְעַל מַלְכוּת בֵּית דָּוִד מְשִׁיחֶךָ, וְעַל הַבַּיִת הַגָּדוֹל וְהַקָּדוֹשׁ שֶׁנִּקְרָא שִׁמְךָ עָלָיו. אֱלֹהֵינוּ, אָבִינוּ, רְעֵנוּ, זוּנֵנוּ, פַּרְנְסֵנוּ, וְכַלְכְּלֵנוּ, וְהַרְוִיחֵנוּ, וְהַרְוַח לָנוּ יְיָ אֱלֹהֵינוּ, מְהֵרָה מִכָּל צָרוֹתֵינוּ. וְנָא אַל תַּצְרִיכֵנוּ, יְיָ אֱלֹהֵינוּ, לֹא לִידֵי מַתְּנַת בָּשָׂר וָדָם, וְלֹא לִידֵי הַלְוָאָתָם, כִּי אִם לְיָדְךָ הַמְּלֵאָה, הַפְּתוּחָה, הַקְּדוֹשָׁה, וְהָרְחָבָה, שֶׁלֹּא נֵבוֹשׁ וְלֹא נִכָּלֵם לְעוֹלָם וָעֶד.

the land of Egypt, and saved us from the house of bondage; for Your promise that You sealed in our flesh, for Your Torah which You taught us, and for Your laws which You let us know; and for the life, kindness and mercy You have granted us; and for the food we eat which You grant and provide for us always, every day, every time, every hour.

And for everything, G-d our Lord, we thank You and bless You. May Your name be blessed by all life always and forever. As it is written "You shall eat and be filled, and you shall bless G-d your Lord for the good land He gave you". Blessed are You G-d, for the land and for the food.

Have mercy, O G-d our Lord, on Your people Israel, on your city Jerusalem, on Zion home of your glory, on the royal house of David Your chosen one, and on the great and holy Temple that bears Your name. Our G-d, our Father, our Shepherd, feed us, support us, nourish us and sustain us. Grant us relief quickly, O G-d our Lord, from all our troubles; and please, O G-d our Lord, do not make us dependent on gifts from flesh and blood, nor upon their loans, but let all come from Your full, open, generous hand, that we not be shamed nor disgraced, forever and ever.

On Sabbath:

רְצֵה וְהַחֲלִיצֵנוּ, יְיָ אֱלֹהֵינוּ, בְּמִצְוֹתֶיךָ, וּבְמִצְוַת יוֹם הַשְּׁבִיעִי הַשַּׁבָּת הַגָּדוֹל וְהַקָּדוֹשׁ הַזֶּה. כִּי יוֹם זֶה גָּדוֹל וְקָדוֹשׁ הוּא לְפָנֶיךָ, לִשְׁבָּת בּוֹ וְלָנוּחַ בּוֹ בְּאַהֲבָה, כְּמִצְוַת רְצוֹנֶךָ. וּבִרְצוֹנְךָ הָנִיחַ לָנוּ, יְיָ אֱלֹהֵינוּ, שֶׁלֹּא תְהֵא צָרָה וְיָגוֹן וַאֲנָחָה בְּיוֹם מְנוּחָתֵנוּ. וְהַרְאֵנוּ, יְיָ אֱלֹהֵינוּ, בְּנֶחָמַת צִיּוֹן עִירֶךָ, וּבְבִנְיַן יְרוּשָׁלַיִם עִיר קָדְשֶׁךָ, כִּי אַתָּה הוּא בַּעַל הַיְשׁוּעוֹת וּבַעַל הַנֶּחָמוֹת.

אֱלֹהֵינוּ וֵאלֹהֵי אֲבוֹתֵינוּ, יַעֲלֶה, וְיָבֹא, וְיַגִּיעַ, וְיֵרָאֶה, וְיֵרָצֶה, וְיִשָּׁמַע, וְיִפָּקֵד, וְיִזָּכֵר, זִכְרוֹנֵנוּ וּפִקְדוֹנֵנוּ, וְזִכְרוֹן אֲבוֹתֵינוּ, וְזִכְרוֹן מָשִׁיחַ בֶּן דָּוִד עַבְדֶּךָ, וְזִכְרוֹן יְרוּשָׁלַיִם עִיר קָדְשֶׁךָ, וְזִכְרוֹן כָּל עַמְּךָ בֵּית יִשְׂרָאֵל, לְפָנֶיךָ, לִפְלֵיטָה, לְטוֹבָה, לְחֵן, וּלְחֶסֶד, וּלְרַחֲמִים, לְחַיִּים וּלְשָׁלוֹם, בְּיוֹם חַג הַמַּצוֹת הַזֶּה. זָכְרֵנוּ, יְיָ אֱלֹהֵינוּ בּוֹ לְטוֹבָה, וּפָקְדֵנוּ בוֹ לִבְרָכָה, וְהוֹשִׁיעֵנוּ בוֹ לְחַיִּים טוֹבִים. וּבִדְבַר יְשׁוּעָה וְרַחֲמִים, חוּס וְחָנֵּנוּ, וְרַחֵם עָלֵינוּ וְהוֹשִׁיעֵנוּ, כִּי אֵלֶיךָ עֵינֵינוּ, כִּי אֵל מֶלֶךְ חַנּוּן וְרַחוּם אָתָּה.

וּבְנֵה יְרוּשָׁלַיִם, עִיר הַקֹּדֶשׁ, בִּמְהֵרָה בְיָמֵינוּ. בָּרוּךְ אַתָּה יְיָ, בּוֹנֵה בְרַחֲמָיו יְרוּשָׁלָיִם. אָמֵן.

On Sabbath:

Be pleased, and strengthen us, G-d our Lord, in Your commandments and in the commandment of the seventh day, this great and holy Sabbath. For this day is great and holy before You for rest and relaxation, in love, as the commandment of Your desire. If it pleases You, let us rest, G-d our Lord, that we not have any trouble or sorrow or grief on our day of rest. Let us see, G-d our Lord, the restoration of Zion Your city, and the building of Jerusalem Your holy city, for You are the master of all help and comfort.

Our Lord and Lord of our fathers: may there go up, come, reach, and be accepted, heard, counted and remembered a reminder of us and our cause, a reminder of our fathers, a reminder of the Mashiach son of David Your servant, a reminder of Jerusalem Your holy city, and a reminder of all Your people the House of Israel, before You, for rescue, kindness, love, and mercy, for life and peace, on this festival of Matzos. Remember us, O G-d our Lord, now for good, recall us now for blessing, and save us for a good life. With a word of hope and mercy have pity and be kind to us; have mercy and save us, for our eyes are lifted to You, for You are a kind and merciful King.

And build Jerusalem the holy city soon in our days. Blessed are You G-d, who builds Jerusalem in His mercy; Amen!

בָּרוּךְ אַתָּה יְיָ, אֱלֹהֵינוּ מֶלֶךְ הָעוֹלָם, הָאֵל
אָבִינוּ, מַלְכֵּנוּ, אַדִּירֵנוּ, בּוֹרְאֵנוּ, גּוֹאֲלֵנוּ,
יוֹצְרֵנוּ, קְדוֹשֵׁנוּ קְדוֹשׁ יַעֲקֹב, רוֹעֵנוּ רוֹעֵה
יִשְׂרָאֵל. הַמֶּלֶךְ הַטּוֹב וְהַמֵּטִיב לַכֹּל, שֶׁבְּכָל יוֹם
וָיוֹם הוּא הֵטִיב, הוּא מֵטִיב, הוּא יֵיטִיב לָנוּ.
הוּא גְמָלָנוּ, הוּא גוֹמְלֵנוּ, הוּא יִגְמְלֵנוּ, לָעַד,
לְחֵן וּלְחֶסֶד וּלְרַחֲמִים וּלְרֶוַח, הַצָּלָה וְהַצְלָחָה,
בְּרָכָה וִישׁוּעָה, נֶחָמָה, פַּרְנָסָה וְכַלְכָּלָה,
וְרַחֲמִים וְחַיִּים וְשָׁלוֹם, וְכָל טוֹב, וּמִכָּל טוֹב
לְעוֹלָם אַל יְחַסְּרֵנוּ.

הָרַחֲמָן, הוּא יִמְלוֹךְ עָלֵינוּ לְעוֹלָם וָעֶד.

הָרַחֲמָן, הוּא יִתְבָּרֵךְ בַּשָּׁמַיִם וּבָאָרֶץ.

הָרַחֲמָן, הוּא יִשְׁתַּבַּח לְדוֹר דּוֹרִים, וְיִתְפָּאַר
בָּנוּ לָעַד וּלְנֵצַח נְצָחִים, וְיִתְהַדַּר בָּנוּ לָעַד
וּלְעוֹלְמֵי עוֹלָמִים.

הָרַחֲמָן, הוּא יְפַרְנְסֵנוּ בְּכָבוֹד.

הָרַחֲמָן, הוּא יִשְׁבּוֹר עֻלֵנוּ מֵעַל צַוָּארֵנוּ,
וְהוּא יוֹלִיכֵנוּ קוֹמְמִיּוּת לְאַרְצֵנוּ.

הָרַחֲמָן, הוּא יִשְׁלַח לָנוּ בְּרָכָה מְרֻבָּה בַּבַּיִת
הַזֶּה, וְעַל שֻׁלְחָן זֶה שֶׁאָכַלְנוּ עָלָיו.

Blessed are You G-d our Lord, King of the world- G-d who is our Father, our King, our Power, our Creator, our Rescuer, our Maker, our Holy One, the Holy One of Jacob; our Shepherd, the Shepherd of Israel; the good King – good to all – who every day was good, is good, and will be good to us. He has granted us, is granting us, and will always grant us our needs, with kindness, love, mercy, and plenty. May help, success, blessing, rescue, comfort, livelihood, support, mercy, life, peace, all good, and all that comes from good, never fail us.

May the Merciful One rule over us for ever and ever.

May the Merciful One be blessed in heaven and earth.

May the Merciful One be praised for all ages, glorified among us for ever and ever, and honored by us until the end of time.

May the Merciful One grant us our needs with honor.

May the Merciful One break our yoke from our necks, and bring us standing tall to our land.

May the Merciful One send a great blessing to this house, and to this table upon which we have eaten.

הָרַחֲמָן, הוּא יִשְׁלַח לָנוּ אֶת אֵלִיָּהוּ הַנָּבִיא
זָכוּר לַטּוֹב, וִיבַשֶּׂר לָנוּ בְּשׂוֹרוֹת טוֹבוֹת יְשׁוּעוֹת
וְנֶחָמוֹת.

*In the following paragraphs, say what is appropriate for the
occasion:*

הָרַחֲמָן, הוּא יְבָרֵךְ אֶת (אָבִי מוֹרִי), בַּעַל
הַבַּיִת הַזֶּה, וְאֶת (אִמִּי מוֹרָתִי), בַּעֲלַת הַבַּיִת
הַזֶּה, אוֹתָם וְאֶת בֵּיתָם וְאֶת זַרְעָם, וְאֶת כָּל
אֲשֶׁר לָהֶם.

הָרַחֲמָן, הוּא יְבָרֵךְ אוֹתִי וְאֶת אִשְׁתִּי וְאֶת
זַרְעִי, וְאֶת כָּל אֲשֶׁר לִי.

אוֹתָנוּ וְאֶת כָּל אֲשֶׁר לָנוּ, כְּמוֹ שֶׁנִּתְבָּרְכוּ
אֲבוֹתֵינוּ אַבְרָהָם יִצְחָק וְיַעֲקֹב, בַּכֹּל מִכֹּל כֹּל,
כֵּן יְבָרֵךְ אוֹתָנוּ, כֻּלָּנוּ יַחַד, בִּבְרָכָה שְׁלֵמָה,
וְנֹאמַר אָמֵן.

בַּמָּרוֹם יְלַמְּדוּ עֲלֵיהֶם וְעָלֵינוּ זְכוּת, שֶׁתְּהֵא
לְמִשְׁמֶרֶת שָׁלוֹם, וְנִשָּׂא בְרָכָה מֵאֵת יְיָ, וּצְדָקָה
מֵאֱלֹהֵי יִשְׁעֵנוּ, וְנִמְצָא חֵן וְשֵׂכֶל טוֹב, בְּעֵינֵי
אֱלֹהִים וְאָדָם.

On Sabbath:

הָרַחֲמָן, הוּא יַנְחִילֵנוּ יוֹם שֶׁכֻּלּוֹ שַׁבָּת וּמְנוּחָה.
לְחַיֵּי הָעוֹלָמִים:

May the Merciful One send us the prophet Eliyahu, remembered for good, and may he bring us good news of hope and comfort.

In the following paragraphs, say what is appropriate for the occasion:

May the Merciful One bless (My honored father) the master of this house, (my honored mother) the lady of this house, their household, their family, and all that is theirs.

May the Merciful One bless me, (my wife, my children,) and all that is mine.

May He bless us and all that is ours, just as our fathers, Abraham, Isaac and Jacob were blessed, with all, from all, and in every way. So may He bless us, all together, with a full blessing, and let us say Amen!

On high may they seek our good, that we should have the protection of peace. Let us receive a blessing from G-d, and charity from the Lord who saves us; and let us find favor and good understanding in the eyes of G-d and man.

On Sabbath:
May the Merciful One grant us a day that will be all Sabbath and rest in eternal life.

הָרַחֲמָן, הוּא יַנְחִילֵנוּ יוֹם שֶׁכֻּלוֹ טוֹב. (יוֹם
שֶׁכֻּלּוֹ אָרוּךְ יוֹם שֶׁצַּדִּיקִים יוֹשְׁבִים וְעַטְרוֹתֵיהֶם
בְּרָאשֵׁיהֶם וְנֶהֱנִים מִזִּיו הַשְּׁכִינָה וִיהִי חֶלְקֵנוּ
עִמָּהֶם.)

הָרַחֲמָן, הוּא יְזַכֵּנוּ לִימוֹת הַמָּשִׁיחַ וּלְחַיֵּי
הָעוֹלָם הַבָּא. מִגְדּוֹל יְשׁוּעוֹת מַלְכּוֹ, וְעֹשֶׂה
חֶסֶד לִמְשִׁיחוֹ, לְדָוִד וּלְזַרְעוֹ עַד עוֹלָם. עֹשֶׂה
שָׁלוֹם בִּמְרוֹמָיו, הוּא יַעֲשֶׂה שָׁלוֹם, עָלֵינוּ וְעַל
כָּל יִשְׂרָאֵל, וְאִמְרוּ אָמֵן.

יְראוּ אֶת יְיָ קְדוֹשָׁיו, כִּי אֵין מַחְסוֹר לִירֵאָיו.
כְּפִירִים רָשׁוּ וְרָעֵבוּ, וְדֹרְשֵׁי יְיָ לֹא יַחְסְרוּ כָל
טוֹב. הוֹדוּ לַיְיָ כִּי טוֹב, כִּי לְעוֹלָם חַסְדּוֹ. פּוֹתֵחַ
אֶת יָדֶךָ, וּמַשְׂבִּיעַ לְכָל חַי רָצוֹן. בָּרוּךְ הַגֶּבֶר
אֲשֶׁר יִבְטַח בַּיְיָ, וְהָיָה יְיָ מִבְטַחוֹ. נַעַר הָיִיתִי גַּם
זָקַנְתִּי, וְלֹא רָאִיתִי צַדִּיק נֶעֱזָב, וְזַרְעוֹ מְבַקֶּשׁ
לָחֶם. יְיָ עֹז לְעַמּוֹ יִתֵּן, יְיָ יְבָרֵךְ אֶת עַמּוֹ
בַשָּׁלוֹם.

הֲרֵינִי רוֹצֶה לְקַיֵּם מִצְוַת כּוֹס שְׁלִישִׁי שֶׁל אַרְבַּע כּוֹסוֹת
לְשֵׁם יְחוּד קוּדְשָׁא בְּרִיךְ הוּא וּשְׁכִינְתֵּיהּ עַל יְדֵי הַהוּא טָמִיר
וְנֶעְלָם בְּשֵׁם כָּל יִשְׂרָאֵל. וִיהִי נֹעַם אֲדֹנָי אֱלֹהֵינוּ עָלֵינוּ
וּמַעֲשֵׂה יָדֵינוּ כּוֹנְנָה עָלֵינוּ, וּמַעֲשֵׂה יָדֵינוּ כּוֹנְנֵהוּ.

May the Merciful One grant us a day that is all good (a day that is always long, a day when the righteous sit with their crowns on their heads, basking in the light of the Divine Presence).

May the Merciful One let us be worthy of the days of the Mashiach and the life of the World to Come. He is a tower of hope to His king, and He shows mercy to His Mashiach, to David and his children forever. He who makes peace in His heights, may He grant peace to us and to all Israel, and say, Amen!

Let His holy ones fear G-d, for those who fear Him will lack nothing. The rich will grow poor and hungry, but those who seek G-d will not lack any good. Give thanks to G-d because He is good, for His love is endless. You open Your hand, and satisfy the desire of all life. Blessed is the man who trusts in G-d, and G-d will be his trust. I have been young and have now grown old, and I have never seen a good man forsaken, or his children begging for bread. G-d will give His people strength, G-d will bless His people with peace.

I am ready and prepared to keep the commandment of drinking the third of the four cups of wine, for the sake of the One G-d and His presence, may it be counted as done in the name of all Israel.

• The third cup should also be drunk while one reclines to his left. However, if one forgets to recline, the cup need not be drunk again (472:7).

בָּרוּךְ אַתָּה יְיָ, אֱלֹהֵינוּ מֶלֶךְ הָעוֹלָם, בּוֹרֵא פְּרִי הַגָּפֶן.

• After the third cup has been drunk, it should be refilled.

• An additional cup, called the *Kos shel Eliyahu*, is also filled at this point (480, [10]).

• The door is opened, and all the Seder participants say שפך חמתך, to show that this night is a ליל שמורים, a night of protection, and that we have no fear. We hope that as a consequence of our trust, we will merit the coming of the Mashiach, when G-d will bring retribution to our enemies (480:1).

13. **Hallel/** Recite the Hallel

• If possible, Hallel should also be completed before halachic midnight (477:1, [7]).

• Although Hallel is usually said standing, during the Seder it is said while sitting as a sign of freedom (480:1, [1]).

• If more than three people – men, women, and children – are at the Seder, the leader should say הודו לה' and אנא ה' aloud, and the other participants answer responsively, in the same manner as in shul (479, [9]).

❖ **Salvation and the Role of Eliyahu**

CUP OF ELIYAHU

At this point in the Seder, a cup of wine is poured for Eliyahu HaNavi, Elijah the Prophet. In keeping with most customs, the cup is poured before saying "Sh'foch chamoscho" – the prayer

Blessed are You O G-d Our Lord, King of the world, Creator of the fruit of the grape- vine.

in which we beseech G-d to usher in the Messianic era, when revenge will be taken on all the enemies of the Jewish people. The filled cup represents both our preparation to celebrate Eliyahu's arrival and our anticipation of his heralding the coming of Mashiach, the Messiah.

Two questions are in order, here. If the significance of Eliyahu's coming is his announcing the advent of Mashiach, would it not make sense to fill a cup for Mashiach himself, not merely for Mashiach's harbinger? And why does Mashiach need a herald, in any case? Why can't he come, by himself, to redeem the Jewish people from exile?

The explanation can be found in Eliyahu's role as *"mal'ach habris"* – the angel of the covenant of circumcision. (See *Pirkei d'Reb Eliezer* 28.)

The Talmud (*Megillah* 17b) explains that the blessing, *"Refoeinu"* – "Please heal us" – was instituted as the eighth blessing in the Amidah, because the mitzvah of circumcision is performed on the eighth day following the birth of a baby boy. Since circumcision wounds need to heal, the Rabbis made the blessing for healing the eighth blessing. What is the relationship between circumcision and all varieties of healing, in general?

In a brilliant exposition, Rav Tzaddok Hakohein (*Pokeid Ikkarim* 13b) explains that the entire concept of healing was presented to the world in the merit of circumcision. This is based on a concept, that the first time an idea is mentioned in the Torah, that is its source. The first mention of healing in the Torah is a consequence of Avraham's circumcision, when G-d sent an angel to heal him. This means that every healing in the world stems from the healing of the circumcision wound. The Rabbis, then, instituted the blessing for healing, in a way that is reminiscent of circumcision.

The *Sifsei Chachamim* (*Bereishis* 18:2) comments that the angel sent to heal Avraham from his circumcision was also sent to save Lot from the destruction of Sodom. He explains that although there is a principle that one angel cannot be subject to more than a single mission, healing and saving are actually one and the same.

From the writings of Rav Tzaddok Hakohain and the *Sifsei Chachamim*, we may deduce that circumcision is the source of other forms of salvation, as well. This is alluded to in the Amidah: After requesting G-d's healing, we also say, *"Hoshe'ainu v'neevoshaia"*: "Save us and we will be saved."

שְׁפֹךְ חֲמָתְךָ אֶל הַגּוֹיִם אֲשֶׁר לֹא יְדָעוּךָ, וְעַל מַמְלָכוֹת אֲשֶׁר בְּשִׁמְךָ לֹא קָרָאוּ: כִּי אָכַל אֶת יַעֲקֹב, וְאֶת נָוֵהוּ הֵשַׁמּוּ: שְׁפָךְ עֲלֵיהֶם זַעְמֶךָ, וַחֲרוֹן אַפְּךָ יַשִּׂיגֵם: תִּרְדֹּף בְּאַף וְתַשְׁמִידֵם, מִתַּחַת שְׁמֵי יְיָ:

לֹא לָנוּ, יְיָ, לֹא לָנוּ, כִּי לְשִׁמְךָ תֵּן כָּבוֹד, עַל חַסְדְּךָ עַל אֲמִתֶּךָ: לָמָּה יֹאמְרוּ הַגּוֹיִם, אַיֵּה נָא

We can now understand Eliyahu's role in the coming of Mashiach. Eliyahu, the angel of circumcision, should precede the healing and salvation that will be brought by Mashiach. A cup is filled for Eliyahu at the Seder, because while we celebrate the salvation from Egypt, we also express hope for, and trust in, the future salvation that he will proclaim.

שפך חמתך אל הגוים

Pour Your anger upon the nations that do not know You...

It is not clear why this paragraph is read during the Seder. What does this prayer for future salvation have to do with the Exodus from Egypt? The answer may be found in a principle cited by the *Noam Elimelech* (*Parshas Bo*). He writes that when G-d performs a miracle for the Jewish people, one that involves saving them from their enemies, a pocket of

compassion is formed. In future moments, when the Jews find themselves in distress, the same pocket of compassion can be used to save them.

Through the mitzvos and the discussion of the Exodus, which have filled the Seder night up to this point, we hope that the pocket of compassion has been energized once more. We therefore take advantage of this propitious moment and request that G-d save us, and take revenge on all our enemies. The remaining part of the Seder is devoted to general praise of G-d.

❖ When Ignorance is no Excuse

אל הגוים אשר לא ידעוך

. . . upon the nations that do not know You...

If the nations truly do not know G-d, why should they be deserving of such harsh treatment?

Pour Your anger [O G-d] upon the nations that do not know you, and upon the kingdoms that do not call Your name. For they have eaten up Jacob, and destroyed his Temple. Pour out Your anger upon them, and let Your raging fury catch them. Chase them in anger and destroy them from under G-d's heaven.

Not to us, O G-d, not to us, but to Your name give glory, for Your mercy and truth. Why

A similar expression is used to describe Pharaoh, at the beginning of the Egyptian persecution: "A new king arose over Egypt, who did not know Yosef" (*Shemos* 1:8). But how is it possible that an Egyptian ruler had not heard of the man, who, a mere 140 years earlier, had saved the Egyptian people and their economy from the Great Famine? Given that Yosef's family still resided in Egypt, how could the Egyptians not have known the amazing saga of the Hebrew slave who had gone from being a prisoner to being appointed viceroy to Pharaoh?

If Pharaoh did not know Yosef, it must have been because he did not *want* to know him. The same is true of the nations of the world. The evidence of G-d's mastery is overwhelming. If there are nations who do not know G-d, it is because they do not *want* to know G-d. It is for that reason that they will be dealt with so severely.

הלל / HALLEL

The commentators ask why no blessing is said on the Hallel that is recited during the Seder. The Ran (*Pesachim* 26b) cites Rav Hai Gaon, who explains that the Seder Hallel is recited for reasons other than those for which the Hallel is ordinarily recited. Here, the Hallel is a form of "*shira*," or song, and no blessing is recited over a song. What exactly is the difference between "*hallel*" and "*shira*?"

"*Shira*" can be understood as a personal and emotional response to an act of kindness. For this reason, the word "*shira*" is often associated with the word "*aniya*," or "answer," because the song is a response of praise to G-d for a kindness He has done us. (See *Bamidbar* 21:17: "*Oz yoshir Yisroel . . . anu lah*": "Then Israel sang this song, 'Arise, O well, respond to it!'" See, also in the *Shacharis* and *Ma'ariv* prayers following the

אֱלֹהֵיהֶם: וֵאלֹהֵינוּ בַשָּׁמַיִם, כֹּל אֲשֶׁר חָפֵץ
עָשָׂה: עֲצַבֵּיהֶם כֶּסֶף וְזָהָב, מַעֲשֵׂה יְדֵי אָדָם:
פֶּה לָהֶם וְלֹא יְדַבֵּרוּ, עֵינַיִם לָהֶם וְלֹא יִרְאוּ:
אָזְנַיִם לָהֶם וְלֹא יִשְׁמָעוּ, אַף לָהֶם וְלֹא יְרִיחוּן:
יְדֵיהֶם וְלֹא יְמִישׁוּן, רַגְלֵיהֶם וְלֹא יְהַלֵּכוּ, לֹא
יֶהְגּוּ בִּגְרוֹנָם: כְּמוֹהֶם יִהְיוּ עֹשֵׂיהֶם, כֹּל אֲשֶׁר
בֹּטֵחַ בָּהֶם: יִשְׂרָאֵל בְּטַח בַּיְיָ, עֶזְרָם וּמָגִנָּם הוּא:
בֵּית אַהֲרֹן בִּטְחוּ בַיְיָ, עֶזְרָם וּמָגִנָּם הוּא: יִרְאֵי
יְיָ בִּטְחוּ בַיְיָ, עֶזְרָם וּמָגִנָּם הוּא:

יְיָ זְכָרָנוּ יְבָרֵךְ, יְבָרֵךְ אֶת בֵּית יִשְׂרָאֵל, יְבָרֵךְ
אֶת בֵּית אַהֲרֹן: יְבָרֵךְ יִרְאֵי יְיָ, הַקְּטַנִּים עִם

Shema: "Lecho anu shira": "To You they responded in song.") Only one who has personally experienced such kindness can be so emotionally affected as to break out in song.

Hallel, on the other hand, is typically a more calculated form of praise. It involves a more analytical appreciation of G-d's kindness to humankind. One need not experience His kindness personally, to appreciate it on an intellectual plane.

It is therefore ordinarily possible to make a blessing on Hallel, because *"kidshonu b'mitzvosav v'tzivanu likro es haHallel"* : "He has commanded us to recite the Hallel." G-d commands us to look deeply into His miracles, so that we can appreciate them and praise His name for them. *"Shira,"* however, cannot be commanded by its very nature, since it is the emotional response to one's own experience.

Rav Hai Gaon's opinion is that the Pesach Hallel is recited as a form of *"shira,"* since one must feel himself as having personally experienced the Exodus. Thus, no blessing should be recited.

We can now address another famous question. The Midrash relates that when the angels witnessed the drowning of the Egyptians at the Sea, they asked

should the nations say, "Where now is their G-d?" Our G-d is in heaven, all that He wants He does. Their idols are silver and gold, the work of human hands. They have a mouth, but cannot speak; they have eyes, but cannot see. They have ears, but cannot hear; they have a nose but cannot smell. They have hands, but cannot feel; they have feet, but cannot walk; they make no sound with their throats. May those who make them be like them, all who trust in them. Let Israel trust in G-d, He is their help and shield. Let the house of Aaron trust in G-d, He is their help and shield. Let the G-d-fearing trust in G-d, He is their help and shield.

G-d will remember us, He will bless. . . . He will bless the house of Israel, He will bless the house of Aaron. He will bless those who fear

permission to sing "*shira.*" G-d told them that since His own handiwork were drowning in the Sea, it was not a proper time to sing His praises. Why were the angels different from the Children of Israel, who sang "*shira*" at the crossing of the Sea?

The answer may be that for the Children of Israel, the song was a personal and emotional reaction to all the miracles that occurred at the Sea. Such a song is permissible, even in the face of the suffering of one's enemies. The angels, however, *asked* if they

could sing "*shira.*" This was not an emotional response, but a calculated expression of appreciation for G-d's miracles, more like a "*hallel.*" This would be improper with respect to the drowning of the Egyptians.

The *Mishna Berura* (490:7) states that on the latter six days of Pesach, only the half-Hallel is said. The reason given is the same Midrash passage: G-d did not allow the angels to sing His praise when His handiwork were drowning. Why is it that Hallel may not be said, yet the shira of "*Oz*

הַגְּדֹלִים: יֹסֵף יְיָ עֲלֵיכֶם, עֲלֵיכֶם וְעַל בְּנֵיכֶם: בְּרוּכִים אַתֶּם לַיְיָ, עֹשֵׂה שָׁמַיִם וָאָרֶץ: הַשָּׁמַיִם שָׁמַיִם לַיְיָ, וְהָאָרֶץ נָתַן לִבְנֵי אָדָם: לֹא הַמֵּתִים יְהַלְלוּ יָהּ, וְלֹא כָּל יֹרְדֵי דוּמָה: וַאֲנַחְנוּ נְבָרֵךְ יָהּ, מֵעַתָּה וְעַד עוֹלָם, הַלְלוּיָהּ:

אָהַבְתִּי כִּי יִשְׁמַע יְיָ, אֶת קוֹלִי תַּחֲנוּנָי: כִּי הִטָּה אָזְנוֹ לִי, וּבְיָמַי אֶקְרָא: אֲפָפוּנִי חֶבְלֵי מָוֶת, וּמְצָרֵי שְׁאוֹל מְצָאוּנִי, צָרָה וְיָגוֹן אֶמְצָא: וּבְשֵׁם יְיָ אֶקְרָא, אָנָּה יְיָ מַלְּטָה נַפְשִׁי: חַנּוּן יְיָ וְצַדִּיק, וֵאלֹהֵינוּ מְרַחֵם: שֹׁמֵר פְּתָאִים יְיָ, דַּלוֹתִי וְלִי יְהוֹשִׁיעַ: שׁוּבִי נַפְשִׁי לִמְנוּחָיְכִי, כִּי יְיָ גָּמַל עָלָיְכִי: כִּי חִלַּצְתָּ נַפְשִׁי מִמָּוֶת, אֶת עֵינִי מִן דִּמְעָה, אֶת רַגְלִי מִדֶּחִי: אֶתְהַלֵּךְ לִפְנֵי יְיָ, בְּאַרְצוֹת הַחַיִּים: הֶאֱמַנְתִּי כִּי אֲדַבֵּר, אֲנִי עָנִיתִי מְאֹד: אֲנִי אָמַרְתִּי בְחָפְזִי, כָּל הָאָדָם כֹּזֵב:

מָה אָשִׁיב לַיְיָ, כָּל תַּגְמוּלוֹהִי עָלָי: כּוֹס

Yashir" is recited daily during prayers? The answer, as we have just explained, is that there is a distinction between "hallel" and "shira."

מה אשיב לה' כל תגמולוהי עלי

What can I repay to G-d, for all His kindness to me? I will lift a

cup of salvation and call in the name of G-d.

The word "oshiv," meaning "repay," can also mean "respond." The Psalmist is saying that when he contemplates everything that G-d has given him, he becomes so overwhelmed, he is incapable of

G-d, great and small alike. May G-d add to you, to you and to your children. Blessed are you by G-d, Maker of heaven and earth. The heaven is the heaven of G-d, but the earth He gave to the sons of man. The dead do not praise G-d, nor those who sink down in silence. But we will bless G-d, now and forever: Halleluyah–Praise G-d!

I love G-d because He heard my voice and my prayer. Because He listened to me on the day I called. The cords of death were around me, the agony of the grave had found me: I was in trouble and sorrow. I called in G-d's name, "G-d, save my soul!" G-d is kind and just; our G-d has pity. G-d watches fools; I was down and He saved me. Rest once again, my soul, for G-d has been good to you. You have delivered my soul from death, my eyes from tears, my foot from stumbling. I will walk before G-d in the world of the living. I had faith, though I spoke– I was in such great trouble that in my panic I said, "All of man is false."

What can I repay to G-d, for all His kindness to

properly expressing his gratitude. Speech is often an inadequate tool for conveying one's most deeply felt feelings.

  The Psalmist continues by asserting that all a person can real- ly do is lift up the cup of salvation and invoke G-d's name in appreci- ation. What is accomplished by invoking G-d's name? How is it that this action is so powerful and expressive?

יְשׁוּעוֹת אֶשָּׂא, וּבְשֵׁם יְיָ אֶקְרָא: נְדָרַי לַיְיָ
אֲשַׁלֵּם, נֶגְדָה נָּא לְכָל עַמּוֹ: יָקָר בְּעֵינֵי יְיָ,
הַמָּוְתָה לַחֲסִידָיו: אָנָּה יְיָ כִּי אֲנִי עַבְדֶּךָ, אֲנִי
עַבְדְּךָ בֶּן אֲמָתֶךָ, פִּתַּחְתָּ לְמוֹסֵרָי: לְךָ אֶזְבַּח
זֶבַח תּוֹדָה, וּבְשֵׁם יְיָ אֶקְרָא: נְדָרַי לַיְיָ אֲשַׁלֵּם,
נֶגְדָה נָּא לְכָל עַמּוֹ: בְּחַצְרוֹת בֵּית יְיָ, בְּתוֹכֵכִי
יְרוּשָׁלָיִם, הַלְלוּיָהּ:

הַלְלוּ אֶת יְיָ כָּל גּוֹיִם, שַׁבְּחוּהוּ כָּל הָאֻמִּים: כִּי
גָבַר עָלֵינוּ חַסְדּוֹ, וֶאֱמֶת יְיָ לְעוֹלָם, הַלְלוּיָהּ:

Imagine a mother returning home after a period of separation from her young child. As she walks through the front doorway, the child flings himself at her with a big hug, and exclaims "Mo-o-o-o-o-ommmmy!" Nothing else need be said, for all the child's pent-up love and longings are released in that one word. Other words might just dilute the intensity of this expression.

Here, too, realizing how poorly words would express profound gratitude, the Psalmist says he will lift up a cup and invoke G-d's name. In that invocation all his true feelings will pour forth.

הללו את ה' כל גוים . . .
כי גבר עלינו חסדו
Let all nations praise G-d . . .

because He has showered His kindness upon us

The commentaries question why other nations should praise G-d for showing kindness to the Jewish people. (See Talmud, *Pesachim* 118b.)

We do find that Yisro, Moshe's father-in-law, praised G-d when he observed the measure-for-measure retribution exacted from the Egyptians. But, Yisro, a gentile, was clearly not the average man. Rashi points out that Yisro was a truth-seeker who had sampled every religion known to man, in order to arrive at the truth. When he saw G-d's justice meted out measure for measure, he praised G-d and accept Him as his own.

Other members of the nations of the world, who had also heard

*me? I will lift the cup of salvation, and call in
the name of G-d. I will honor my promises to
G-d in the presence of all His people. Precious
in G-d's eyes is the death of His saints. O G-d,
I am Your servant; I am Your servant, son of
Your maidservant; You have opened my chains.
I will sacrifice a thanksgiving offering to You; I
will call in the name of G-d. I will pay up my
promises to G-d, yes in the presence of all His
people. In the courts of G-d's Temple, in the
middle of Jerusalem; Halleluyah– Praise G-d!*

*Let all nations praise G-d, let all governments
glorify Him. For He has showered His kindness
upon us, Halleluyah– Praise G-d!*

about the Children of Israel's miraculous salvation, were not motivated to praise G-d, as witnessed by the Song of the Sea: "The nations heard and were disturbed. Fear grabbed the dwellers of Philistia. The noblemen of Edom were overwhelmed, and trembling grabbed the leaders of Moab, all the dwellers of Canaan melted. . . ."(*Shemos* 15:14-15). The nations were all frightened, but no mention is made of their praising G-d. But then, why should we expect them to?

The Talmud (*Chullin* 7a) relates the following. Rav Pinchas ben Yair once came to a river and could not find a way to cross it. He offered a prayer to G-d, and the river miraculously split for him to cross. An Arab standing nearby was also waiting to cross the river. Rav Pinchas ben Yair prayed that the Arab be allowed to cross as well, in order that he not be suspected of selfishness, thereby causing a desecration of G-d's name. The river split again to allow the Arab to cross. Hence we see that a person may sometimes experience G-d's kindness undeservedly – on the shoulders, so to speak, of somebody else who *does* deserve it.

This may explain why the other nations should praise G-d. They too may have benefited from G-d's kindness to the Jewish people. Even a person who has bene-

Responsively:

הוֹדוּ לַיְיָ כִּי טוֹב, כִּי לְעוֹלָם חַסְדּוֹ
הוֹדוּ לַיְיָ כִּי טוֹב, כִּי לְעוֹלָם חַסְדּוֹ
יֹאמַר נָא יִשְׂרָאֵל, כִּי לְעוֹלָם חַסְדּוֹ

יֹאמַר נָא יִשְׂרָאֵל, כִּי לְעוֹלָם חַסְדּוֹ
הוֹדוּ לַיְיָ כִּי טוֹב, כִּי לְעוֹלָם חַסְדּוֹ
יֹאמְרוּ נָא בֵית אַהֲרֹן, כִּי לְעוֹלָם חַסְדּוֹ

יֹאמְרוּ נָא בֵית אַהֲרֹן, כִּי לְעוֹלָם חַסְדּוֹ
הוֹדוּ לַיְיָ כִּי טוֹב, כִּי לְעוֹלָם חַסְדּוֹ
יֹאמְרוּ נָא יִרְאֵי יְיָ, כִּי לְעוֹלָם חַסְדּוֹ

יֹאמְרוּ נָא יִרְאֵי יְיָ, כִּי לְעוֹלָם חַסְדּוֹ
הוֹדוּ לַיְיָ כִּי טוֹב, כִּי לְעוֹלָם חַסְדּוֹ

fited indirectly from G-d's kindness must still express the proper thank-you.

Perhaps the expectation of the other nations' praise may have an alternative explanation. I remember hearing about a Torah scholar sitting in a doctor's waiting room. The doctor was running late, and the scholar was impatient to get back to his yeshiva in time for class. He stood up to reschedule his appointment with the receptionist. He had just left his seat, when outside the office, a car on the street lost control and crashed into the waiting room – right where the scholar had been sitting.

Had he not gotten up when he did, he would have been killed or badly hurt.

On his return to the yeshiva, the scholar asked the Rosh Yeshiva if he should say the *Birchas HaGomel*, the special prayer recited at the Torah reading for a person miraculously spared in a life-threatening situation. To his surprise, the Rosh Yeshiva told him not to say the blessing. The Rosh Yeshiva explained that only one who had actually lived through a dangerous situation and been spared, should recite the *Birchas HaGomel*. In this instance, however-er, the scholar was never in any

Responsively

Thank G-d for He is good;
for His kindness lasts forever.
Thank G-d for He is good; for His kindness lasts forever.
Now let Israel say it:
for His kindness lasts forever.

Now let Israel say it:
for His kindness lasts forever.
Thank G-d for He is good; for His kindness lasts forever.
Now let the house of Aaron say it:
for His kindness lasts forever.

Now let the house of Aaron say it:
for His kindness lasts forever.
Thank G-d for He is good; for His kindness lasts forever.
Now let those who fear G-d say it:
for His kindness lasts forever.

Now let those who fear G-d say it:
for His kindness lasts forever.
Thank G-d for He is good;
for His kindness lasts forever.

real jeopardy, because he had left his seat before the danger was present. The Rosh Yeshiva compared him to a person whose clothing fell out of a window. In those circumstances, the person would not make this special blessing, despite the fact that had he been wearing the clothes, he would have been severely hurt!

The Hallel can best be appreciated either by a person who had personally experienced danger and was miraculously spared, or by one who had witnessed such a miracle. The other nations that had been in the latter situation – those that had witnessed the Egyptian campaign to harm the Jewish people, and their miraculous rescue by G-d – were, in fact, in a better position to want to praise G-d than the Jews themselves. Many of the Jews may not have been fully aware of the danger that had faced them.

מִן הַמֵּצַר קָרָאתִי יָּה, עָנָנִי בַמֶּרְחָב יָה: יְיָ לִי
לֹא אִירָא, מַה יַּעֲשֶׂה לִי אָדָם: יְיָ לִי בְּעֹזְרָי,
וַאֲנִי אֶרְאֶה בְשֹׂנְאָי: טוֹב לַחֲסוֹת בַּיְיָ, מִבְּטֹחַ
בָּאָדָם: טוֹב לַחֲסוֹת בַּיְיָ, מִבְּטֹחַ בִּנְדִיבִים: כָּל
גּוֹיִם סְבָבוּנִי, בְּשֵׁם יְיָ כִּי אֲמִילַם: סַבּוּנִי גַם
סְבָבוּנִי, בְּשֵׁם יְיָ כִּי אֲמִילַם: סַבּוּנִי כִדְבֹרִים,
דֹּעֲכוּ כְּאֵשׁ קוֹצִים, בְּשֵׁם יְיָ כִּי אֲמִילַם: דָּחֹה
דְחִיתַנִי לִנְפֹּל, וַיְיָ עֲזָרָנִי: עָזִּי וְזִמְרָת יָה, וַיְהִי
לִי לִישׁוּעָה: קוֹל רִנָּה וִישׁוּעָה בְּאָהֳלֵי צַדִּיקִים,
יְמִין יְיָ עֹשָׂה חָיִל: יְמִין יְיָ רוֹמֵמָה, יְמִין יְיָ עֹשָׂה
חָיִל: לֹא אָמוּת כִּי אֶחְיֶה, וַאֲסַפֵּר מַעֲשֵׂי יָה:
יַסֹּר יִסְּרַנִי יָּה, וְלַמָּוֶת לֹא נְתָנָנִי: פִּתְחוּ לִי
שַׁעֲרֵי צֶדֶק, אָבֹא בָם אוֹדֶה יָּה: זֶה הַשַּׁעַר לַיְיָ,
צַדִּיקִים יָבֹאוּ בוֹ:

אוֹדְךָ כִּי עֲנִיתָנִי, וַתְּהִי לִי לִישׁוּעָה:
אוֹדְךָ כִּי עֲנִיתָנִי, וַתְּהִי לִי לִישׁוּעָה:

אֶבֶן מָאֲסוּ הַבּוֹנִים, הָיְתָה לְרֹאשׁ פִּנָּה:
אֶבֶן מָאֲסוּ הַבּוֹנִים, הָיְתָה לְרֹאשׁ פִּנָּה:

מֵאֵת יְיָ הָיְתָה זֹּאת, הִיא נִפְלָאת בְּעֵינֵינוּ:
מֵאֵת יְיָ הָיְתָה זֹּאת, הִיא נִפְלָאת בְּעֵינֵינוּ:

In my stress I called to G-d, He answered me openly. G-d is with me, I will not fear; what can man do to me? G-d is with me as my helper, I can overlook my enemies. It is better to rely on G-d than to trust in princes. All the nations surround me; in G-d's name I will destroy them. They surround me like bees, but they burned out like burning thorns, for I shall destroy them in G-d's name. They shoved and pushed me to fall, but G-d helped me. G-d is my strength and song, He has become my hope. A sound of joy and hope in the tents of the righteous; G-d's right hand makes an army. G-d's right hand is lifted high; G-d's right hand makes an army. I will not die; I will live and speak of G-d's deeds. Let me suffer, O G-d, but do not let me die. Open for me the gates of righteousness; let me come through and thank G-d. This is G-d's gate, the righteous shall come through it.

I will thank You, for You answered me, and You became my hope.
I will thank You, for You answered me, and You became my hope.

The stone discarded by the builders has become the main cornerstone.
The stone discarded by the builders has become the main cornerstone.

This was indeed from G-d, it is a wonder in our eyes.
This was indeed from G-d, it is a wonder in our eyes.

זֶה הַיּוֹם עָשָׂה יְיָ, נָגִילָה וְנִשְׂמְחָה בּוֹ:

זֶה הַיּוֹם עָשָׂה יְיָ, נָגִילָה וְנִשְׂמְחָה בּוֹ:

Responsively:

אָנָּא יְיָ הוֹשִׁיעָה נָּא: אָנָּא יְיָ הוֹשִׁיעָה נָּא:

אָנָּא יְיָ הוֹשִׁיעָה נָּא: אָנָּא יְיָ הוֹשִׁיעָה נָּא:

אָנָּא יְיָ הַצְלִיחָה נָא: אָנָּא יְיָ הַצְלִיחָה נָא:

אָנָּא יְיָ הַצְלִיחָה נָא: אָנָּא יְיָ הַצְלִיחָה נָא:

בָּרוּךְ הַבָּא בְּשֵׁם יְיָ, בֵּרַכְנוּכֶם מִבֵּית יְיָ:

בָּרוּךְ הַבָּא בְּשֵׁם יְיָ, בֵּרַכְנוּכֶם מִבֵּית יְיָ:

אֵל יְיָ וַיָּאֶר לָנוּ, אִסְרוּ חַג בַּעֲבֹתִים עַד קַרְנוֹת הַמִּזְבֵּחַ:

אֵל יְיָ וַיָּאֶר לָנוּ, אִסְרוּ חַג בַּעֲבֹתִים עַד קַרְנוֹת הַמִּזְבֵּחַ:

אֵלִי אַתָּה וְאוֹדֶךָּ, אֱלֹהַי אֲרוֹמְמֶךָּ:

אֵלִי אַתָּה וְאוֹדֶךָּ, אֱלֹהַי אֲרוֹמְמֶךָּ:

הוֹדוּ לַיְיָ כִּי טוֹב, כִּי לְעוֹלָם חַסְדּוֹ:

הוֹדוּ לַיְיָ כִּי טוֹב, כִּי לְעוֹלָם חַסְדּוֹ:

הוֹדוּ לַיְיָ כִּי טוֹב,   כִּי לְעוֹלָם חַסְדּוֹ

הוֹדוּ לֵאלֹהֵי הָאֱלֹהִים,   כִּי לְעוֹלָם חַסְדּוֹ

הודו לה' כי טוב כי לעולם חסדו
Thank G-d for He is good — for His kindness lasts forever.

This psalm is referred to as "Hallel Hagadol," "the great Hallel" (*Pesachim* 118a). As the Talmud

This is the day G-d did it, we will be happy and rejoice in Him.
This is the day G-d did it, we will be happy and rejoice in Him.

Responsively:

O G-d, save us!   *O G-d, save us!*
O G-d, save us!   O G-d, save us!

O G-d, help us!   *O G-d, help us!*
O G-d, help us!   O G-d, help us!

Welcome in G-d's name, we bless you from the house of G-d.
Welcome in G-d's name, we bless you from the house of G-d.

Mighty is G-d, He gives us light; bind the feast with myrtle on the horns of the Altar.
Mighty is G-d, He gives us light; bind the feast with myrtle on the horns of the Altar.

You are my G-d, and I thank You; my G-d, to all heights I praise You.
You are my G-d, and I thank You; my G-d, to all heights I praise You.

Thank G-d because He is good; for His kindness lasts forever.
Thank G-d because He is good; for His kindness lasts forever.

❦

Thank G-d for He is good;
            for His kindness lasts forever.
Thank the G-d of gods;
            for His kindness lasts forever.

הוֹדוּ לַאֲדֹנֵי הָאֲדֹנִים,   כִּי לְעוֹלָם חַסְדּוֹ

לְעֹשֵׂה נִפְלָאוֹת גְּדֹלוֹת לְבַדּוֹ, כִּי לְעוֹלָם חַסְדּוֹ

לְעֹשֵׂה הַשָּׁמַיִם בִּתְבוּנָה,   כִּי לְעוֹלָם חַסְדּוֹ

לְרוֹקַע הָאָרֶץ עַל הַמָּיִם,   כִּי לְעוֹלָם חַסְדּוֹ

לְעֹשֵׂה אוֹרִים גְּדֹלִים,   כִּי לְעוֹלָם חַסְדּוֹ

אֶת הַשֶּׁמֶשׁ לְמֶמְשֶׁלֶת בַּיּוֹם, כִּי לְעוֹלָם חַסְדּוֹ

אֶת הַיָּרֵחַ וְכוֹכָבִים לְמֶמְשְׁלוֹת בַּלָּיְלָה,

כִּי לְעוֹלָם חַסְדּוֹ

לְמַכֵּה מִצְרַיִם בִּבְכוֹרֵיהֶם,   כִּי לְעוֹלָם חַסְדּוֹ

---

explains, this psalm praises G-d for His great kindness, "*nosain lechem l'chol basar*" – "in giving sustenance to all flesh."

It is puzzling that the psalm limits itself to three primary themes: the wonders of Creation, the Exodus, and the conquest of Canaan. How are these three events connected?

The psalm reads:
> For. . . delivering Israel from among them,
> His kindness lasts forever.
> With a strong hand and an outstretched arm,
> His kindness lasts forever.
> For splitting the Sea of Reeds into lanes,
> His kindness lasts forever.
> And leading Israel through it,
> His kindness lasts forever. . . .

Why does the Psalmist interrupt each statement or thought with the common refrain, "for His kindness lasts forever"? Would it not have made more sense to have written, for example, "He took Israel out with a strong hand, for His kindness lasts forever. He divided the Sea

Thank the Lord of lords;
*   for His kindness lasts forever.*
For doing great wonders all alone;
*   for His kindness lasts forever.*
For making the heavens with wisdom;
*   for His kindness lasts forever.*
For spreading the land over the waters;
*   for His kindness lasts forever.*
For making great lights;
*   for His kindness lasts forever.*
The sun to rule by day;
*   for His kindness lasts forever.*
The moon and stars to rule by night;
*   for His kindness lasts forever.*
For striking Egypt through their first-born;
*   for His kindness lasts forever.*
And delivering Israel from among them;
*   for His kindness lasts forever.*

and passed Israel through it, for His kindness lasts forever. . ."[20]

The refrain, "for His kindness lasts forever," implies that each of the miracles and events – and even each *part* of the miracles and events – about which the Psalmist writes, has a dimension of eternity. Each of these events had repercussions that are still with us today. The sun and moon, for example, were set in place during Creation, and still serve as manifestations of G-d's munificence.

---

20. The psalm actually has twenty-six verses. The Talmud (Pesachim 118a) explains that the verses correspond to the first twenty-six generations of the world, until the Giving of the Torah. Each of these generations was sustained by G-d's kindness, not through its virtues or merits. This may be one explanation for the continual repetition of the phrase: For twenty-six generations He was kind, even though the generations were undeserving.

וַיּוֹצֵא יִשְׂרָאֵל מִתּוֹכָם,   כִּי לְעוֹלָם חַסְדּוֹ

בְּיָד חֲזָקָה וּבִזְרוֹעַ נְטוּיָה,   כִּי לְעוֹלָם חַסְדּוֹ

לְגֹזֵר יַם סוּף לִגְזָרִים,   כִּי לְעוֹלָם חַסְדּוֹ

וְהֶעֱבִיר יִשְׂרָאֵל בְּתוֹכוֹ,   כִּי לְעוֹלָם חַסְדּוֹ

וְנִעֵר פַּרְעֹה וְחֵילוֹ בְיַם סוּף,   כִּי לְעוֹלָם חַסְדּוֹ

לְמוֹלִיךְ עַמּוֹ בַּמִּדְבָּר,   כִּי לְעוֹלָם חַסְדּוֹ

לְמַכֵּה מְלָכִים גְּדֹלִים,   כִּי לְעוֹלָם חַסְדּוֹ

וַיַּהֲרֹג מְלָכִים אַדִּירִים,   כִּי לְעוֹלָם חַסְדּוֹ

לְסִיחוֹן מֶלֶךְ הָאֱמֹרִי,   כִּי לְעוֹלָם חַסְדּוֹ

וּלְעוֹג מֶלֶךְ הַבָּשָׁן,   כִּי לְעוֹלָם חַסְדּוֹ

וְנָתַן אַרְצָם לְנַחֲלָה,   כִּי לְעוֹלָם חַסְדּוֹ

נַחֲלָה לְיִשְׂרָאֵל עַבְדּוֹ,   כִּי לְעוֹלָם חַסְדּוֹ

שֶׁבְּשִׁפְלֵנוּ זָכַר לָנוּ,   כִּי לְעוֹלָם חַסְדּוֹ

וַיִּפְרְקֵנוּ מִצָּרֵינוּ,   כִּי לְעוֹלָם חַסְדּוֹ

נֹתֵן לֶחֶם לְכָל בָּשָׂר,   כִּי לְעוֹלָם חַסְדּוֹ

הוֹדוּ לְאֵל הַשָּׁמָיִם,   כִּי לְעוֹלָם חַסְדּוֹ:

Thus, the Plague of the First-born figures more prominently than the other plagues, because there G-d's eternal kindness is clearest. It was the eternal sanctity of the Jewish firstborn that resulted from their being saved during this plague.

The long-term ramifications of the other events and miracles may not be as clear, but the Psalmist obviously understood them.

The twenty-six repetitions of the refrain, both from their meaning and their *sound*, remind us of G-d's sustained and eternal kindness.

With a strong hand and outstretched arm;
                    for His kindness lasts forever.
For splitting the Sea of Reeds into lanes;
                    for His kindness lasts forever.
And leading Israel through it;
                    for His kindness lasts forever.
For casting Pharaoh and his army in the Sea of Reeds;
                    for His kindness lasts forever.
For leading His people in the desert;
                    for His kindness lasts forever.
For striking down great kings;
                    for His kindness lasts forever.
And killing mighty rulers;
                    for His kindness lasts forever.
Sichon, king of the Amorites;
                    for His kindness lasts forever.
And Og, king of the Bashan;
                    for His kindness lasts forever.
He gave us their land to keep;
                    for His kindness lasts forever.
For Israel, His servant, to keep;
                    for His kindness lasts forever.
When we were low He remembered us;
                    for His kindness lasts forever.
And saved us from our enemies;
                    for His kindness lasts forever.
He gives bread to all flesh;
                    for His kindness lasts forever.
Thank the G-d of heaven;
                    for His kindness lasts forever.

נִשְׁמַת כָּל חַי. תְּבָרֵךְ אֶת שִׁמְךָ יְיָ אֱלֹהֵינוּ, וְרוּחַ כָּל בָּשָׂר תְּפָאֵר וּתְרוֹמֵם זִכְרְךָ מַלְכֵּנוּ תָּמִיד. מִן הָעוֹלָם וְעַד הָעוֹלָם אַתָּה אֵל, וּמִבַּלְעָדֶיךָ אֵין לָנוּ מֶלֶךְ גּוֹאֵל וּמוֹשִׁיעַ, פּוֹדֶה וּמַצִּיל וּמְפַרְנֵס וּמְרַחֵם בְּכָל עֵת צָרָה וְצוּקָה, אֵין לָנוּ מֶלֶךְ אֶלָּא אָתָּה:

אֱלֹהֵי הָרִאשׁוֹנִים וְהָאַחֲרוֹנִים. אֱלוֹהַּ כָּל בְּרִיוֹת, אֲדוֹן כָּל תּוֹלָדוֹת: הַמְהֻלָּל בְּרוֹב הַתִּשְׁבָּחוֹת. הַמְנַהֵג עוֹלָמוֹ בְּחֶסֶד, וּבְרִיּוֹתָיו בְּרַחֲמִים. וַיְיָ לֹא יָנוּם וְלֹא יִישָׁן, הַמְעוֹרֵר יְשֵׁנִים, וְהַמֵּקִיץ נִרְדָּמִים. וְהַמֵּשִׂיחַ אִלְּמִים. וְהַמַּתִּיר אֲסוּרִים. וְהַסּוֹמֵךְ נוֹפְלִים. וְהַזּוֹקֵף כְּפוּפִים. לְךָ לְבַדְּךָ אֲנַחְנוּ מוֹדִים:

אִלּוּ פִינוּ מָלֵא שִׁירָה כַּיָּם, וּלְשׁוֹנֵנוּ רִנָּה כַּהֲמוֹן גַּלָּיו. וְשִׂפְתוֹתֵינוּ שֶׁבַח כְּמֶרְחֲבֵי רָקִיעַ. וְעֵינֵינוּ מְאִירוֹת כַּשֶּׁמֶשׁ וְכַיָּרֵחַ. וְיָדֵינוּ פְרוּשׂוֹת כְּנִשְׁרֵי שָׁמָיִם. וְרַגְלֵינוּ קַלּוֹת כָּאַיָּלוֹת. אֵין אֲנַחְנוּ מַסְפִּיקִים לְהוֹדוֹת לָךְ, יְיָ אֱלֹהֵינוּ וֵאלֹהֵי אֲבוֹתֵינוּ, וּלְבָרֵךְ אֶת שְׁמֶךָ, עַל אַחַת מֵאֶלֶף אֶלֶף אַלְפֵי אֲלָפִים וְרִבֵּי רְבָבוֹת פְּעָמִים, הַטּוֹבוֹת שֶׁעָשִׂיתָ עִם אֲבוֹתֵינוּ, וְעִמָּנוּ:

The soul of all life shall bless Your name, O G-d our Lord, and the spirit of all flesh shall always praise and glorify Your fame, our King. From the beginning to the end of time, You are G-d. Besides You we have no king who saves and helps; who frees and rescues, who grants our needs and has mercy in all time of trouble and pain. We have no king other than You!

G-d, first and last, G-d of all creatures; Master of all history, praised in many songs, who guides His world with mercy, and His creatures with pity. G-d does not slumber, nor does He sleep. He awakes those who sleep, arouses those who slumber, makes the dumb speak, releases prisoners, supports the fallen, and raises the depressed. To You alone we give thanks.

If our mouths were filled with singing like the sea, and our tongues filled with song like its many waves; if our lips were filled with praise as broad as the sky, and our eyes could shine like the sun and the moon; if our hands were spread out like the eagles of the sky, and our feet could run lightly as the deer; it would still not be enough to thank You, O G-d Our Lord and Lord of our fathers; or to bless Your name for even one thousandth– one millionth or billionth of all the good You have done for our fathers and for ourselves.

מִמִּצְרַיִם גְּאַלְתָּנוּ, יְיָ אֱלֹהֵינוּ, וּמִבֵּית עֲבָדִים פְּדִיתָנוּ. בְּרָעָב זַנְתָּנוּ, וּבְשָׂבָע כִּלְכַּלְתָּנוּ, מֵחֶרֶב הִצַּלְתָּנוּ, וּמִדֶּבֶר מִלַּטְתָּנוּ, וּמֵחֳלָיִם רָעִים וְנֶאֱמָנִים דִּלִּיתָנוּ: עַד הֵנָּה עֲזָרוּנוּ רַחֲמֶיךָ, וְלֹא עֲזָבוּנוּ חֲסָדֶיךָ, וְאַל תִּטְּשֵׁנוּ יְיָ אֱלֹהֵינוּ לָנֶצַח:

עַל כֵּן אֵבָרִים שֶׁפִּלַּגְתָּ בָּנוּ, וְרוּחַ וּנְשָׁמָה שֶׁנָּפַחְתָּ בְּאַפֵּינוּ, וְלָשׁוֹן אֲשֶׁר שַׂמְתָּ בְּפִינוּ: הֵן הֵם יוֹדוּ וִיבָרְכוּ, וִישַׁבְּחוּ וִיפָאֲרוּ, וִירוֹמְמוּ וְיַעֲרִיצוּ, וְיַקְדִּישׁוּ וְיַמְלִיכוּ אֶת שִׁמְךָ מַלְכֵּנוּ: כִּי כָל פֶּה לְךָ יוֹדֶה, וְכָל לָשׁוֹן לְךָ תִשָּׁבַע. וְכָל בֶּרֶךְ לְךָ תִכְרַע. וְכָל קוֹמָה לְפָנֶיךָ תִשְׁתַּחֲוֶה. וְכָל לְבָבוֹת יִירָאוּךָ. וְכָל קֶרֶב וּכְלָיוֹת יְזַמְּרוּ לִשְׁמֶךָ. כַּדָּבָר שֶׁכָּתוּב, כָּל עַצְמֹתַי תֹּאמַרְנָה יְיָ מִי כָמוֹךָ: מַצִּיל עָנִי מֵחָזָק מִמֶּנּוּ, וְעָנִי וְאֶבְיוֹן מִגֹּזְלוֹ.

מִי יִדְמֶה לָּךְ, וּמִי יִשְׁוֶה לָּךְ, וּמִי יַעֲרָךְ לָךְ. הָאֵל הַגָּדוֹל, הַגִּבּוֹר וְהַנּוֹרָא, אֵל עֶלְיוֹן, קוֹנֵה שָׁמַיִם וָאָרֶץ: נְהַלֶּלְךָ, וּנְשַׁבֵּחֲךָ וּנְפָאֶרְךָ וּנְבָרֵךְ אֶת שֵׁם קָדְשֶׁךָ: כָּאָמוּר: לְדָוִד, בָּרְכִי נַפְשִׁי אֶת יְיָ, וְכָל קְרָבַי אֶת שֵׁם קָדְשׁוֹ:

You delivered us from Egypt, O G-d our Lord, and rescued us from the house of slaves. When we were in hunger, You fed us; in plenty, You provided for us. You saved us from the sword, delivered us from the plague, and safeguarded us from serious sickness. Until now Your mercy has saved us, and Your kindness has not let us down; May You not forsake us, O G-d our Lord, forever.

Therefore, the limbs You gave us, the breath and soul You breathed in our nostrils, the tongue You placed in our mouths— all of them will thank, bless, be grateful, praise, uplift, revere, make holy and crown Your name, our King. For every mouth shall thank You, every tongue shall promise to be loyal; every knee shall bow to You, and all who stand shall kneel before You; every heart shall fear You, and every man's inner self shall sing praises to Your name; as the word that is written "All my bones shall say, 'O G-d, who is like You? [You] help the poor from those stronger than him, the poor and beggar from those who would rob them'".

Who is like You? Who is equal? Who can be compared? The great, mighty and fearful G-d, G-d most high, Owner of heaven and earth! We will praise You, glorify You, be grateful to You, and we will bless Your holy name, as it is written, "By David, may my soul bless G-d, and may everything in me bless His holy name".

הָאֵל, בְּתַעֲצֻמוֹת עֻזֶּךָ. הַגָּדוֹל, בִּכְבוֹד שְׁמֶךָ. הַגִּבּוֹר, לָנֶצַח, וְהַנּוֹרָא, בְּנוֹרְאוֹתֶיךָ: הַמֶּלֶךְ, הַיּוֹשֵׁב עַל כִּסֵּא, רָם וְנִשָּׂא:

שׁוֹכֵן עַד, מָרוֹם וְקָדוֹשׁ שְׁמוֹ. וְכָתוּב, רַנְּנוּ צַדִּיקִים בַּיְיָ, לַיְשָׁרִים נָאוָה תְהִלָּה. בְּפִי יְשָׁרִים תִּתְהַלָּל. וּבְדִבְרֵי צַדִּיקִים תִּתְבָּרַךְ. וּבִלְשׁוֹן חֲסִידִים תִּתְרוֹמָם. וּבְקֶרֶב קְדוֹשִׁים תִּתְקַדָּשׁ :

וּבְמַקְהֵלוֹת רִבְבוֹת עַמְּךָ בֵּית יִשְׂרָאֵל. בְּרִנָּה יִתְפָּאַר שִׁמְךָ מַלְכֵּנוּ, בְּכָל דּוֹר וָדוֹר. שֶׁכֵּן חוֹבַת כָּל הַיְצוּרִים, לְפָנֶיךָ יְיָ אֱלֹהֵינוּ, וֵאלֹהֵי אֲבוֹתֵינוּ, לְהוֹדוֹת לְהַלֵּל לְשַׁבֵּחַ לְפָאֵר לְרוֹמֵם לְהַדֵּר לְבָרֵךְ לְעַלֵּה וּלְקַלֵּס, עַל כָּל דִּבְרֵי שִׁירוֹת וְתִשְׁבְּחוֹת דָּוִד בֶּן יִשַׁי עַבְדְּךָ מְשִׁיחֶךָ:

יִשְׁתַּבַּח שִׁמְךָ לָעַד מַלְכֵּנוּ, הָאֵל הַמֶּלֶךְ הַגָּדוֹל וְהַקָּדוֹשׁ, בַּשָּׁמַיִם וּבָאָרֶץ. כִּי לְךָ נָאֶה יְיָ

ובמקהלות רבבות עמך בית ישראל
In the assemblies of the myriads of Your people, the house of Israel, they praise Your Name in song....

The Talmud (*Berachos* 50a) understands from the words "*in the assemblies you should bless* G-d" (*Tehillim* 68:27), that even the fetus in its mother's womb sang G-d's praises at the crossing of the Sea.

In Egypt, the fetus had been at great risk. In his campaign against the Jewish nation, Pharaoh's first decree was leveled at the Jewish

O G-d, in Your tremendous power, great in the glory of Your name, mighty forever and feared for Your deeds, the King who sits on a high and lofty throne!

You dwell in eternity on high, and Holy in Your name. It is written, "Let saints rejoice in G-d, for the just it is good to praise Him". By the mouth of the just You are praised; by the words of saints You are blessed; by the tongue of the pious You are raised high, and among the holy, You are sanctified.

And in the assemblies of the myriads of Your nation, the house of Israel, they praise Your name in song, O King, in every generation. For this is the duty of all creatures, before You, G-d our Lord and Lord of our fathers, to thank, praise, show gratitude, glorify, raise high, beautify, bless and uplift, and to sing out above all the songs and praise of [even] David, son of Yishai, Your chosen servant.

Praised be Your name forever, King, the great and holy G-d and King in heaven and earth. For

---

unborn. He had ordered the midwives to kill the male children during their birth. Pharaoh had thought this would be a discreet form of murder. It would go unnoticed by his people, and he would not have to justify himself to them. Only after the midwives refused to obey Pharaoh's orders, did he order the public execution of Jewish baby boys.

Accordingly, at the revelation of G-d's mighty Hand at the Sea, even the fetus in the most discreet of places – the womb itself – opened its mouth and joined in the people's recognition and praise of G-d.

אֱלֹהֵינוּ וֵאלֹהֵי אֲבוֹתֵינוּ, שִׁיר וּשְׁבָחָה, הַלֵּל
וְזִמְרָה, עֹז וּמֶמְשָׁלָה, נֵצַח. גְּדֻלָּה וּגְבוּרָה,
תְּהִלָּה וְתִפְאֶרֶת קְדֻשָׁה וּמַלְכוּת: בְּרָכוֹת
וְהוֹדָאוֹת מֵעַתָּה וְעַד עוֹלָם.

יְהַלְלוּךָ יְיָ אֱלֹהֵינוּ כָּל מַעֲשֶׂיךָ. וַחֲסִידֶיךָ
צַדִּיקִים עוֹשֵׂי רְצוֹנֶךָ. וְכָל עַמְּךָ בֵּית יִשְׂרָאֵל,
בְּרִנָּה יוֹדוּ וִיבָרְכוּ. וִישַׁבְּחוּ וִיפָאֲרוּ. וִירוֹמְמוּ
וְיַעֲרִיצוּ. וְיַקְדִּישׁוּ וְיַמְלִיכוּ אֶת שִׁמְךָ מַלְכֵּנוּ. כִּי
לְךָ טוֹב לְהוֹדוֹת וּלְשִׁמְךָ נָאֶה לְזַמֵּר. כִּי מֵעוֹלָם
וְעַד עוֹלָם אַתָּה אֵל. בָּרוּךְ אַתָּה יְיָ, מֶלֶךְ
מְהֻלָּל בַּתִּשְׁבָּחוֹת:

הֲרֵינִי רוֹצֶה לְקַיֵּים מִצְוַת כּוֹס רְבִיעִי שֶׁל אַרְבַּע כּוֹסוֹת לְשֵׁם
יִחוּד קוּדְשָׁא בְּרִיךְ הוּא וּשְׁכִינְתֵּיהּ עַל יְדֵי הַהוּא טָמִיר
וְנֶעְלָם בְּשֵׁם כָּל יִשְׂרָאֵל. וִיהִי נֹעַם אֲדֹנָי אֱלֹהֵינוּ עָלֵינוּ
וּמַעֲשֵׂה יָדֵינוּ כּוֹנְנָה עָלֵינוּ, וּמַעֲשֵׂה יָדֵינוּ כּוֹנְנֵהוּ.

• After the completion of the Hallel, the *bracha* is made
on the fourth cup of wine. It is drunk while reclining. If one
did not recline, it need not be drunk again (472:7).

• Although one need only drink the majority of a *revi'is*
for each of the first three cups, a full *revi'is* must be drunk
for the fourth cup in order to be able to make the *bracha*
על הגפן afterwards (472, [30]).

בָּרוּךְ אַתָּה יְיָ, אֱלֹהֵינוּ מֶלֶךְ הָעוֹלָם, בּוֹרֵא פְּרִי
הַגָּפֶן.

to You it is fitting, G-d our Lord and Lord of our fathers, song and praise, hymn and psalm, power and dominion, victory, greatness and strength, and prayer, beauty, holiness, and royalty, blessing and thanks, now and forever.

All Your works shall praise You, O G-d our Lord, along with all Your righteous saints, who do Your will. All Your people, the house of Israel, shall give thanks in song, and bless and show gratitude, glorify, uplift, revere, sanctify, and crown Your name, our King. For it is good to thank You, and it is pleasant to sing praise to Your name, because from the beginning to the end of time You are G-d. Blessed are You, G-d a King praised in prayer.

I am ready and prepared to keep the commandment of drinking the fourth of the four cups of wine, for the sake of the One G-d and His presence, may it be counted as done in the name of all Israel.

Blessed are You G-d our Lord, King of the world, Creator of the fruit of the grape- vine.

בָּרוּךְ אַתָּה יְיָ, אֱלֹהֵינוּ מֶלֶךְ הָעוֹלָם, עַל הַגֶּפֶן
וְעַל פְּרִי הַגֶּפֶן, וְעַל תְּנוּבַת הַשָּׂדֶה, וְעַל אֶרֶץ
חֶמְדָּה טוֹבָה וּרְחָבָה, שֶׁרָצִיתָ וְהִנְחַלְתָּ
לַאֲבוֹתֵינוּ, לֶאֱכוֹל מִפִּרְיָהּ וְלִשְׂבּוֹעַ מִטּוּבָהּ.
רַחֵם נָא יְיָ אֱלֹהֵינוּ, עַל יִשְׂרָאֵל עַמֶּךָ, וְעַל
יְרוּשָׁלַיִם עִירֶךָ, וְעַל צִיּוֹן מִשְׁכַּן כְּבוֹדֶךָ, וְעַל
מִזְבְּחֶךָ, וְעַל הֵיכָלֶךָ, וּבְנֵה יְרוּשָׁלַיִם, עִיר
הַקּוֹדֶשׁ, בִּמְהֵרָה בְיָמֵינוּ, וְהַעֲלֵנוּ לְתוֹכָהּ,
וְשַׂמְּחֵנוּ בְּבִנְיָנָהּ, וְנֹאכַל מִפִּרְיָהּ, וְנִשְׂבַּע
מִטּוּבָהּ, וּנְבָרֶכְךָ עָלֶיהָ בִּקְדוּשָׁה וּבְטָהֳרָה:
(On Sabbath: וּרְצֵה וְהַחֲלִיצֵנוּ בְּיוֹם הַשַּׁבָּת הַזֶּה)
וְשַׂמְּחֵנוּ בְּיוֹם חַג הַמַּצּוֹת הַזֶּה, כִּי אַתָּה יְיָ טוֹב
וּמֵטִיב לַכֹּל, וְנוֹדֶה לְּךָ עַל הָאָרֶץ וְעַל פְּרִי
הַגֶּפֶן. בָּרוּךְ אַתָּה יְיָ עַל הָאָרֶץ וְעַל פְּרִי הַגֶּפֶן:

14. Nirtzah / Our Observance is Accepted

חֲסַל סִדּוּר פֶּסַח כְּהִלְכָתוֹ.
כְּכָל מִשְׁפָּטוֹ וְחֻקָּתוֹ.
כַּאֲשֶׁר זָכִינוּ לְסַדֵּר אוֹתוֹ.
כֵּן נִזְכֶּה לַעֲשׂוֹתוֹ.
זָךְ שׁוֹכֵן מְעוֹנָה.
קוֹמֵם קְהַל עֲדַת מִי מָנָה.
בְּקָרוֹב נַהֵל נִטְעֵי כַנָּה.
פְּדוּיִם לְצִיּוֹן בְּרִנָּה:

Blessed are You, Lord our G-d, King of the world, for the vine, for the fruit of the vine, for the crops of the field, and for the lovely, good spacious land that You desired and granted to our fathers [that they should] eat its fruits and be satisfied with its good. Have mercy, Lord our G-d, on Your people Israel, on Your city Jerusalem, on Zion, home of Your glory, and on Your altar and on Your Temple. Build Jerusalem, the holy city, soon, in our days, and bring us up into it. Let us rejoice when it is built, let us eat its fruit and be satisfied with its good, and let us bless You for it in holiness and purity. (On Sabbath: Be pleased and strengthen us on this Sabbath day.) *Let us rejoice on this feast of Matzos. For You, G-d, are good, and You do good to all, so we will thank You for the land and for the fruit of the vine. Blessed are You, G-d, for the land and for the fruit of the grape- vine.*

Chasal Siddur Pesach

Ended is the Seder as the Law commands,
Its symbols and rules done by our hands;
> *As we were worthy*
> *To set up here,*
> *So may we do it next year!*

Pure One who dwells in the heavens on high,
Raise up Your people, countless to the eye,
> *Soon may You guide*
> *The ones You planted strong*
> *Free again in Zion in joyous song!*

לְשָׁנָה הַבָּאָה בִּירוּשָׁלָיִם.

On the First Night:

וּבְכֵן וַיְהִי בַּחֲצִי הַלַּיְלָה:

בַּלַּיְלָה. אָז רוֹב נִסִּים הִפְלֵאתָ

הַלַּיְלָה. בְּרֹאשׁ אַשְׁמוֹרֶת זֶה

לָיְלָה: גֵּר צֶדֶק נִצַּחְתּוֹ כְּנֶחֱלַק לוֹ

וַיְהִי בַּחֲצִי הַלַּיְלָה:

נרצה / NIRTZAH

לשנה הבאה בירושלים
Next year in Jerusalem!

After completing the mitzvos of the Seder and the Hallel, we are filled with a sense of fulfillment. Yet, we also realize that we cannot fool ourselves into believing that everything is perfect. Despite our celebration of freedom, we still suffer the ravages of exile. For this reason, the first and last paragraphs of the Haggadah, "*Ha lachma anya*" and "*Chad Gadya*", are both written in Aramaic, the language of the Babylonian exile: to remind us, both at the beginning and the end of the evening, that – despite the festivities – we are still in exile.

However, we can feel the certainty of G-d's guarantee that, just as He redeemed the Jews from

Egypt, He will redeem us from the present exile. For this reason, the last part of the Seder is called Nirtzah, which means, "it has been accepted." "Has been" is the present perfect tense: G-d has *already* accepted our service this evening, and will surely send Mashiach soon.

This explains the difference between the expression used at the Seder's conclusion – "Next year in Jerusalem! – and the statement made at the Seder's beginning – "Now we are here; next year we should be in the Land of Israel." At the beginning of the Seder, we express our hopes and prayers to G-d for the redemption of the Jewish people. After we have completed the mitzvos of the Seder, however, we declare – with total confidence and joy – that next year we will *indeed* be in Jerusalem!

Next year in Jerusalem!

On the First Night

And now –" And it was at midnight!"

The many, many miracles
Were performed by You   *at night;*
At the beginning of watches
On this very   *night;*
You made the righteous convert win
[When Avraham] divided his men   *at night;*
And it was at midnight!

❖ **Never Despair!**

ובכן ויהי בחצי הלילה

It was in the middle of the night. . . .

The Haggadah speaks of the many miracles that G-d performed for the Jewish people in the middle of the night. Avraham was victorious at war during the night. Yaakov won the struggle with the angel during the night. Pharaoh and the Egyptians, and the armies of Sisera and Sancheriv, all suffered their downfall during the night. Why has G-d chosen the middle of the night, as a time to have worked so many miracles?

Night may be seen as a symbol of the darkness of exile, in contrast to morning, which represents the light and dawn of redemption. The middle of the night is the darkest and bleakest time of exile, when no hope of salvation remains. It is specifically at this time that G-d performed miracles, so they would serve as a source of comfort and encouragement to the Jew in exile.

Even in the darkest gloom of night, G-d makes his presence felt. He shows that He has not forgotten His people. Since we end the Seder on a note of confidence and hope for the future, this poem is recited to remind us that G-d has brought salvation to His people, and will continue to do so, in the bleakest of circumstances.

דָּנְתָּ מֶלֶךְ גְּרָר בַּחֲלוֹם   הַלַּיְלָה.

הִפְחַדְתָּ אֲרַמִּי בְּאֶמֶשׁ   לַיְלָה.

וַיָּשַׂר יִשְׂרָאֵל לְמַלְאָךְ וַיּוּכַל לוֹ   לַיְלָה:

וַיְהִי בַּחֲצִי הַלַּיְלָה:

זֶרַע בְּכוֹרֵי פַתְרוֹס מָחַצְתָּ בַּחֲצִי   הַלַּיְלָה.

חֵילָם לֹא מָצְאוּ בְּקוּמָם   בַּלַּיְלָה.

טִיסַת נְגִיד חֲרוֹשֶׁת סִלִּיתָ בְּכוֹכְבֵי   לַיְלָה:

וַיְהִי בַּחֲצִי הַלַּיְלָה:

יָעַץ מְחָרֵף לְנוֹפֵף אִוּוּי, הוֹבַשְׁתָּ פְּגָרָיו בַּלַּיְלָה.

כָּרַע בֵּל וּמַצָּבוֹ בְּאִישׁוֹן   לַיְלָה.

לְאִישׁ חֲמוּדוֹת נִגְלָה רָז חֲזוֹת   לַיְלָה:

וַיְהִי בַּחֲצִי הַלַּיְלָה:

מִשְׁתַּכֵּר בִּכְלֵי קֹדֶשׁ נֶהֱרַג בּוֹ   בַּלַּיְלָה.

נוֹשַׁע מִבּוֹר אֲרָיוֹת פּוֹתֵר בְּעֲתוּתֵי   לַיְלָה.

שִׂנְאָה נָטַר אֲגָגִי וְכָתַב סְפָרִים   בַּלַּיְלָה:

וַיְהִי בַּחֲצִי הַלַּיְלָה:

You judged the king of Gerar (Avimelech)
    In a dream   *at night;*
You made the Aramean (Lavan) tremble
    In the darkness   *of night;*
And Israel struggled with an angel
    And won him too,   *at night;*
    And it was at midnight!

the first born of Pathros (Egypt)
    You demolished in the middle of the night;
They could not find their wealth
    When they woke up   *at night;*
The forces of the prince of Charosheth (Sisera)
    Were swept away by the stars of the night
    And it was at midnight!

Without respect [Sancheriv] sieged Jerusalem
    But You dried up his corpse   *at night;*
Ba'al and its pedestal were thrown down
    In the darkness   *of night;*
To the beloved [Daniel]
    You revealed mysteries in a vision at night;
    And it was at midnight!

He drank from the holy vessels
    And so [Belshazzar] was killed at night;
[Daniel] was saved from the lion's den
And interpreted fearsome dreams of the night;
[Haman] of Agag kept up his hate
    And wrote letters   *at night;*
    And it was at midnight!

עוֹרַרְתָּ נִצְחֲךָ עָלָיו בְּנֶדֶד שְׁנַת   לַיְלָה.
פּוּרָה תִדְרוֹךְ לְשׁוֹמֵר מַה   מִלַּיְלָה.
צָרַח כַּשּׁוֹמֵר וְשָׂח אָתָא בוֹקֶר וְגַם   לַיְלָה:

וַיְהִי בַּחֲצִי הַלַּיְלָה:

קָרֵב יוֹם אֲשֶׁר הוּא לֹא יוֹם וְלֹא   לַיְלָה.
רָם הוֹדַע כִּי לְךָ הַיּוֹם אַף לְךָ   הַלַּיְלָה.
שׁוֹמְרִים הַפְקֵד לְעִירְךָ כָּל הַיּוֹם וְכָל   הַלַּיְלָה.   הַלַּיְלָה.
תָּאִיר כְּאוֹר יוֹם חֶשְׁכַּת   לַיְלָה.

וַיְהִי בַּחֲצִי הַלַּיְלָה:

On the Second Night:

וּבְכֵן וַאֲמַרְתֶּם זֶבַח פֶּסַח:

אֹמֶץ גְּבוּרוֹתֶיךָ הִפְלֵאתָ   בַּפֶּסַח.
בְּרֹאשׁ כָּל מוֹעֲדוֹת נִשֵּׂאתָ   פֶּסַח.
גִּלִּיתָ לְאֶזְרָחִי חֲצוֹת לֵיל   פֶּסַח:

וַאֲמַרְתֶּם זֶבַח פֶּסַח:

You rose and beat Haman
         By not letting the king sleep   at night;
You crushed the wicked
         To protect us from the forces   of night;
He cried out like the watchman:
         Morning is coming, and also   the night;
         And it was at midnight!

May the day soon come
         When it is no longer day   or night;
That all shall know
         That day is Yours, and also   the night;
Set up guards for Your city
         For all the day and all   the night;
That bright as day may be
         The darkness of   the night;
         And it was at midnight!

On the Second Night

And now– "So declare the Pesach feast!"
Mighty acts of power
         Were done by You   on Pesach;
To the head of all festivals
         You raised the feast   of Pesach;
You revealed Yourself to the Eastern one
         [To Abraham] on the midnight of Pesach;
         So declare the Pesach feast!

דְּלָתָיו דָּפַקְתָּ כְּחוֹם הַיּוֹם בַּפֶּסַח.

הִסְעִיד נוֹצְצִים עֻגוֹת מַצּוֹת בַּפֶּסַח.

וְאֶל הַבָּקָר רָץ זֵכֶר לְשׁוֹר עֵרֶךְ פֶּסַח:

וַאֲמַרְתֶּם זֶבַח פֶּסַח:

זֹעֲמוּ סְדוֹמִים וְלֹהֲטוּ בָּאֵשׁ בַּפֶּסַח.

חֻלַּץ לוֹט מֵהֶם וּמַצּוֹת אָפָה בְּקֵץ פֶּסַח.

טֵאטֵאתָ אַדְמַת מוֹף וְנוֹף בְּעָבְרְךָ בַּפֶּסַח:

וַאֲמַרְתֶּם זֶבַח פֶּסַח:

יָהּ רֹאשׁ כָּל אוֹן מָחַצְתָּ בְּלֵיל שִׁמּוּר פֶּסַח.

כַּבִּיר, עַל בֵּן בְּכוֹר פָּסַחְתָּ בְּדַם פֶּסַח.

לְבִלְתִּי תֵת מַשְׁחִית לָבֹא בִּפְתָחַי בַּפֶּסַח:

וַאֲמַרְתֶּם זֶבַח פֶּסַח:

מְסֻגֶּרֶת סֻגְּרָה בְּעִתּוֹתֵי פֶּסַח.

נִשְׁמְדָה מִדְיָן בִּצְלִיל שְׂעוֹרֵי עֹמֶר פֶּסַח.

שֹׂרְפוּ מִשְׁמַנֵּי פּוּל וְלוּד בִּיקַד יְקוֹד פֶּסַח:

וַאֲמַרְתֶּם זֶבַח פֶּסַח:

You knocked at Abraham's door
    In the heat of day   *on Pesach;*
He fed the angels
    cakes of Matza   *on Pesach;*
He ran to the cattle
Recalling the ox prepared   *on Pesach;*
    So declare the Pesach feast!

The men of Sodom angered [G-d]
    And were destroyed by fire *on Pesach;*
Lot took off from them
    And baked Matzos   *on Pesach;*
You swept the land of Mof and Nof
  When You passed through [Egypt]
                    on Pesach;
    So declare the Pesach feast!

G-d, You demolished the first born
On the guarded night   *of Pesach;*
Mighty One, You passed over Israel
Your own first-born   *on Pesach;*
You let no destruction come
To enter my doors   *on Pesach;*
    So declare the Pesach feast!

The strong walled city (Jericho)
[Fell] at the season   *of Pesach;*
Midian was destroyed [by Gideon]
Through [a dream of] a barley loaf on Pesach;
The fat Pul and Lud (Sancheriv's chiefs)
Were burned in a blazing flame *on Pesach;*
    So declare the Pesach feast!

עוֹד הַיּוֹם בְּנוֹב לַעֲמוֹד עַד גָּעָה עוֹנַת   פֶּסַח.

פַּס יָד כָּתְבָה לְקַעֲקֵעַ צוּל   בַּפֶּסַח.

צָפֹה הַצָּפִית עָרוֹךְ הַשֻּׁלְחָן   בַּפֶּסַח:

וַאֲמַרְתֶּם זֶבַח פֶּסַח:

קָהָל כִּנְּסָה הֲדַסָּה לְשַׁלֵּשׁ צוֹם   בַּפֶּסַח:

רֹאשׁ מִבֵּית רָשָׁע מָחַצְתָּ בְּעֵץ חֲמִשִּׁים   בַּפֶּסַח.

שְׁתֵּי אֵלֶּה רֶגַע תָּבִיא לְעוּצִית   בַּפֶּסַח.

תָּעֹז יָדְךָ וְתָרוּם יְמִינְךָ כְּלֵיל הִתְקַדֶּשׁ חַג

פֶּסַח:

וַאֲמַרְתֶּם זֶבַח פֶּסַח:

כִּי לוֹ נָאֶה כִּי לוֹ יָאֶה

אַדִּיר בִּמְלוּכָה. בָּחוּר כַּהֲלָכָה. גְּדוּדָיו יֹאמְרוּ
לוֹ. לְךָ וּלְךָ. לְךָ כִּי לְךָ. לְךָ אַף לְךָ. לְךָ יְיָ
הַמַּמְלָכָה: כִּי לוֹ נָאֶה. כִּי לוֹ יָאֶה:

דָּגוּל בִּמְלוּכָה. הָדוּר כַּהֲלָכָה. וָתִיקָיו יֹאמְרוּ
לוֹ. לְךָ וּלְךָ. לְךָ כִּי לְךָ. לְךָ אַף לְךָ. לְךָ יְיָ
הַמַּמְלָכָה: כִּי לוֹ נָאֶה. כִּי לוֹ יָאֶה:

[Sancheriv] stood and waited in Nob
            For a day until the feast   of Pesach;
A hand wrote [for Belshazzar]
      Tattooing a shadow on the wall on Pesach;
They lit the lamps
            And prepared the table   on Pesach;
      So declare the Pesach feast!

Hadassah (Esther) gathered a congregation
            For a three day fast   on Pesach;
The head of the evil house (Haman)
      Was hung on a fifty foot gallows on Pesach;
Two punishments You shall suddenly bring
            Upon the wicked kingdom   on Pesach;
Raise Your mighty hand in strength
      As on the night You made holy   as Pesach;
      So declare the Pesach feast!

∾⌀⟨⟩⌀∾

Ki Lo Na'eh
For His delight, and for His right!

Mighty as a King, Supreme in everything,
His armies say to Him:

Chorus:

To You and just You, To You for just You, To
You, yes just You, To You O G-d the throne
is due, for His delight, and for His right!

Famous as a King, Brilliant in everything,
His good ones say to Him:

Ki Lo Na'eh etc.

זַכַּאי בִּמְלוּכָה. חָסִין כַּהֲלָכָה. טַפְסְרָיו יֹאמְרוּ
לוֹ. לְךָ וּלְךָ. לְךָ כִּי לְךָ. לְךָ אַף לְךָ. לְךָ יְיָ
הַמַּמְלָכָה: כִּי לוֹ נָאֶה. כִּי לוֹ יָאֶה:

יָחִיד בִּמְלוּכָה. כַּבִּיר כַּהֲלָכָה. לִמּוּדָיו יֹאמְרוּ
לוֹ. לְךָ וּלְךָ. לְךָ כִּי לְךָ. לְךָ אַף לְךָ. לְךָ יְיָ
הַמַּמְלָכָה: כִּי לוֹ נָאֶה. כִּי לוֹ יָאֶה:

מוֹשֵׁל בִּמְלוּכָה. נוֹרָא כַּהֲלָכָה. סְבִיבָיו יֹאמְרוּ
לוֹ. לְךָ וּלְךָ. לְךָ כִּי לְךָ. לְךָ אַף לְךָ. לְךָ יְיָ
הַמַּמְלָכָה: כִּי לוֹ נָאֶה. כִּי לוֹ יָאֶה:

עָנָיו בִּמְלוּכָה. פּוֹדֶה כַּהֲלָכָה. צַדִּיקָיו יֹאמְרוּ
לוֹ. לְךָ וּלְךָ. לְךָ כִּי לְךָ. לְךָ אַף לְךָ. לְךָ יְיָ
הַמַּמְלָכָה: כִּי לוֹ נָאֶה. כִּי לוֹ יָאֶה:

קָדוֹשׁ בִּמְלוּכָה. רַחוּם כַּהֲלָכָה. שִׁנְאַנָּיו יֹאמְרוּ
לוֹ. לְךָ וּלְךָ. לְךָ כִּי לְךָ. לְךָ אַף לְךָ. לְךָ יְיָ
הַמַּמְלָכָה: כִּי לוֹ נָאֶה. כִּי לוֹ יָאֶה:

תַּקִּיף בִּמְלוּכָה. תּוֹמֵךְ כַּהֲלָכָה. תְּמִימָיו יֹאמְרוּ
לוֹ. לְךָ וּלְךָ. לְךָ כִּי לְךָ. לְךָ אַף לְךָ. לְךָ יְיָ
הַמַּמְלָכָה: כִּי לוֹ נָאֶה. כִּי לוֹ יָאֶה:

Purest as a King, Sturdy in everything,
His servants say to Him:

Ki Lo Na'eh etc.

Alone as a King, Strongest in everything,
His wise ones say to Him:

Ki Lo Na'eh etc.

Ruling as a King, Fearsome in everything,
His suburbs say to Him:

Ki Lo Na'eh etc.

Humble as a King, Helping in everything,
His righteous say to Him:

Ki Lo Na'eh etc.

Holy as a King, Tender in everything,
His angels say to Him:

Ki Lo Na'eh etc.

Forceful as a King, Support in everything,
His true ones say to Him:

Ki Lo Na'eh etc.

אַדִּיר הוּא

אַדִּיר הוּא. יִבְנֶה בֵיתוֹ בְּקָרוֹב. בִּמְהֵרָה,
בִּמְהֵרָה, בְּיָמֵינוּ, בְּקָרוֹב. אֵל, בְּנֵה, אֵל, בְּנֵה.
בְּנֵה בֵיתְךָ בְּקָרוֹב:

בָּחוּר הוּא. גָּדוֹל הוּא. דָּגוּל הוּא. יִבְנֶה בֵיתוֹ
בְּקָרוֹב. בִּמְהֵרָה, בִּמְהֵרָה, בְּיָמֵינוּ, בְּקָרוֹב. אֵל,
בְּנֵה, אֵל, בְּנֵה. בְּנֵה בֵיתְךָ בְּקָרוֹב:

הָדוּר הוּא. וָתִיק הוּא. זַכַּאי הוּא. **חָסִיד** הוּא.
יִבְנֶה בֵיתוֹ בְּקָרוֹב. בִּמְהֵרָה, בִּמְהֵרָה, בְּיָמֵינוּ,
בְּקָרוֹב. אֵל, בְּנֵה, אֵל, בְּנֵה. בְּנֵה בֵיתְךָ בְּקָרוֹב:

טָהוֹר הוּא. יָחִיד הוּא. כַּבִּיר הוּא. **לָמוּד** הוּא.
מֶלֶךְ הוּא. **נוֹרָא** הוּא. סַגִּיב הוּא. עִזּוּז הוּא.
פּוֹדֶה הוּא. **צַדִּיק** הוּא. יִבְנֶה בֵיתוֹ בְּקָרוֹב:
בִּמְהֵרָה, בִּמְהֵרָה, בְּיָמֵינוּ, בְּקָרוֹב. אֵל, בְּנֵה,
אֵל, בְּנֵה. בְּנֵה בֵיתְךָ בְּקָרוֹב:

קָדוֹשׁ הוּא **רַחוּם** הוּא. **שַׁדַּי** הוּא. **תַּקִּיף** הוּא.
יִבְנֶה בֵיתוֹ בְּקָרוֹב. בִּמְהֵרָה בִּמְהֵרָה בְּיָמֵינוּ
בְּקָרוֹב. אֵל בְּנֵה אֵל בְּנֵה. בְּנֵה בֵיתְךָ בְּקָרוֹב:

ADIR HU

Mighty One, Mighty One

Chorus:
Build Your Temple soon, speedily, speedily, in our days, soon, O G-d build, O G-d build, build Your Temple soon.

Chosen One, Greatest One, Famous One, **(Chorus:)** Build Your Temple soon, speedily, speedily, in our days, soon, O G-d build, O G-d build, build Your Temple soon.

Brilliant One, Faithful One, Blameless One, Kindest One, **(Chorus:)** Build Your Temple soon, speedily, speedily, in our days, soon, O G-d build, O G-d build, build Your Temple soon.

Purest One, Only One, Sturdy One, Wisest One, Royal One, Fearsome One, Highest One, Boldest One, Saving One, Righteous One, **(Chorus:)** Build Your Temple soon, speedily, speedily, in our days, soon, O G-d build, O G-d build, build Your Temple soon.

Holy One, Tender One, Almighty One, Forceful One, **(Chorus:)** Build Your Temple soon, speedily, speedily, in our days, soon, O G-d build, O G-d build, build Your Temple soon.

אֶחָד מִי יוֹדֵעַ.

אֶחָד מִי יוֹדֵעַ. אֶחָד אֲנִי יוֹדֵעַ. אֶחָד אֱלֹהֵינוּ
שֶׁבַּשָּׁמַיִם וּבָאָרֶץ:

שְׁנַיִם מִי יוֹדֵעַ. שְׁנַיִם אֲנִי יוֹדֵעַ. שְׁנֵי לֻחוֹת
הַבְּרִית. אֶחָד אֱלֹהֵינוּ שֶׁבַּשָּׁמַיִם וּבָאָרֶץ.

שְׁלֹשָׁה מִי יוֹדֵעַ. שְׁלֹשָׁה אֲנִי יוֹדֵעַ. שְׁלֹשָׁה
אָבוֹת. שְׁנֵי לֻחוֹת הַבְּרִית. אֶחָד אֱלֹהֵינוּ
שֶׁבַּשָּׁמַיִם וּבָאָרֶץ.

אַרְבַּע מִי יוֹדֵעַ. אַרְבַּע אֲנִי יוֹדֵעַ. אַרְבַּע
אִמָּהוֹת. שְׁלֹשָׁה אָבוֹת. שְׁנֵי לֻחוֹת הַבְּרִית.
אֶחָד אֱלֹהֵינוּ שֶׁבַּשָּׁמַיִם וּבָאָרֶץ.

אחד מי יודע...
Who knows One?...

חד גדיא ...
One little kid, One little kid, . . .

In the earlier section, **Kadesh**, we have described the connection that *Echod Me Yodaia* ("Who knows one?") and *Chad Gadya* ("One little kid, One little kid") have with the rest of the Haggadah. However, another reason may explain why these two songs were chosen for the conclusion to the Haggadah.

The mitzvah of discussing the

Exodus must be fulfilled in such a way as makes it most likely that the lessons will be absorbed and retained. For this reason, as we suggested above, the discussion has a question-and-answer format. For this reason, as well, we begin with our disgrace and conclude with G-d's praise.

Through these two songs, the Haggadah recapitulates the format. *Echod Me Yodaia* has a series of questions and answers. The first verse is composed of a question and an answer. The second verse is a new question and its answer,

Who Knows One

Who knows One? I know One! One is our G-d, Who is in heaven and in earth!

Who knows two? I know two! Two tablets G-d gave Moshe, One is our G-d, Who is in heaven and in earth!

Who knows three? I know three! Three fathers of our people, Two tablets G-d gave Moshe, One is our G-d, Who is in heaven and in earth!

Who knows four? I know four! Four are the mothers of our nation, Three fathers of our people, Two tablets G-d gave Moshe, One is our G-d, Who is in heaven and in earth!

and then reiterates the answer to the first question. To each new verse, with its question and answer, is appended all the previous answers, so we are always brought full circle, back to the beginning.

Chad Gadya begins with disgrace: Each creature or object, introduced in the previous verse, is conquered by the newcomer of the most current verse. In the next-to-last verse, comes the Angel of Death, as victor over the slaughterer. But, in the final verse, it is the Holy One, Blessed is He, Who destroys the Angel of Death. So we begin with defeat and end with praise. Here, too, to each verse the action of all the previous verses is appended, an ever-growing refrain. Thus, ultimately, all the previous struggles are recounted, as they are subsumed under the dominion of the Holy One.

We learn from both songs that the lessons of the Haggadah – with the proper format and the continual repetition of the story – can become part and parcel of our lives throughout the year. May it indeed be so!

חֲמִשָׁה מִי יוֹדֵעַ. חֲמִשָׁה אֲנִי יוֹדֵעַ. חֲמִשָׁה חוּמְשֵׁי תוֹרָה. אַרְבַּע אִמָּהוֹת. שְׁלֹשָׁה אָבוֹת. שְׁנֵי לֻחוֹת הַבְּרִית. אֶחָד אֱלֹהֵינוּ שֶׁבַּשָּׁמַיִם וּבָאָרֶץ.

שִׁשָׁה מִי יוֹדֵעַ. שִׁשָׁה אֲנִי יוֹדֵעַ. שִׁשָׁה סִדְרֵי מִשְׁנָה. חֲמִשָׁה חוּמְשֵׁי תוֹרָה. אַרְבַּע אִמָּהוֹת. שְׁלֹשָׁה אָבוֹת. שְׁנֵי לֻחוֹת הַבְּרִית. אֶחָד אֱלֹהֵינוּ שֶׁבַּשָּׁמַיִם וּבָאָרֶץ.

שִׁבְעָה מִי יוֹדֵעַ. שִׁבְעָה אֲנִי יוֹדֵעַ. שִׁבְעָה יְמֵי שַׁבַּתָּא. שִׁשָׁה סִדְרֵי מִשְׁנָה. חֲמִשָׁה חוּמְשֵׁי תוֹרָה. אַרְבַּע אִמָּהוֹת. שְׁלֹשָׁה אָבוֹת. שְׁנֵי לֻחוֹת הַבְּרִית. אֶחָד אֱלֹהֵינוּ שֶׁבַּשָּׁמַיִם וּבָאָרֶץ.

שְׁמוֹנָה מִי יוֹדֵעַ. שְׁמוֹנָה אֲנִי יוֹדֵעַ. שְׁמוֹנָה יְמֵי מִילָה. שִׁבְעָה יְמֵי שַׁבַּתָּא. שִׁשָׁה סִדְרֵי מִשְׁנָה. חֲמִשָׁה חוּמְשֵׁי תוֹרָה. אַרְבַּע אִמָּהוֹת. שְׁלֹשָׁה אָבוֹת. שְׁנֵי לֻחוֹת הַבְּרִית. אֶחָד אֱלֹהֵינוּ שֶׁבַּשָּׁמַיִם וּבָאָרֶץ.

תִּשְׁעָה מִי יוֹדֵעַ. תִּשְׁעָה אֲנִי יוֹדֵעַ. תִּשְׁעָה יַרְחֵי לֵידָה. שְׁמוֹנָה יְמֵי מִילָה. שִׁבְעָה יְמֵי שַׁבַּתָּא. שִׁשָׁה סִדְרֵי מִשְׁנָה. חֲמִשָׁה חוּמְשֵׁי תוֹרָה.

Who knows five? I know five! Five books of the Torah, Four are the mothers of our nation, Three fathers of our people, Two tablets G-d gave Moshe, One is our G-d, Who is in heaven and in earth!

Who knows six? I know six! Six parts of the Mishna, Five books of the Torah, Four are the mothers of our nation, Three fathers of our people, Two tablets G-d gave Moshe, One is our G-d, Who is in heaven and in earth!

Who knows seven? I know seven! Seven days for the Sabbath, Six parts of the Mishna, Five books of the Torah, Four are the mothers of our nation, Three fathers of our people, Two tablets G-d gave Moshe, One is our G-d, Who is in heaven and in earth!

Who knows eight? I know eight! Eight days to the circumcision, Seven days for the Sabbath, Six parts of the Mishna, Five books of the Torah, Four are the mothers of our nation, Three fathers of our people, Two tablets G-d gave Moshe, One is our G-d, Who is in heaven and in earth!

Who knows nine? I know nine! Nine months to childbirth, Eight days to the circumcision, Seven days for the Sabbath, Six parts of the Mishna, Five books of the Torah, Four are the mothers of our nation, Three fathers of our

אַרְבַּע אִמָּהוֹת. שְׁלֹשָׁה אָבוֹת. שְׁנֵי לֻחוֹת
הַבְּרִית. אֶחָד אֱלֹהֵינוּ שֶׁבַּשָּׁמַיִם וּבָאָרֶץ.

עֲשָׂרָה מִי יוֹדֵעַ. עֲשָׂרָה אֲנִי יוֹדֵעַ. עֲשָׂרָה
דִּבְּרַיָּא. תִּשְׁעָה יַרְחֵי לֵידָה. שְׁמוֹנָה יְמֵי מִילָה.
שִׁבְעָה יְמֵי שַׁבַּתָּא. שִׁשָּׁה סִדְרֵי מִשְׁנָה. חֲמִשָּׁה
חוּמְשֵׁי תוֹרָה. אַרְבַּע אִמָּהוֹת. שְׁלֹשָׁה אָבוֹת.
שְׁנֵי לֻחוֹת הַבְּרִית. אֶחָד אֱלֹהֵינוּ שֶׁבַּשָּׁמַיִם
וּבָאָרֶץ.

אַחַד עָשָׂר מִי יוֹדֵעַ. אַחַד עָשָׂר אֲנִי יוֹדֵעַ. אַחַד
עָשָׂר כּוֹכְבַיָּא. עֲשָׂרָה דִּבְּרַיָּא. תִּשְׁעָה יַרְחֵי
לֵידָה. שְׁמוֹנָה יְמֵי מִילָה. שִׁבְעָה יְמֵי שַׁבַּתָּא.
שִׁשָּׁה סִדְרֵי מִשְׁנָה. חֲמִשָּׁה חוּמְשֵׁי תוֹרָה.
אַרְבַּע אִמָּהוֹת. שְׁלֹשָׁה אָבוֹת. שְׁנֵי לֻחוֹת
הַבְּרִית. אֶחָד אֱלֹהֵינוּ שֶׁבַּשָּׁמַיִם וּבָאָרֶץ.

שְׁנֵים עָשָׂר מִי יוֹדֵעַ. שְׁנֵים עָשָׂר אֲנִי יוֹדֵעַ.
שְׁנֵים עָשָׂר שִׁבְטַיָּא. אַחַד עָשָׂר כּוֹכְבַיָּא. עֲשָׂרָה
דִּבְּרַיָּא. תִּשְׁעָה יַרְחֵי לֵידָה. שְׁמוֹנָה יְמֵי מִילָה.
שִׁבְעָה יְמֵי שַׁבַּתָּא. שִׁשָּׁה סִדְרֵי מִשְׁנָה. חֲמִשָּׁה
חוּמְשֵׁי תוֹרָה. אַרְבַּע אִמָּהוֹת. שְׁלֹשָׁה אָבוֹת.
שְׁנֵי לֻחוֹת הַבְּרִית. אֶחָד אֱלֹהֵינוּ שֶׁבַּשָּׁמַיִם
וּבָאָרֶץ.

people, Two tablets G-d gave Moshe, One is our G-d, Who is in heaven and in earth!

Who knows ten? I know ten! Ten Commandments at Mount Sinai, Nine months to childbirth, Eight days to the circumcision, Seven days for the Sabbath, Six parts of the Mishna, Five books of the Torah, Four are the mothers of our nation, Three fathers of our people, Two tablets G-d gave Moshe, One is our G-d, Who is in heaven and in earth!

Who knows eleven? I know eleven! Eleven stars in Joseph's dream, Ten Commandments at Mount Sinai, Nine months to childbirth, Eight days to the circumcision, Seven days for the Sabbath, Six parts of the Mishna, Five books of the Torah, Four are the mothers of our nation, Three fathers of our people, Two tablets G-d gave Moshe, One is our G-d, Who is in heaven and in earth!

Who knows twelve? I know twelve! Twelve tribes of Israel, Eleven stars in Joseph's dream, Ten Commandments at Mount Sinai, Nine months to childbirth, Eight days to the circumcision, Seven days for the Sabbath, Six parts of the Mishna, Five books of the Torah, Four are the mothers of our nation, Three fathers of our people, Two tablets G-d gave Moshe, One is our G-d, Who is in heaven and in earth!

שְׁלֹשָׁה עָשָׂר מִי יוֹדֵעַ. שְׁלֹשָׁה עָשָׂר אֲנִי יוֹדֵעַ. שְׁלֹשָׁה עָשָׂר מִדַּיָּא. שְׁנֵים עָשָׂר שִׁבְטַיָּא. אַחַד עָשָׂר כּוֹכְבַיָּא. עֲשָׂרָה דִבְּרַיָּא. תִּשְׁעָה יַרְחֵי לֵידָה. שְׁמוֹנָה יְמֵי מִילָה. שִׁבְעָה יְמֵי שַׁבַּתָּא. שִׁשָּׁה סִדְרֵי מִשְׁנָה. חֲמִשָּׁה חוּמְשֵׁי תוֹרָה. אַרְבַּע אִמָּהוֹת. שְׁלֹשָׁה אָבוֹת. שְׁנֵי לֻחוֹת הַבְּרִית. אֶחָד אֱלֹהֵינוּ שֶׁבַּשָּׁמַיִם וּבָאָרֶץ.

⋯⟨ᘓᗅᘔ⟩⋯

חַד גַּדְיָא. חַד גַּדְיָא.

דְּזַבִּין אַבָּא בִּתְרֵי זוּזֵי, חַד גַּדְיָא. חַד גַּדְיָא:

וְאָתָא שׁוּנְרָא, וְאָכְלָה לְגַדְיָא. דְּזַבִּין אַבָּא בִּתְרֵי זוּזֵי. חַד גַּדְיָא. חַד גַּדְיָא:

וְאָתָא כַלְבָּא, וְנָשַׁךְ לְשׁוּנְרָא. דְּאָכְלָה לְגַדְיָא. דְּזַבִּין אַבָּא בִּתְרֵי זוּזֵי. חַד גַּדְיָא. חַד גַּדְיָא:

וְאָתָא חוּטְרָא, וְהִכָּה לְכַלְבָּא. דְּנָשַׁךְ לְשׁוּנְרָא. דְּאָכְלָה לְגַדְיָא. דְּזַבִּין אַבָּא בִּתְרֵי זוּזֵי. חַד גַּדְיָא. חַד גַּדְיָא:

Who knows thirteen? I know thirteen! Thirteen ways of G-d's mercy, Twelve tribes of Israel, Eleven stars in Joseph's dream, Ten Commandments at Mount Sinai, Nine months to childbirth, Eight days to the circumcision, Seven days for the Sabbath, Six parts of the Mishna, Five books of the Torah, Four are the mothers of our nation, Three fathers of our people, Two tablets G-d gave Moshe, One is our G-d, Who is in heaven and in earth!

⸻

Chad Gadya– One Little Kid

One little Kid, One little kid!
> Chorus:
> *That daddy bought for two zuzim,*
> *One little kid, one little kid!*

Then along came a cat
> *And ate the little kid,*
> Chorus

Then along came a dog
> *And bit the cat,*
That ate the little kid,
> Chorus

Then along came a stick
> *And beat the dog*
> *That bit the cat*
That ate the little kid,
> Chorus

וְאָתָא נוּרָא, וְשָׂרַף לְחוּטְרָא. דְהִכָּה לְכַלְבָּא. דְנָשַׁךְ לְשׁוּנְרָא. דְאָכְלָה לְגַדְיָא. דְזַבִּין אַבָּא בִּתְרֵי זוּזֵי. חַד גַּדְיָא. חַד גַּדְיָא:

וְאָתָא מַיָּא, וְכָבָה לְנוּרָא. דְשָׂרַף לְחוּטְרָא. דְהִכָּה לְכַלְבָּא. דְנָשַׁךְ לְשׁוּנְרָא. דְאָכְלָה לְגַדְיָא. דְזַבִּין אַבָּא בִּתְרֵי זוּזֵי. חַד גַּדְיָא. חַד גַּדְיָא:

וְאָתָא תוֹרָא, וְשָׁתָא לְמַיָּא. דְכָבָה לְנוּרָא. דְשָׂרַף לְחוּטְרָא. דְהִכָּה לְכַלְבָּא. דְנָשַׁךְ לְשׁוּנְרָא. דְאָכְלָה לְגַדְיָא. דְזַבִּין אַבָּא בִּתְרֵי זוּזֵי. חַד גַּדְיָא. חַד גַּדְיָא:

וְאָתָא הַשּׁוֹחֵט, וְשָׁחַט לְתוֹרָא. דְשָׁתָא לְמַיָּא. דְכָבָה לְנוּרָא. דְשָׂרַף לְחוּטְרָא. דְהִכָּה לְכַלְבָּא. דְנָשַׁךְ לְשׁוּנְרָא. דְאָכְלָה לְגַדְיָא. דְזַבִּין אַבָּא בִּתְרֵי זוּזֵי. חַד גַּדְיָא. חַד גַּדְיָא:

Then along came a fire
    And burned the stick
    That beat the dog
    That bit the cat
That ate the little kid,
    Chorus

Then along came some water
    And put out the fire
    That burned the stick
    That beat the dog
    That bit the cat
That ate the little kid,
    Chorus

Then along came an ox
    And drank the water
    That put out the fire
    That burned the stick
    That beat the dog
    That bit the cat
That ate the little kid,
    Chorus

Then along came a slaughterer
    And killed the ox
    That drank the water
    That put out the fire
    That burned the stick
    That beat the dog
    That bit the cat
That ate the little kid,
    Chorus

וְאָתָא מַלְאַךְ הַמָּוֶת, וְשָׁחַט לְשׁוֹחֵט. דְּשָׁחַט
לְתוֹרָא. דְּשָׁתָא לְמַיָּא. דְּכָבָה לְנוּרָא. דְּשָׂרַף
לְחוּטְרָא. דְּהִכָּה לְכַלְבָּא. דְּנָשַׁךְ לְשׁוּנְרָא.
דְּאָכְלָה לְגַדְיָא. דְּזַבִּין אַבָּא בִּתְרֵי זוּזֵי. חַד
גַּדְיָא. חַד גַּדְיָא:

וְאָתָא הַקָּדוֹשׁ בָּרוּךְ הוּא. וְשָׁחַט לְמַלְאַךְ
הַמָּוֶת. דְּשָׁחַט לְשׁוֹחֵט. דְּשָׁחַט לְתוֹרָא. דְּשָׁתָא
לְמַיָּא. דְּכָבָה לְנוּרָא. דְּשָׂרַף לְחוּטְרָא. דְּהִכָּה
לְכַלְבָּא. דְּנָשַׁךְ לְשׁוּנְרָא. דְּאָכְלָה לְגַדְיָא. דְּזַבִּין
אַבָּא בִּתְרֵי זוּזֵי. חַד גַּדְיָא. חַד גַּדְיָא:

⁌⁌⁌

• After completing the Seder, a person should continue
to discuss the Exodus and the Halachos of Pesach, until
overcome by sleep (481:2).

• Only the first paragraph of the שמע and ברכת המפיל are
said before going to sleep as a demonstration of our trust in
G-d on this night of protection (ibid.,[4]).

Then along came the Angel of Death
> *And killed the slaughterer*
> *That killed the ox*
> *That drank the water*
> *That put out the fire*
> *That burned the stick*
> *That beat the dog*
> *That bit the cat*

That ate the little kid,
> *Chorus*

Then along came the Holy One Blessed be He
> *And killed the Angel of Death*
> *That killed the slaughterer*
> *That killed the ox*
> *That drank the water*
> *That put out the fire*
> *That burned the stick*
> *That beat the dog*
> *That bit the cat*

That ate the little kid,
> *Chorus*

שִׁיר הַשִּׁירִים

[א]

שִׁיר הַשִּׁירִים אֲשֶׁר לִשְׁלֹמֹה. יִשָּׁקֵנִי מִנְּשִׁיקוֹת פִּיהוּ, כִּי טוֹבִים דֹּדֶיךָ מִיָּיִן. לְרֵיחַ שְׁמָנֶיךָ טוֹבִים, שֶׁמֶן תּוּרַק שְׁמֶךָ, עַל כֵּן עֲלָמוֹת אֲהֵבוּךָ. מָשְׁכֵנִי אַחֲרֶיךָ נָּרוּצָה, הֱבִיאַנִי הַמֶּלֶךְ חֲדָרָיו, נָגִילָה וְנִשְׂמְחָה בָּךְ,

שיר השירים

❖ An Expression of Holy Love

There is a wide-spread custom of reading *Shir HaShirim* ("The Song of Songs") after finishing the Haggadah. What is the connection between *Shir HaShirim* and the Pesach Seder?

Rambam *(Teshuva 10:3)* explains the romantic dialogue of *Shir HaShirim* as an allegory describing the love between G-d and the Jewish people. Rav Mordechai Gifter *(Divrei Pesicha,* ArtScroll *Shir HaShirim)* explains that the intensity of emotion in the relationship between G-d and Israel is such that it can *only* be understood by means of allegory. The male-female relationship, and more specifically marriage, provides such an allegory.

The Talmud *(Yoma 54a)* relates that the *keruvim*, the carved human images atop the Aron in the Beis HaMikdash, one male and one female, clasped each other in an embrace. When Jews made their pilgrimage to Jerusalem, the kohanim would pull aside the curtains of the *Kodesh Kodashim* ("Holy of Holies") and display the *keruvim* to the assemblage. They would tell those gathered that the embracing *keruvim* represented the love of G-d for the Jewish people, as the love between a husband and wife.

This is the meaning of Rabbi Akiva's enigmatic statement, that if all of the Scriptures are holy, *Shir HaShirim* is the holiest of them all *(Midrash Tanchuma, Tetzaveh 5)*. *Shir HaShirim* represents the love of G-d for Israel, which was represented in the holiest place on earth – the *keruvim* in the *Kodesh Kodoshim*.

For this reason, the wedding day is considered so holy, that the bride and groom spend it fasting and reciting the Yom Kippur confession. Since marriage is the model for the love of G-d, as represented in the *Kodesh Kodoshim*, the wedding day is on the same plane as Yom Kippur – the day

נַזְכִּירָה דֹדֶיךָ מִיַּיִן, מֵישָׁרִים אֲהֵבוּךָ. שְׁחוֹרָה אֲנִי
וְנָאוָה, בְּנוֹת יְרוּשָׁלָיִם, כְּאָהֳלֵי קֵדָר, כִּירִיעוֹת
שְׁלֹמֹה. אַל תִּרְאֻנִי שֶׁאֲנִי שְׁחַרְחֹרֶת, שֶׁשְּׁזָפַתְנִי
הַשָּׁמֶשׁ, בְּנֵי אִמִּי נִחֲרוּ בִי, שָׂמֻנִי נֹטֵרָה אֶת־הַכְּרָמִים,
כַּרְמִי שֶׁלִּי לֹא נָטָרְתִּי. הַגִּידָה לִּי, שֶׁאָהֲבָה נַפְשִׁי,
אֵיכָה תִרְעֶה, אֵיכָה תַּרְבִּיץ בַּצָּהֳרָיִם, שַׁלָּמָה אֶהְיֶה

that the *Kohain Gadol* was permitted to enter the *Kodesh Kodoshim*, as an expression of the love to be seen there.

This may help us understand a surprising statement in the Talmud (*Ta'anis* 26b): "There were no happier days for the Jewish people than the fifteenth day of Av and Yom Kippur, for on these days the eligible young women of Jerusalem would go out dressed in borrowed white dresses. . . ." The Talmud goes on to describe how eligible young men and women would meet on these two days for the purpose of marriage.

It is difficult to imagine that people in Jerusalem spent the afternoon of such an auspicious day as Yom Kippur fraternizing for the purpose of getting married.(See *Tiferes Yisrael* for an alternative interpretation.) However, Yom Kippur and marriage actually complement each other perfectly: They both represent the opportunity for men and women to develop an intimate relationship with G-d. Rav

Avraham Chaim Levin put it succinctly: For a nation that views the wedding day as Yom Kippur, there is no contradiction in having Yom Kippur as a day to prepare for weddings!

The Pesach Seder is also meant as a vehicle for bringing the Jewish people "into the *Kodesh Kodoshim*," as a means for them to gain a deeper appreciation of G-d's love. *Seder HeAruch* (ch.114) cites sources that explain the wearing of a "kittel," or white robe, at the Seder, as a way of recalling the white garments of the Kohain Gadol, as he entered the *Kodesh Kodoshim* on Yom Kippur.

After we have discussed the great miracles of the Exodus, and after we have drunk the four cups of wine that represent the four stages of elevation from Egyptian bondage – which culminated in the "marriage to G-d" at Mount Sinai – it is certainly appropriate to recite *Shir HaShirim*, to evoke the intense passion of the G-d-Israel relationship.

כְּעֶטְיָה עַל עֶדְרֵי חֲבֵרֶיךָ. אִם לֹא תֵדְעִי לָךְ, הַיָּפָה
בַּנָּשִׁים, צְאִי לָךְ בְּעִקְבֵי הַצֹּאן, וּרְעִי אֶת־גְּדִיֹּתַיִךְ עַל
מִשְׁכְּנוֹת הָרֹעִים. לְסֻסָתִי בְּרִכְבֵי פַרְעֹה, דִּמִּיתִיךְ
רַעְיָתִי. נָאווּ לְחָיַיִךְ בַּתֹּרִים, צַוָּארֵךְ בַּחֲרוּזִים. תּוֹרֵי
זָהָב נַעֲשֶׂה לָּךְ, עִם נְקֻדּוֹת הַכָּסֶף. עַד שֶׁהַמֶּלֶךְ
בִּמְסִבּוֹ, נִרְדִּי נָתַן רֵיחוֹ. צְרוֹר הַמֹּר דּוֹדִי לִי, בֵּין שָׁדַי
יָלִין. אֶשְׁכֹּל הַכֹּפֶר דּוֹדִי לִי, בְּכַרְמֵי עֵין גֶּדִי. הִנָּךְ יָפָה
רַעְיָתִי, הִנָּךְ יָפָה עֵינַיִךְ יוֹנִים. הִנְּךָ יָפֶה דוֹדִי אַף
נָעִים, אַף עַרְשֵׂנוּ רַעֲנָנָה. קֹרוֹת בָּתֵּינוּ אֲרָזִים, רַהִיטֵנוּ
בְּרוֹתִים.

[ב]

אֲנִי חֲבַצֶּלֶת הַשָּׁרוֹן, שׁוֹשַׁנַּת הָעֲמָקִים. כְּשׁוֹשַׁנָּה
בֵּין הַחוֹחִים, כֵּן רַעְיָתִי בֵּין הַבָּנוֹת. כְּתַפּוּחַ בַּעֲצֵי
הַיַּעַר, כֵּן דּוֹדִי בֵּין הַבָּנִים, בְּצִלּוֹ חִמַּדְתִּי וְיָשַׁבְתִּי,
וּפִרְיוֹ מָתוֹק לְחִכִּי. הֱבִיאַנִי אֶל בֵּית הַיַּיִן, וְדִגְלוֹ עָלַי
אַהֲבָה. סַמְּכוּנִי בָּאֲשִׁישׁוֹת, רַפְּדוּנִי בַּתַּפּוּחִים, כִּי
חוֹלַת אַהֲבָה אָנִי. שְׂמֹאלוֹ תַּחַת לְרֹאשִׁי, וִימִינוֹ
תְּחַבְּקֵנִי. הִשְׁבַּעְתִּי אֶתְכֶם, בְּנוֹת יְרוּשָׁלַ͏ִם, בִּצְבָאוֹת,
אוֹ בְּאַיְלוֹת הַשָּׂדֶה, אִם תָּעִירוּ וְאִם תְּעוֹרְרוּ אֶת־
הָאַהֲבָה עַד שֶׁתֶּחְפָּץ. קוֹל דּוֹדִי הִנֵּה־זֶה בָּא, מְדַלֵּג
עַל הֶהָרִים, מְקַפֵּץ עַל הַגְּבָעוֹת. דּוֹמֶה דוֹדִי לִצְבִי, אוֹ
לְעֹפֶר הָאַיָּלִים, הִנֵּה־זֶה עוֹמֵד אַחַר כָּתְלֵנוּ, מַשְׁגִּיחַ
מִן הַחַלֹּנוֹת, מֵצִיץ מִן הַחֲרַכִּים. עָנָה דוֹדִי וְאָמַר לִי,
קוּמִי לָךְ רַעְיָתִי יָפָתִי וּלְכִי לָךְ. כִּי הִנֵּה הַסְּתָו עָבַר,

הַגֶּשֶׁם חָלַף הָלַךְ לוֹ. הַנִּצָּנִים נִרְאוּ בָאָרֶץ, עֵת הַזָּמִיר
הִגִּיעַ, וְקוֹל הַתּוֹר נִשְׁמַע בְּאַרְצֵנוּ. הַתְּאֵנָה חָנְטָה
פַגֶּיהָ, וְהַגְּפָנִים סְמָדַר נָתְנוּ רֵיחַ, קוּמִי לָךְ רַעְיָתִי יָפָתִי
וּלְכִי לָךְ. יוֹנָתִי, בְּחַגְוֵי הַסֶּלַע, בְּסֵתֶר הַמַּדְרֵגָה,
הַרְאִינִי אֶת־מַרְאַיִךְ, הַשְׁמִיעִנִי אֶת־קוֹלֵךְ, כִּי קוֹלֵךְ
עָרֵב וּמַרְאֵיךְ נָאוֶה. אֶחֱזוּ לָנוּ שׁוּעָלִים, שֻׁעָלִים
קְטַנִּים מְחַבְּלִים כְּרָמִים, וּכְרָמֵינוּ סְמָדַר. דּוֹדִי לִי וַאֲנִי
לוֹ, הָרֹעֶה בַּשּׁוֹשַׁנִּים. עַד שֶׁיָּפוּחַ הַיּוֹם, וְנָסוּ הַצְּלָלִים,
סֹב דְּמֵה לְךָ דוֹדִי, לִצְבִי, אוֹ לְעֹפֶר הָאַיָּלִים עַל הָרֵי
בָתֶר.

[ג]

עַל מִשְׁכָּבִי בַּלֵּילוֹת, בִּקַּשְׁתִּי, אֵת שֶׁאָהֲבָה נַפְשִׁי,
בִּקַּשְׁתִּיו וְלֹא מְצָאתִיו. אָקוּמָה נָּא, וַאֲסוֹבְבָה בָעִיר,
בַּשְּׁוָקִים וּבָרְחֹבוֹת, אֲבַקְשָׁה, אֵת שֶׁאָהֲבָה נַפְשִׁי,
בִּקַּשְׁתִּיו וְלֹא מְצָאתִיו. מְצָאוּנִי הַשֹּׁמְרִים, הַסֹּבְבִים
בָּעִיר, אֵת שֶׁאָהֲבָה נַפְשִׁי רְאִיתֶם. כִּמְעַט שֶׁעָבַרְתִּי
מֵהֶם, עַד שֶׁמָּצָאתִי אֵת שֶׁאָהֲבָה נַפְשִׁי, אֲחַזְתִּיו וְלֹא
אַרְפֶּנּוּ, עַד שֶׁהֲבֵיאתִיו אֶל בֵּית אִמִּי, וְאֶל חֶדֶר
הוֹרָתִי. הִשְׁבַּעְתִּי אֶתְכֶם, בְּנוֹת יְרוּשָׁלַ͏ִם, בִּצְבָאוֹת,
אוֹ בְּאַיְלוֹת הַשָּׂדֶה, אִם תָּעִירוּ וְאִם תְּעוֹרְרוּ אֶת־
הָאַהֲבָה עַד שֶׁתֶּחְפָּץ. מִי זֹאת, עֹלָה מִן הַמִּדְבָּר,
כְּתִימְרוֹת עָשָׁן, מְקֻטֶּרֶת מֹר וּלְבוֹנָה, מִכֹּל אַבְקַת
רוֹכֵל. הִנֵּה, מִטָּתוֹ שֶׁלִּשְׁלֹמֹה, שִׁשִּׁים גִּבֹּרִים סָבִיב
לָהּ, מִגִּבֹּרֵי יִשְׂרָאֵל. כֻּלָּם אֲחֻזֵי חֶרֶב, מְלֻמְּדֵי

מִלְחָמָה, אִישׁ חַרְבּוֹ עַל יְרֵכוֹ, מִפַּחַד בַּלֵּילוֹת.
אַפִּרְיוֹן, עָשָׂה לוֹ הַמֶּלֶךְ שְׁלֹמֹה, מֵעֲצֵי הַלְּבָנוֹן.
עַמּוּדָיו עָשָׂה כֶסֶף, רְפִידָתוֹ זָהָב, מֶרְכָּבוֹ אַרְגָּמָן,
תּוֹכוֹ רָצוּף אַהֲבָה, מִבְּנוֹת יְרוּשָׁלָ͏ִם. צְאֶינָה וּרְאֶינָה
בְּנוֹת צִיּוֹן בַּמֶּלֶךְ שְׁלֹמֹה, בָּעֲטָרָה, שֶׁעִטְּרָה לּוֹ אִמּוֹ
בְּיוֹם חֲתֻנָּתוֹ, וּבְיוֹם שִׂמְחַת לִבּוֹ.

[ד]

הִנָּךְ יָפָה רַעְיָתִי הִנָּךְ יָפָה, עֵינַיִךְ יוֹנִים, מִבַּעַד
לְצַמָּתֵךְ, שַׂעְרֵךְ כְּעֵדֶר הָעִזִּים, שֶׁגָּלְשׁוּ מֵהַר גִּלְעָד.
שִׁנַּיִךְ כְּעֵדֶר הַקְּצוּבוֹת שֶׁעָלוּ מִן הָרַחְצָה, שֶׁכֻּלָּם
מַתְאִימוֹת, וְשַׁכֻּלָה אֵין בָּהֶם. כְּחוּט הַשָּׁנִי שִׂפְתוֹתַיִךְ,
וּמִדְבָּרֵךְ נָאוֶה, כְּפֶלַח הָרִמּוֹן רַקָּתֵךְ, מִבַּעַד לְצַמָּתֵךְ.
כְּמִגְדַּל דָּוִיד צַוָּארֵךְ, בָּנוּי לְתַלְפִּיּוֹת, אֶלֶף הַמָּגֵן תָּלוּי
עָלָיו, כֹּל שִׁלְטֵי הַגִּבֹּרִים. שְׁנֵי שָׁדַיִךְ כִּשְׁנֵי עֳפָרִים
תְּאוֹמֵי צְבִיָּה, הָרֹעִים בַּשּׁוֹשַׁנִּים. עַד שֶׁיָּפוּחַ הַיּוֹם,
וְנָסוּ הַצְּלָלִים, אֵלֶךְ לִי אֶל הַר הַמּוֹר, וְאֶל גִּבְעַת
הַלְּבוֹנָה. כֻּלָּךְ יָפָה רַעְיָתִי, וּמוּם אֵין בָּךְ. אִתִּי מִלְּבָנוֹן
כַּלָּה, אִתִּי מִלְּבָנוֹן תָּבוֹאִי, תָּשׁוּרִי ׀ מֵרֹאשׁ אֲמָנָה,
מֵרֹאשׁ שְׂנִיר וְחֶרְמוֹן, מִמְּעֹנוֹת אֲרָיוֹת, מֵהַרְרֵי
נְמֵרִים. לִבַּבְתִּנִי אֲחֹתִי כַלָּה, לִבַּבְתִּנִי בְּאַחַת מֵעֵינַיִךְ,
בְּאַחַד עֲנָק מִצַּוְּרֹנָיִךְ. מַה יָּפוּ דֹדַיִךְ אֲחֹתִי כַלָּה, מַה
טֹּבוּ דֹדַיִךְ מִיָּיִן, וְרֵיחַ שְׁמָנַיִךְ מִכָּל־בְּשָׂמִים. נֹפֶת
תִּטֹּפְנָה שִׂפְתוֹתַיִךְ כַּלָּה, דְּבַשׁ וְחָלָב תַּחַת לְשׁוֹנֵךְ,

וְרֵיחַ שַׁלְמֹתַיִךְ כְּרֵיחַ לְבָנוֹן. גַּן ׀ נָעוּל אֲחֹתִי כַלָּה,
גַּל נָעוּל מַעְיָן חָתוּם. שְׁלָחַיִךְ פַּרְדֵּס רִמּוֹנִים, עִם פְּרִי
מְגָדִים, כְּפָרִים עִם נְרָדִים. נֵרְדְּ וְכַרְכֹּם, קָנֶה וְקִנָּמוֹן,
עִם כָּל־עֲצֵי לְבוֹנָה, מֹר וַאֲהָלוֹת, עִם כָּל־רָאשֵׁי
בְשָׂמִים. מַעְיַן גַּנִּים, בְּאֵר מַיִם חַיִּים, וְנֹזְלִים מִן לְבָנוֹן.
עוּרִי צָפוֹן וּבוֹאִי תֵימָן, הָפִיחִי גַנִּי יִזְּלוּ בְשָׂמָיו, יָבֹא
דוֹדִי לְגַנּוֹ, וְיֹאכַל פְּרִי מְגָדָיו.

[ה]

בָּאתִי לְגַנִּי אֲחֹתִי כַלָּה, אָרִיתִי מוֹרִי עִם בְּשָׂמִי,
אָכַלְתִּי יַעְרִי עִם דִּבְשִׁי, שָׁתִיתִי יֵינִי עִם חֲלָבִי, אִכְלוּ
רֵעִים, שְׁתוּ וְשִׁכְרוּ דּוֹדִים. אֲנִי יְשֵׁנָה וְלִבִּי עֵר, קוֹל ׀
דּוֹדִי דוֹפֵק, פִּתְחִי לִי, אֲחֹתִי רַעְיָתִי יוֹנָתִי תַמָּתִי,
שֶׁרֹאשִׁי נִמְלָא טָל, קְוֻצּוֹתַי רְסִיסֵי לָיְלָה. פָּשַׁטְתִּי אֶת־
כֻּתָּנְתִּי, אֵיכָכָה אֶלְבָּשֶׁנָּה, רָחַצְתִּי אֶת־רַגְלַי אֵיכָכָה
אֲטַנְּפֵם. דּוֹדִי, שָׁלַח יָדוֹ מִן הַחֹר, וּמֵעַי הָמוּ עָלָיו.
קַמְתִּי אֲנִי לִפְתֹּחַ לְדוֹדִי, וְיָדַי נָטְפוּ מוֹר, וְאֶצְבְּעֹתַי
מוֹר עֹבֵר, עַל כַּפּוֹת הַמַּנְעוּל. פָּתַחְתִּי אֲנִי לְדוֹדִי,
וְדוֹדִי חָמַק עָבָר, נַפְשִׁי יָצְאָה בְדַבְּרוֹ, בִּקַּשְׁתִּיהוּ וְלֹא
מְצָאתִיהוּ, קְרָאתִיו וְלֹא עָנָנִי. מְצָאֻנִי הַשֹּׁמְרִים
הַסֹּבְבִים בָּעִיר הִכּוּנִי פְצָעוּנִי, נָשְׂאוּ אֶת־רְדִידִי
מֵעָלַי, שֹׁמְרֵי הַחֹמוֹת. הִשְׁבַּעְתִּי אֶתְכֶם בְּנוֹת
יְרוּשָׁלַ͏ִם, אִם תִּמְצְאוּ אֶת־דּוֹדִי, מַה תַּגִּידוּ לוֹ שֶׁחוֹלַת
אַהֲבָה אָנִי. מַה דּוֹדֵךְ מִדּוֹד, הַיָּפָה בַּנָּשִׁים, מַה דּוֹדֵךְ

מָדוֹד, שֶׁכָּכָה הִשְׁבַּעְתָּנוּ. דּוֹדִי צַח וְאָדוֹם, דָּגוּל מֵרְבָבָה. רֹאשׁוֹ כֶּתֶם פָּז, קְוֻצּוֹתָיו תַּלְתַּלִּים, שְׁחֹרוֹת כָּעוֹרֵב. עֵינָיו כְּיוֹנִים עַל אֲפִיקֵי מָיִם, רֹחֲצוֹת בֶּחָלָב, יֹשְׁבוֹת עַל מִלֵּאת. לְחָיָו כַּעֲרוּגַת הַבֹּשֶׂם, מִגְדְּלוֹת מֶרְקָחִים, שִׂפְתוֹתָיו שׁוֹשַׁנִּים, נֹטְפוֹת מוֹר עֹבֵר. יָדָיו גְּלִילֵי זָהָב, מְמֻלָּאִים בַּתַּרְשִׁישׁ, מֵעָיו עֶשֶׁת שֵׁן, מְעֻלֶּפֶת סַפִּירִים. שׁוֹקָיו עַמּוּדֵי שֵׁשׁ, מְיֻסָּדִים עַל אַדְנֵי פָז, מַרְאֵהוּ כַּלְּבָנוֹן, בָּחוּר כָּאֲרָזִים. חִכּוֹ מַמְתַקִּים, וְכֻלּוֹ מַחֲמַדִּים, זֶה דוֹדִי וְזֶה רֵעִי, בְּנוֹת יְרוּשָׁלָם.

[ו]

אָנָה הָלַךְ דּוֹדֵךְ, הַיָּפָה בַּנָּשִׁים, אָנָה פָּנָה דוֹדֵךְ, וּנְבַקְשֶׁנּוּ עִמָּךְ. דּוֹדִי יָרַד לְגַנּוֹ, לַעֲרֻגוֹת הַבֹּשֶׂם, לִרְעוֹת בַּגַּנִּים, וְלִלְקֹט שׁוֹשַׁנִּים. אֲנִי לְדוֹדִי וְדוֹדִי לִי, הָרֹעֶה בַּשׁוֹשַׁנִּים. יָפָה אַתְּ רַעְיָתִי כְּתִרְצָה, נָאוָה כִּירוּשָׁלָם, אֲיֻמָּה כַּנִּדְגָּלוֹת. הָסֵבִּי עֵינַיִךְ מִנֶּגְדִּי, שֶׁהֵם הִרְהִיבֻנִי, שַׂעְרֵךְ כְּעֵדֶר הָעִזִּים, שֶׁגָּלְשׁוּ מִן הַגִּלְעָד. שִׁנַּיִךְ כְּעֵדֶר הָרְחֵלִים, שֶׁעָלוּ מִן הָרַחְצָה, שֶׁכֻּלָּם מַתְאִימוֹת, וְשַׁכֻּלָה אֵין בָּהֶם. כְּפֶלַח הָרִמּוֹן רַקָּתֵךְ, מִבַּעַד לְצַמָּתֵךְ. שִׁשִּׁים הֵמָּה מְלָכוֹת, וּשְׁמֹנִים פִּילַגְשִׁים, וַעֲלָמוֹת אֵין מִסְפָּר. אַחַת הִיא יוֹנָתִי תַמָּתִי, אַחַת הִיא לְאִמָּהּ, בָּרָה הִיא לְיוֹלַדְתָּהּ, רָאוּהָ בָנוֹת וַיְאַשְּׁרוּהָ, מְלָכוֹת וּפִילַגְשִׁים וַיְהַלְלוּהָ. מִי זֹאת

הַנִּשְׁקָפָה כְּמוֹ שָׁחַר, יָפָה כַלְּבָנָה, בָּרָה כַּחַמָּה, אֲיֻמָּה כַּנִּדְגָּלוֹת. אֶל גִּנַּת אֱגוֹז יָרַדְתִּי לִרְאוֹת בְּאִבֵּי הַנָּחַל, לִרְאוֹת הֲפָרְחָה הַגֶּפֶן, הֵנֵצוּ הָרִמֹּנִים. לֹא יָדַעְתִּי, נַפְשִׁי שָׂמַתְנִי, מַרְכְּבוֹת עַמִּי נָדִיב.

[ז]

שׁוּבִי שׁוּבִי הַשּׁוּלַמִּית, שׁוּבִי שׁוּבִי וְנֶחֱזֶה בָּךְ, מַה תֶּחֱזוּ בַּשּׁוּלַמִּית, כִּמְחֹלַת הַמַּחֲנָיִם. מַה יָּפוּ פְעָמַיִךְ בַּנְּעָלִים בַּת נָדִיב, חַמּוּקֵי יְרֵכַיִךְ כְּמוֹ חֲלָאִים, מַעֲשֵׂה יְדֵי אָמָּן. שָׁרְרֵךְ אַגַּן הַסַּהַר, אַל יֶחְסַר הַמָּזֶג, בִּטְנֵךְ עֲרֵמַת חִטִּים, סוּגָה בַּשּׁוֹשַׁנִּים. שְׁנֵי שָׁדַיִךְ כִּשְׁנֵי עֳפָרִים, תָּאֳמֵי צְבִיָּה. צַוָּארֵךְ כְּמִגְדַּל הַשֵּׁן, עֵינַיִךְ בְּרֵכוֹת בְּחֶשְׁבּוֹן, עַל שַׁעַר בַּת רַבִּים, אַפֵּךְ כְּמִגְדַּל הַלְּבָנוֹן, צוֹפֶה פְּנֵי דַמָּשֶׂק. רֹאשֵׁךְ עָלַיִךְ כַּכַּרְמֶל, וְדַלַּת רֹאשֵׁךְ כָּאַרְגָּמָן, מֶלֶךְ אָסוּר בָּרְהָטִים. מַה יָּפִית וּמַה נָּעַמְתְּ, אַהֲבָה בַּתַּעֲנוּגִים. זֹאת קוֹמָתֵךְ דָּמְתָה לְתָמָר, וְשָׁדַיִךְ לְאַשְׁכֹּלוֹת. אָמַרְתִּי אֶעֱלֶה בְתָמָר, אֹחֲזָה בְּסַנְסִנָּיו, וְיִהְיוּ נָא שָׁדַיִךְ כְּאֶשְׁכְּלוֹת הַגֶּפֶן, וְרֵיחַ אַפֵּךְ כַּתַּפּוּחִים. וְחִכֵּךְ כְּיֵין הַטּוֹב הוֹלֵךְ לְדוֹדִי לְמֵישָׁרִים, דּוֹבֵב שִׂפְתֵי יְשֵׁנִים. אֲנִי לְדוֹדִי, וְעָלַי תְּשׁוּקָתוֹ. לְכָה דוֹדִי נֵצֵא הַשָּׂדֶה, נָלִינָה בַּכְּפָרִים. נַשְׁכִּימָה לַכְּרָמִים, נִרְאֶה אִם פָּרְחָה הַגֶּפֶן פִּתַּח הַסְּמָדַר, הֵנֵצוּ הָרִמּוֹנִים, שָׁם אֶתֵּן אֶת־דֹּדַי לָךְ.

הַדּוּדָאִים נָתְנוּ רֵיחַ, וְעַל פְּתָחֵינוּ כָּל־מְגָדִים, חֲדָשִׁים גַּם יְשָׁנִים, דּוֹדִי צָפַנְתִּי לָךְ.

[ח]

מִי יִתֶּנְךָ כְּאָח לִי, יוֹנֵק שְׁדֵי אִמִּי, אֶמְצָאֲךָ בַחוּץ אֶשָּׁקְךָ, גַּם לֹא יָבֻזוּ לִי. אֶנְהָגֲךָ, אֲבִיאֲךָ אֶל בֵּית אִמִּי תְּלַמְּדֵנִי, אַשְׁקְךָ מִיַּיִן הָרֶקַח, מֵעֲסִיס רִמֹּנִי. שְׂמֹאלוֹ תַּחַת רֹאשִׁי, וִימִינוֹ תְּחַבְּקֵנִי. הִשְׁבַּעְתִּי אֶתְכֶם בְּנוֹת יְרוּשָׁלָ͏ִם, מַה תָּעִירוּ ׀ וּמַה תְּעֹרְרוּ אֶת־הָאַהֲבָה עַד שֶׁתֶּחְפָּץ. מִי זֹאת, עֹלָה מִן הַמִּדְבָּר, מִתְרַפֶּקֶת עַל דּוֹדָהּ, תַּחַת הַתַּפּוּחַ עוֹרַרְתִּיךָ, שָׁמָּה חִבְּלַתְךָ אִמֶּךָ, שָׁמָּה חִבְּלָה יְלָדַתְךָ. שִׂימֵנִי כַחוֹתָם עַל לִבֶּךָ, כַּחוֹתָם עַל זְרוֹעֶךָ, כִּי עַזָּה כַמָּוֶת אַהֲבָה, קָשָׁה כִשְׁאוֹל קִנְאָה, רְשָׁפֶיהָ, רִשְׁפֵּי, אֵשׁ שַׁלְהֶבֶתְיָה. מַיִם רַבִּים, לֹא יוּכְלוּ לְכַבּוֹת אֶת־הָאַהֲבָה, וּנְהָרוֹת לֹא יִשְׁטְפוּהָ, אִם יִתֵּן אִישׁ אֶת־כָּל־הוֹן בֵּיתוֹ בָּאַהֲבָה, בּוֹז יָבוּזוּ לוֹ. אָחוֹת לָנוּ קְטַנָּה, וְשָׁדַיִם אֵין לָהּ, מַה נַּעֲשֶׂה לַאֲחֹתֵנוּ, בַּיּוֹם שֶׁיְּדֻבַּר בָּהּ. אִם חוֹמָה הִיא, נִבְנֶה עָלֶיהָ טִירַת כָּסֶף, וְאִם דֶּלֶת הִיא, נָצוּר עָלֶיהָ לוּחַ אָרֶז. אֲנִי חוֹמָה, וְשָׁדַי כַּמִּגְדָּלוֹת, אָז הָיִיתִי בְעֵינָיו כְּמוֹצְאֵת שָׁלוֹם. כֶּרֶם הָיָה לִשְׁלֹמֹה בְּבַעַל הָמוֹן, נָתַן אֶת־הַכֶּרֶם לַנֹּטְרִים, אִישׁ יָבִא בְּפִרְיוֹ אֶלֶף כָּסֶף. כַּרְמִי שֶׁלִּי לְפָנָי, הָאֶלֶף לְךָ שְׁלֹמֹה, וּמָאתַיִם לְנֹטְרִים

אֶת־פִּרְיוֹ. הַיּוֹשֶׁבֶת בַּגַּנִּים, חֲבֵרִים מַקְשִׁיבִים לְקוֹלֵךְ הַשְׁמִיעִנִי. בְּרַח דּוֹדִי, וּדְמֵה לְךָ לִצְבִי אוֹ לְעֹפֶר הָאַיָּלִים, עַל הָרֵי בְשָׂמִים.

רִבּוֹן כָּל הָעוֹלָמִים, יְהִי רָצוֹן מִלְּפָנֶיךָ, יְיָ אֱלֹהַי וֵאלֹהֵי אֲבוֹתַי, שֶׁבִּזְכוּת שִׁיר הַשִּׁירִים אֲשֶׁר קָרִיתִי וְלָמַדְתִּי, שֶׁהוּא קֹדֶשׁ קָדָשִׁים, בִּזְכוּת פְּסוּקָיו, וּבִזְכוּת תֵּבוֹתָיו, וּבִזְכוּת אוֹתִיּוֹתָיו, וּבִזְכוּת נְקֻדּוֹתָיו, וּבִזְכוּת טְעָמָיו, וּבִזְכוּת שְׁמוֹתָיו, וְצֵרוּפָיו וּרְמָזָיו וְסוֹדוֹתָיו הַקְּדוֹשִׁים וְהַטְּהוֹרִים הַנּוֹרָאִים הַיּוֹצְאִים מִמֶּנּוּ. שֶׁתְּהֵא שָׁעָה זוֹ שְׁעַת רַחֲמִים, שְׁעַת הַקְשָׁבָה, שְׁעַת הָאֲזָנָה, וְנִקְרָאֲךָ וְתַעֲנֵנוּ. נַעְתִּיר לְךָ וְהֵעָתֵר לָנוּ, שֶׁיִּהְיֶה עוֹלֶה לְפָנֶיךָ קְרִיאַת וְלִמּוּד שִׁיר הַשִּׁירִים, כְּאִלּוּ הִשַּׂגְנוּ כָּל הַסּוֹדוֹת הַנִּפְלָאוֹת וְהַנּוֹרָאוֹת אֲשֶׁר הֵם חֲתוּמִים בּוֹ, בְּכָל תְּנָאָיו. וְנִזְכֶּה לְמָקוֹם שֶׁהָרוּחוֹת וְהַנְּשָׁמוֹת נֶחְצָבוֹת מִשָּׁם. וּכְאִלּוּ עָשִׂינוּ כָּל מַה שֶּׁמּוּטָל עָלֵינוּ לְהַשִּׂיג, בֵּין בְּגִלְגּוּל זֶה בֵּין בְּגִלְגּוּל אַחֵר. וְלִהְיוֹת מִן הָעוֹלִים וְהַזּוֹכִים לָעוֹלָם הַבָּא עִם שְׁאָר צַדִּיקִים וַחֲסִידִים. וּמַלֵּא כָּל מִשְׁאֲלוֹת לִבֵּנוּ לְטוֹבָה, וְתִהְיֶה עִם לְבָבֵנוּ וְאִמְרֵי פִינוּ, בְּעֵת מַחְשְׁבוֹתֵינוּ. וְעִם יָדֵינוּ, בְּעֵת מַעְבָּדֵינוּ. וְתִשְׁלַח בְּרָכָה וְהַצְלָחָה וְהַרְוָחָה, בְּכָל מַעֲשֵׂה יָדֵינוּ. וּמֵעָפָר תְּקִימֵנוּ, וּמֵאַשְׁפּוֹת דַּלּוּתֵנוּ תְּרוֹמְמֵנוּ, וְתָשִׁיב שְׁכִינָתְךָ לְעִיר קָדְשֶׁךָ, בִּמְהֵרָה בְיָמֵינוּ. אָמֵן.

✦